The Hidden Text of Mill's *Liberty*

The Hidden Text of Mill's *Liberty*

Stewart Justman

Rowman & Littlefield Publishers, Inc.

ROWMAN & LITTLEFIELD PUBLISHERS, INC.

Published in the United States of America
by Rowman & Littlefield Publishers, Inc.
8705 Bollman Place, Savage, Maryland 20763

British Cataloging in Publication Information Available

Library of Congress Cataloging-in-Publication Data

Justman, Stewart.
The hidden text of Mill's Liberty / Stewart Justman.
p.   cm.
Includes bibliographical references (p.   ) and index.
1. Mill, John Stuart, 1806-1873.   On Liberty.   I. Title.
JC585.M75J87   1990
323.44—dc20   90-9131 CIP

ISBN 0–8476–7654–4 (alk. paper)

Quotations from *The Collected Works of John Stuart Mill, On
Liberty* are reproduced with the kind permission of the
publisher, University of Toronto Press, Canada.

5   4   3   2   1

Printed in the United States of America

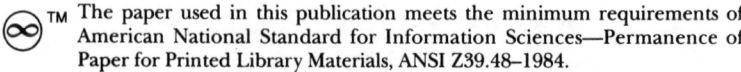

TM The paper used in this publication meets the minimum requirements of
American National Standard for Information Sciences—Permanence of
Paper for Printed Library Materials, ANSI Z39.48–1984.

Contents

Introduction

WHEN I FIRST read Mill's *On Liberty*[1] as a student of Victorian literature, I was dispirited by what seemed the lifelessness of his prose, moved at the same time by his defense of a private sphere within which people are free to do as they choose, and struck by his ability to anticipate topics of my own time, such as victimless crime and the other-directed individual. When I went on to teach *On Liberty* in my own right, I naturally organized my lectures around these points. In addition, I held up *On Liberty* as a model of argumentation, citing Mill's abstention from the use of slogans and epithets, and his decision to challenge and encourage rational thought, not kill it. And yet it appeared that my students were not much challenged by *On Liberty*. None of them had any real argument with the essay. It seemed to fall right in with their own thinking. Over the years it became clear to me that my students were reading *On Liberty* as a philosophical charter of consumer values they generally subscribed to, values like free choice, much as I had brought my own prepossessions to the text when I had read it as a criticism of conformity.

When *On Liberty* was written, to argue that we are bound neither by tradition nor dogma nor the opinions of our neighbors was to take a stance. But in a society where political choice itself is patterned after choices of consumption (where political candidates, for example, are marketed by the same advertising agencies that vend soft drinks and beer), the idea that people are entitled to make their own choices in whatever concerns themselves has become a sort of cliché in its own

1

right. Maybe it was an impulse of contrariety that made me question whether *On Liberty* does no more than affirm the commonplaces of a consumer society. Frustration at my own inability to teach the text well also entered in. For I knew that unlike a consumer—who is inclined to identify freedom with private consumption itself and to see the public world as so much mummery—Mill was intensely public-spirited. Somehow a man with an elevated conception of the public good wrote the pre-eminent defense of the individual's right to pursue his or her own good. Teaching *On Liberty*, I sensed too that the libertarian precepts of that text provide no antidote to the mass influences Mill wanted to check. In contemporary America, the belief that everyone has a right to pursue happiness in his or her own way— the libertarian thesis of *On Liberty*—has wide currency, but America is a mass society for all that, agencies like the mass media having grown immeasurably more powerful than they were in Mill's time. People may give broad acceptance to libertarian notions without being any less subject to mass influences. Those notions may be marketed by the mass media themselves.

At the time I was teaching *On Liberty* I was also reading the writings of Hannah Arendt, who brought home my own society's radical depreciation of the public realm. Arendt is unclassifiable, but her idealization of an order of law within which our nature as acting beings is realized, her reference to ancient models, and perhaps too her distrust of socio-economic forces ally her with the more classical strains of the republican tradition. I was recalled again to the tradition of republicanism by *Habits of the Heart*, a 1985 inquiry into the state of American values.[2] The authors of that study don't seem to share my sense of the conflict between civic and consumer ideals, and they permit themselves to hope for a revival of republican values in the very midst of a consumer society, a hope I find improbable. Even so, *Habits of the Heart* quickened my desire to learn more about the republican tradition that I sensed working in the argumentation of John Stuart Mill and that survives vestigially in the public discourse of our own society. And so I came around to J. G. A. Pocock's study of *The Machiavellian Moment: Florentine Political Thought and the Atlantic Republican Tradition*, an erudite volume wherein I learned about the history of the ideal of a republic sustained by the active virtue of its citizens. Elsewhere Pocock cautions against the conclusion that the ideal of the classical citizen (the man of active virtue) was killed off at some point in the eighteenth century by the rise of commercial society. That ideal "refused to disappear," he says,[3] and I think it enjoys a pallid afterlife in *On Liberty*, which criticizes the morality of passivity, obedience, and private accumulation in the name of the active virtue that realizes the citizen. If the republican tradition warns of the "enfeeblement" of the citizenry that sacrifices public to private interests,[4] Mill himself complains of an enfeeblement of the Victorian middle class, a loss of vigor and capacity—a loss accompanied, moreover, by just that kind of mental narrowness we would expect to result from the single-minded devotion to private interests. But is it not then ironic that Mill defended the private sphere so emphatically?

So forcible, in fact, is Mill's defense of the private sphere in *On Liberty* that it overbears the republican principles informing his argument as a whole. In his most famous volume, Mill drew on a republican notion of self-realization that stresses citizenly duty, armed virtue and the active life (a notion variously employed, for example, by Machiavelli, Milton and radical republicans in Mill's own day) and bleached it almost to invisibility; perhaps this bleaching is responsible in some degree for the pallor of Mill's prose. In *On Liberty*, self-realization suggests less the active pursuit of a common good in company with others than the pursuit of happiness in one's own way and noninterference with others as they do the same. That is, self-realization almost loses its political charge, almost becomes identical with the bourgeois ideal of private happiness.[5] Perhaps because Mill tempered his republican principles, and in any case didn't placard them as at a political meeting in the open air, readers have been able to ignore them entirely. An exception, Bernard Semmel, classes Mill with "the defenders of civic virtue from the Florentine thinkers of the Renaissance to the British and American Whigs of the seventeenth and eighteenth centuries"[6]—places Mill, that is, in the tradition Pocock has studied.

There can be no doubt Mill did esteem civic virtue, however poorly this value consists with the notion of suiting ourselves and tending closely to our own interests. If advocacy of a citizen militia is the mark of a republican, then Mill was one, for he opposed standing armies and favored a citizen militia in their place. He wanted people trained to fight. *On Liberty* calls—in passing—for each person to share in the common defense. And to me this provision of *On Liberty*, so little commented on in the literature, characterizes the argument as a whole. Almost invisibly, the author weaves into *On Liberty* a republican principle that runs aslant to his libertarian thesis; for as a member of a militia one is *not* sovereign over one's body, nor is one free to pursue an exclusively private happiness. In the militia "the individual loses his personal identity," although the loss is handsomely compensated, for one gains in virtue what one gave up in rights.[7] The militia is an academy of civic virtue. The foremost advocate of the citizen militia was Machiavelli, whose "republican doctrine, throughout all his writings, is based on an expanded body of people politically active and militarily participant"[8]—a highly charged ideal that survives into the writings of John Stuart Mill, modified and much weakened. I think that in the little he says about the citizen army Mill looks backward to the virtue of the Romans (as did Machiavelli), not forward to the conscripted armies, and the mass production of death, that we know in the twentieth century.

In muting the ideal of an active citizenry, Mill follows the example of Bentham, who would have liked to do away with the rhetoric of political liberty (as being emotive and dangerous, a kind of firewater) and who resolved liberty into security. The idea that liberty might consist not in being well governed but in sharing in government itself— this Bentham considered a crazy fallacy. In his horror of the idea he called up the specter of

> the exercise of the powers of government on every occasion by every member of the community, by every one of the persons to be governed, by every member of the community men and women [sic], adults and minors, sane and insane, convicts and unconvicted, without exception made of a single individual.[9]

Bentham much preferred to understand liberty as security against coercion—a "negative" conception of liberty inherited by Mill. But as is well known, Mill broke from Benthamism in some degree, and we read evidence of that break not so much perhaps in Mill's advocacy of political participation (which he prescribes in the smallest doses) as in his rhetoric of liberty as the exercise of powers. A free person, as Mill envisions this individual in *On Liberty*, is an able being, an agent, just as the conformist is lacking in agency, maimed, incapable. The conformist may enjoy secure expectations, but that hardly makes him or her a model of a free person in the mind of Mill. Mill rebelled against Bentham not only in the name of a romantic ideal of personality, but in the name of a roughly civic-humanist ideal of political personality. At the same time, he departed from Bentham only so far; thus, for example, the notion of "self-regarding acts"—the centerpiece of *On Liberty*—derives from Bentham himself. In all, Mill's attitudes toward the republican tradition are just as vexed as his attitudes toward Bentham.

Mill detests corruption both in the classical republican sense of a loss of independence, and in the vernacular sense of the taking of public funds or the use of public office for private ends—the more familiar sense of "corruption" broadly shared by radical movements in his era. A loose as well as an evocative term, "corruption" serves different masters. In the adulation of the rich, Adam Smith saw the cause of "the corruption of our moral sentiments,"[10] a subject Mill takes up 100 years later. The corruption of the rich themselves is a theme of eighteenth-century anti-establishment thinking; Mary Wollstonecraft gave that theme her own turn when she declaimed against the corruption of women, pampered and cretinized like the rich.[11] In turn, Mill extended the range of the notion of corruption to take in the very class Mary Wollstonecraft saw as the bearer of virtue, the middle class. Bentham and James Mill abominated a corrupt government that multiplied places and bought parliamentary majorities;[12] the younger Mill entered into this feeling while reviving an antique meaning of "corruption" as a vitiation of the person, a moral debility, a loss of the power of action. Moreover, quite as though Mill shared the civic humanist obsession with the return to original principles and the "renovation of virtue," he speaks repeatedly in *On Liberty* of renewal and beginning. Radical utilitarianism may have had nothing to do with civic humanism and its stress on the "renovation of virtue,"[13] but Mill evidently did, and in his vocabulary of reviving/expiring, flourishing/decaying, acting/failing, we may trace some of his differences with the way of thinking that he grew up with and that in many ways he retained.

As belated as it is, Mill's republicanism also belongs to his own time. He took the part of the French republicans, and when the revolution of 1848 brought Lamartine into power in France (putting an end to the July Monarchy and its infamous corruption), he was moved to prophesy liberty for Europe, even hazarding the prediction that England itself would be "republicanised." By this he can hardly have meant that security of property and person would one day come to England, for it existed in England already; he must have meant that the English would one day abolish privilege and at last begin to concern themselves with the common good. As Mill loved France (on and off) for giving a home to those elevated sentiments that could find no place in the meanness and narrowness of English life, so in his polemic on behalf of French republicanism he wrote with all the feeling he is often thought to lack. The French republicans in their turn were animated by the memory of 1789. Mill also drew on the writing of an arch-republican who figured in the first of the great revolutions—Milton. In ways that I hadn't recognized and that he himself does not quite avow, Mill's thought is underwritten by the revolutionary tradition.

That *On Liberty* bears a strong relation to Milton's "Areopagitica" none dispute. Evidently, however, Mill thought better to play down his debt to Milton, for he nowhere acknowledges it, and I have come to think that this dynamic stands for Mill's tense relation to the republican tradition. On the one hand, Mill dreams of a polity founded not on subordination or custom but on the active virtue of citizens (a polity freestanding and autonomous); on the other hand, he is extremely wary of the dangers of republicanism, among them the danger of mobilizing people whose capacity for political virtue he trusted little. In any case, reading convinced me that Mill's relation to Milton went deeper than I had supposed, and needs to be brought to light if *On Liberty* is to be understood; in later pages—especially Chapter 2—I make some assays at determining how Mill stands to Milton. The Milton problem itself suggests how it is that Mill's republicanism has gone so largely unregarded. Political theorists and philosophers commenting on *On Liberty* are apt to ignore Mill's debts to the famous republican, which may appear to them a "merely literary" question. Literary people commenting on *On Liberty* are apt to ignore the republican tradition, as my instructors did, perhaps considering the issue "merely political." (Mill himself, a nonsectarian, put up no barbed wire between fields of discourse.) Perhaps, too, we are loath to recognize that the most celebrated exponent of "negative liberty"— liberty as noninterference—builds on the work of a man who saw the freedom to do what you like as a kind of servitude.[14]

In history, republican and liberal ideas are sometimes bound together like strands in a rope, or indeed a knot. Locke, traditionally seen as the author of liberalism, holds much in common with republicans like Milton, as Richard Ashcraft has persuasively argued.[15] We read of liberal republicanism in the nineteenth century. But at least in the abstract, republican and liberal principles are not one and the same. Milton we designate not a liberal but a republican; so too Rousseau; both enter into *On Liberty*, Rousseau by name and Milton invisibly. Again, Mill himself noted that espousing republican ideas requires caution, probably because of the insurrectionary ring of the word itself. (Certainly Mill's own republicanism was a rarified thing compared to the ideology of the barricades; still, he was broadly in sympathy with those more radical than himself, "sympathy" being important in his theory of mental culture.) But if republican principles had to be voiced cautiously, the doctrine of noninterference for which Mill is known—that we do best to mind what we know best, namely our own business—this doctrine requires no such special handling. *On Liberty* states it verbatim. It is so far from being a novel or daring proposition that Adam Smith considered the habit of concerning oneself with one's own business as a mark of prudence, and Lewis Carroll's Alice—a schoolgirl—knows that what makes the world go round is " 'everybody minding their own business!' "[16] In 1831 Mill himself observed with contempt that "nine-tenths of the men who can read or write" subscribe to the notion that "every person . . . is the best judge of what is most for his own advantage";[17] I doubt the doctrine was any less commonplace or any more ennobling when Mill made it the stated premise of *On Liberty* a quarter century later.

In politics, liberals and republicans may find themselves in disagreement, as following the 1830 revolution in France, when the young republicans admired by Mill opposed the timorous, and older, liberals. More generally we might say that liberalism can tolerate kings and republicanism can't.[18] Again, where liberalism sees progress, civility, and improved manners, republicanism may see decadence and corruption.[19] (Not given to one-eyed views, Mill sees civilization as both improving and corrupt.) Above all, a distinction can be drawn between the liberal principle respecting people's right to judge of their own interests and seek their own good, and the traditional republican principle of the superior claim of the public good, or what Mill in *On Liberty* calls "the idea of obligation to the public" (OL 256). These incongruous doctrines played happily together in the thought of Benjamin Franklin. Franklin advised people to watch over their material interests with a sort of sacred vigilance, for that was the way to get rich, at the same time that he preached (and himself possessed) public spirit, helped organize a citizen militia, and joined enthusiastically in the use of the republican vocabulary of Virtue versus Corruption. The unlikelihood of all this doesn't seem to have bothered Franklin, who for all his waggishness and wit was something of a Polonius—what no one can say of Mill. Mill had to struggle with his conflicting loyalties to liberal and republican principles, and in the end I think his struggle was unsuccessful. By crossing the language of noninterference and the language of high republicanism in *On Liberty*, Mill implies that consumers who choose as they like are somehow carrying forward a valorous tradition, a claim I find without merit. Mill's implicit argument that self-regarding acts awaken public spirit is really no less odd than William Cobbett's claim that shoemakers "show more public spirit

than any other men" because they never have to go begging for
business, that is, because they don't have to care about the public at
all.[20]

On Liberty is usually placed near the center of the liberal tradition,
and it stands as the cardinal defense of people's right to pursue their
own good in their own way. And yet in many passages throughout his
writings, Mill evidences a disapproval of private interests as well as a
belief that the morality of self-interest (say, Poor Richard's morality)
has extinguished public spirit and the courage to act. In both of these
beliefs Mill was less a liberal than a republican. Mill's republican
principles led him to interpret the French revolution of 1848 as practically a millennial event and to defend the French republicans to an
English audience. Moreover, to Mill republicanism was no mere slogan
or war-cry but a classically inspired set of values including the abolition
of privilege, service in a citizen militia, political participation (occasional and closely watched), and above all devotion to the public good.
I find that republicanism underlies *On Liberty*, which draws distantly
on the Aristotelian conception of the citizen whose nature is fully
achieved and more proximately on the republicanism of Milton; and
that Mill's republican values conflict with his own defense of the freest
possible pursuit of private happiness. In *On Liberty*, I conceive, Mill
tries but fails to contain the contradiction between a republican code
of public good, and a liberalism that would leave people to the pursuit
of their own goods; between stilted classical values and values proper
to a commercial society. Intending to revive the classical value of
"obligation to the public," Mill unwittingly gave a philosophical sanction to the values now reigning in consumer society, a society in which
the public realm itself lacks credit. My sense is that Mill got himself
into these embarrassments because he was both drawn to the tradition
of republicanism and wary of its dangers. In the end, Mill's republicanism proves as innocuous as the conventional morality he scorns. Of
three republican topics I mentioned above—citizenly duty, armed
virtue, the active life—the first is poorly integrated into the argument
of *On Liberty*, the second mentioned as an aside, the third reduced to
self-regarding acts. A protest against narrowness, *On Liberty* itself
narrows republicanism. How otherwise could that various tradition,[21]
with all its archaism and militancy, its ties both to ancient virtue and
modern radicalism—how could it be fitted into what Mill calls the "one
very simple principle" of noninterference (OL 223)? Having once

complained that in order to persuade the English "we must contract our reasoning into the most confined limits,"[22] Mill did just that in *On Liberty*: he retrenched the republican tradition.

It would be fine if we could say Mill concerned himself with private affairs in *On Liberty* and public responsibilities in *Considerations on Representative Government* (1861), and so reconciled the two. Possibly he himself mapped out his work this way. What spoils the neatness of this scheme is that in *On Liberty* itself Mill laments the loss of a sense of "obligation to the public" (OL 256), and furthermore lets us understand that the general debility he deplores is another name for the waning of public spirit. But more significant than any particular clause of *On Liberty* is the sense of the whole, and as I have said, the essay is filled with the republican sentiment that the "virtue" (strength, capacity) of Mill's fellow-citizens has expired. Both in *On Liberty* and in the later volume Mill makes carefully measured references to the kind of activity we might expect to revive those citizens—political participation. Mill didn't reconcile republicanism (which sees the citizen as "directly participant" in the life of the polity) with liberalism (which sees the citizen as dedicated first and foremost to private concerns) so much as he crossed them up, dignified the second by means of the first, and curbed the first by means of the second.[23]

Once we let go of the notion that Mill's sole intention in *On Liberty* was to secure freedom of choice, we are in a position to see that specific topics in that essay were also topics in a republican discourse dedicated less to the security of the individual than to the transformation of society through action. The legitimacy of tyrannicide and the decadence of Christianity had been asserted for all to hear by the indescribable Richard Carlile in his journal the *Republican* well before Mill mused on the killing of tyrants in a mystifying footnote, cautiously exploded Christian morality, and called Jesus a "man" (OL 235). (Among Mill's earliest publications are open letters on freedom of the press inspired by the prosecution of Carlile and his wife and sister.) Other topics of *On Liberty* as well, from the liberalization of divorce to the importance of self-realization, have analogues in republican discussion and journalism. Where one acquaintance of Mill's worked up the principles of duty and altruism into a "distinctive mystical republicanism,"[24] Mill broke with a Benthamite philosophy that couldn't conceive of altruism and was himself enough of a republican to recall us in *On Liberty* to our neglected "obligation to the public"— a point eclipsed by the rest of his argument, with its emphatic defense of a private sphere within which we are *not* obligated to the public. It seems that in one way or another—by guarded language or passing references or unrecorded debts—Mill keeps the banner of republicanism from quite coming into sight in *On Liberty*. When he argues, albeit in a kind of parenthesis, that people need to learn to "guide their conduct by aims which unite instead of isolating them from one another" (OL 305), he does voice one of the animating principles of working-class republicanism: that political transformation is to be brought about by acting in common cause, and not, for example, by leaving matters to an administrative state or a political engineer (such as Bentham fancied himself to be). And yet, characteristically, while Mill maintains that learning to act for public ends is vital to liberty, *On Liberty* says next to nothing about it. Prudence, indeed, characterizes Mill's handling not only of the fighting words of radical republicanism but even of the more classical republican values he himself preferred. If the spirit of self-interest makes us (as Mill says) "slavish," then surely an essay on liberty ought to lay some stress on the sort of political participation that (as Mill believes) frees us from that sorry state. (Ought to, unless words like "slavish" are considered as mere "poetry." But Mill learned to respect poetry.) In point of fact, not only is *On Liberty* virtually mute on this point, but it presents itself as a defense of the pursuit of an exclusively private happiness. Even though Mill despises the meanness of soul bred by a way of life that "fasten[s] [one's] attention and interest exclusively upon"[25] oneself—even though *On Liberty* itself springs from Mill's contempt for all such littleness—he makes his stand on self-regarding, or exclusively private, acts. So it is that Mill's complex response to the republican tradition, the tradition concerned with our capacity to advance the general good, is recorded in *On Liberty*.

Where before Mill's prose had seemed lifeless to me, I now see it as the prose of a man of strong feeling who deplored the sacrifice of the more heroic virtues to the morality of self-interest, who sometimes used Miltonic idioms himself, but who generally practiced what he calls in *On Liberty* a "studied moderation of language" (OL 259). Where before I was amazed at Mill's prescience, I now perceive that he looked backward as well: in the spirit of those republicans who returned in imagination to classical antiquity, Mill was mounting the steps of the Capitol in Rome when he conceived the idea of writing a volume on liberty. Where before I was stirred by his argument securing the private realm against the encroachments of government and society, I now perceive that Mill defused the language of republicanism and argued at some cost to his own more public-spirited principles—for he was also concerned to draw people out of the smallness of their private interests, by which means alone he thought we could achieve the full measure of our being. I find that Mill was scarcely better able to reconcile the claims of private interest and public responsibility than we ourselves, who possess at best a dim memory of the republican tradition.

In one sense, Mill's argument for liberty has been claimed by consumer society. In a different sense, the claimants to *On Liberty* are the brilliant eccentric and the sexual dissenter, whose loyalty is not to the public (which is liable to be hostile) but to their fellows and friends. The ethical style of private loyalty is set out in E. M. Forster's "What I Believe," an essay so clearly and consciously in the line of John Stuart Mill that it could be placed side-by-side with *On Liberty*. Free speech; tolerance of diversity; an allegiance to democracy on the one hand and a nonhereditary "aristocracy" on the other; a discountenancing of hero-worship—many of Forster's positions directly match Mill's. And yet the retreat into "personal relationships" that is defended in this essay—the repudiation of any obligation to the public—marks a definitive break with the republican ideal of public spirit that still animated Mill. Writes Forster:

> Personal relations are despised today. They are regarded as bourgeois luxuries, as products of a time of fair weather which is now past, and we are urged to get rid of them, and to dedicate ourselves to some movement or cause instead. I hate the idea of causes, and if I had to choose between betraying my country and betraying my friend, I hope I should have the guts to betray my country.[26]

This in 1939, with Hitler in full view. At such a time the author can talk complacently of betraying his country. But the same honesty that compels us to reject altogether a line of thinking that would condone betraying England to Hitler or Stalin also compels us to recognize that the retreat from the political, the seclusion of the individual within the private sphere, has already begun in *On Liberty*; that is perhaps why Forster can place himself in the tradition of Mill at all. In *On Liberty* it is as though the politically charged values of republicanism were being transposed into exclusively private terms.

I think Mill's belief that there really exists a public good above private interests spared him the more radical implications of the consumer model of liberty that he uses in chapter 4 of *On Liberty*. Consumer society (a society infatuated with personal relationships, let it be said) likes to picture just about all decisions as open choices;

under such a doctrine, how are we to avoid the linguistic dead-end of
"My choice is right because I made it—right for me"? In truth, the
word "choice" *has* come to connote an act incapable of rational
defense, an act at once inarguable, arbitrary, and final. As consumers,
too, we choose without any sense that in so doing we are responsible
to the public. In an argument drawing on the liberal principle of
respecting the otherness of others, Samuel Gorovitz profiles for us the
life of responsibility-free choice. Reflecting on the difficulty of remem-
bering the reasons for our choices, he asks us to review the choices
that have made our lives what they are. Think

> why you chose the career you did, or the spouse you have, let alone the
> car you drive or the neighborhood you live in, and you will be reminded
> of the difficulty of being able, after the fact, to give a clear account of the
> reasons that led to decisions that constitute a major influence on the
> course of our lives.[27]

Perhaps unintentionally, Gorovitz has sketched out the sort of life
constantly celebrated for us in the mass media, the life of a middle-
class consumer. Let me suggest that the consumer model stifles ethical
inquiry and deters us from connecting the indefensibility of choices to
the isolation of individuals; from exploring the implications of politics
as a form of consumption; and from questioning consumerism itself as
a fitting model for a human life. While Mill framed the classic argument
for free choice, and while parts of that argument do look forward to
consumerism, he could not discard the concept of the individual as
responsible to others and as acting with others as a political being. In
essential respects, too, Mill's concept of choice was not our own. It is
clear, for example, that he never considered choice as lying outside
the jurisdiction of rational argument. He believed it can be shown (not
mathematically but discursively) that there are better and poorer
choices, one main difference between them being that a choice that
promotes the public good is better than a choice that disserves it. A
vote honestly cast is better than a bought vote, Mill judged, and a vote
arising out of impartial reflection is better than a vote arising out of
private interest. As skeptics, we naturally want Mill to tell us what is
to stop people from voting their interest and claiming they did so after
impartial reflection, and what entitles someone, anyway, to the claim
of being impartial. These are good questions. Mill might have retorted
that appealing to the private interest of voters is simply bribery, the
worse for being public. Some say Reagan clinched the 1980 election

when in a "debate" with Carter he asked voters whether they were better off than they had been in 1976, that is, whether they had more purchasing power. Reagan asked us to consult our private interest— "the bottom line," as it is said.

Most seem to agree that our public discourse these days is simply a sham. But what else could it be if we possess not even the concept of discourse (choices being inarguable, like points of taste), nor yet the concept of a public realm in which we ourselves act? Finally what I admire in Mill is that he never calls on us to "consume" what he has to say—that is, to accept it passively—just as he can't really bring himself to abandon once and for all the conception of humans as acting beings. Perhaps just because of his conflicts and struggles, Mill gives us an example of political argumentation worthy of a human being. He does not try to induce primitive responses and never gives in to the fallacious notion that about disputed questions nothing can rationally be said. In Mill's view, far from marking the end of rationality, disputed questions seem to call for the highest rationality of all. His own fell short, but how could it not?

ACKNOWLEDGMENTS

Finally some words of thanks. To my colleagues Gerry Brenner, Robert Johnstone, and Doug Purl I owe thanks for the gift of intellectual companionship. Gerry in particular I thank for the example of his moral courage; Bob (my Milton tutor) for embodying the spirit of learning; Doug for his intolerance of cant and his keen editorial eye. I thank the Interlibrary Loan Office of the University of Montana Library, without whose help, so cheerfully tendered, I would have been unable to complete my task. Sigyn Minier came to the aid of my French. The Philosophy Forum of the University of Montana gave me the chance to present a germinal version of my thinking about Mill. I benefited from the meticulous workmanship of Pat Merrill, my copy editor. Thanks are due also to the Rockefeller Foundation for a fellowship some ten years ago that started me on my way, mapless and stumbling, to this manuscript. And to my wife—the ideal reader—and my children I owe thanks beyond words, not only for tolerating but for teaching me.

NOTES

1. I take Mill to have been the author of *On Liberty*, even though he credited this work in large part to Harriet Taylor Mill. I do not intend this judgment as a slight of women.

2. Robert N. Bellah, Richard Madsen, William M. Sullivan, Ann Swidler, and Steven M. Tipton, *Habits of the Heart: Individualism and Commitment in American Life* (Berkeley: University of California Press, 1985).

3. J. G. A. Pocock, *Virtue, Commerce, and History: Essays on Political Thought and History, Chiefly in the Eighteenth Century* (Cambridge, U.K.: Cambridge University Press, 1985), p. 122.

4. Donald Winch, *Adam Smith's Politics: An Essay in Historiographic Revision* (Cambridge, U.K.: Cambridge University Press, 1978), p. 30.

5. While not without metaphor, *On Liberty* does more or less lack the verbal equivalents of banners, cockades, emblems, the insignia of political association. On the role of political symbolism, see James Epstein, "Understanding the Cap of Liberty: Symbolic Practice and Social Conflict in Early Nineteenth-Century England," *Past and Present* 122 (1989), 75–118.

6. Bernard Semmel, *John Stuart Mill and the Pursuit of Virtue* (New Haven, Conn.: Yale University Press, 1984), p. 110.

7. See Judith N. Shklar, *Men & Citizens: A Study of Rousseau's Social Theory* (Cambridge, U.K.: Cambridge University Press, 1985), p. 15.

8. Sebastian de Grazia, *Machiavelli in Hell* (Princeton, N.J.: Princeton University Press, 1989), p. 291.

9. Cited in Douglas G. Long, *Bentham on Liberty: Jeremy Bentham's Idea of Liberty in Relation to His Utilitarianism* (Toronto: University of Toronto Press, 1977), p. 174.

10. Adam Smith, *The Theory of Moral Sentiments*, ed. D. D. Raphael and A. L. Macfie (Indianapolis: Liberty Classics, 1982), p. 61.

11. See G. J. Barker-Benfield, "Mary Wollstonecraft: Eighteenth-Century Commonwealthwoman," *Journal of the History of Ideas* 50 (1989), 95–115.

12. On this point see Joseph Hamburger, *Intellectuals in Politics: John Stuart Mill and the Philosophic Radicals* (New Haven, Conn.: Yale University Press, 1965), pp. 40, 42, 57.

13. J. G. A. Pocock, *The Machiavellian Moment: Florentine Political Thought and the Atlantic Republican Tradition* (Princeton, N.J.: Princeton University Press, 1975), pp. 547–48.

14. On this point, see Stanley Fish, *Surprised by Sin: The Reader in Paradise Lost* (London: Macmillan, 1967), p. 337.

15. Richard Ashcraft, *Revolutionary Politics and Locke's Two Treatises of Government* (Princeton, N.J.: Princeton University Press, 1986), p. 212n. For the opposite view—that Locke was nothing of a republican—see Pocock, *Machiavellian Moment*, pp. 424, 436.

16. Lewis Carroll, *Alice in Wonderland*, ed. Donald J. Gray (New York: Norton, 1971), p. 70.

17. See volume XXII, p. 320, of the University of Toronto edition of Mill's *Collected Works*. All of my references to Mill are taken from his *Collected Works*, abbreviated CW. In the case of *On Liberty*, I use "OL" rather than the number of the volume (XVIII) in which the essay appears; thus "OL 254"

means "page 254 of volume XVIII of Mill's *Collected Works*." This is awkward, but *On Liberty* is so well known that readers shouldn't have trouble looking up quoted material, even in another edition.

18. Not an absolute distinction. Mill himself once spoke of republican institutions with a hereditary chief. See CW XXII, lxii along with footnote; CW XXIII, 530.

19. In the opinion of Pocock, this antithesis is of determining importance in British political discourse in the eighteenth century. See *Virtue, Commerce, and History*, p. 231.

20. William Cobbett, *Advice to Young Men* (London: Routledge, 1892), p. 264.

21. On the difference between "classical" and "Jeffersonian" (or "liberal") styles of republicanism, see Joyce Appleby, *Capitalism and a New Social Order: The Republican Vision of the 1790s* (New York: New York University Press, 1984), e.g., p. 14. If Appleby is right in saying that the new republicans in America "placed the personal ahead of the political" (p. 96), then there is a precedent within the history of republicanism itself for the privatization of action that is seen in *On Liberty*. But this needs qualification, for the new republicans created robust forms of political association well beyond the closely measured, and closely watched, political participation that Mill allows.

22. See CW XXIII, 446.

23. "Directly participant": Pocock, *Machiavellian Moment*, p. 523. On the shift from classical republicanism to liberalism in America, see a critic of Pocock: Joyce Appleby, "Republicanism in Old and New Contexts," *William and Mary Quarterly* 3rd ser., 43 (1986), 20–34. On Jefferson's ideal of citizen participation, see Bellah et al., *Habits of the Heart*, pp. 30–31.

24. F. B. Smith, *Radical Artisan: William James Linton, 1812–97* (Manchester, U.K.: Manchester University Press, 1973), p. 30. Like Mill, Linton was connected to the circle of W. J. Fox, noted Unitarian.

25. The source is Mill's "De Tocqueville on Democracy in America [II]," in CW XVIII, 169. The same passage describes the commercial spirit as "slavish," among other things.

26. E. M. Forster, *Two Cheers for Democracy* (New York: Harcourt, Brace, 1951), p. 68. Forster's sense of living in the last hours of the liberal era was shared by George Orwell, who defended such values as personal decency without renouncing his citizenship.

27. Samuel Gorovitz, *Doctors' Dilemmas: Moral Conflict and Medical Care* (New York: Oxford University Press, 1982), p. 47.

1

Mill and Republicanism

IN NONE OF his writings, perhaps, does John Stuart Mill impress us more favorably than in his companion-essays on Bentham (1838) and Coleridge (1840). Mill honors each of these mighty opposites without sacrificing his critical judgment to either. He writes with grace and civility and no trace of party spirit. Bentham, the patron of James Mill and a sort of intellectual godfather to Mill himself, is praised as the great demystifier of established doctrine and the scourge of corrupt institutions. By the same token, he is criticized for his prejudice against the past. Bentham disregarded historical experience and other minds, Mill tells us; he was a man of one dimension whose conceptions, too, lack depth. Coleridge is presented by Mill as the corrective to Bentham—a man who viewed people not as units but as members of a historical community, and who looked to a cultural establishment to define and conserve the values of the community. Coleridge is faulted, however, for being too much given to transcendent notions and for writing on political economy "like an arrant driveller" (CW X, 155; see the Introduction of this book, note 17). Mill leans a little to Coleridge in this adjudication, but even so he appears to be fairness itself. He seems to have freed himself from the limitations of each of the parties' perspectives and, in so doing, to have found his intellectual independence. So masterfully executed are the essays on Bentham and Coleridge that a reader may conclude Mill has actually reconciled these philosophical opponents, and this in a way they themselves would probably not have been able to achieve. A reader is meant to have this impression.

In "Coleridge" Mill presents the idea that partial truths can be stitched into a whole truth comprehending the parts, like political positions that are mutually correcting if the debaters but knew it. Actually this doctrine itself isn't neutral with respect to Bentham and Coleridge, but comes from Coleridge, as Mill duly reports. Mill took it over and made it his, and nearly 20 years later, in his essay *On Liberty* (1859), he still asserts that

> Truth, in the great practical concerns of life, is so much a question of the reconciling and combining of opposites, that very few have minds suffi-ciently capacious and impartial to make the adjustment with an approach to correctness, and it has to be made by the rough process of a struggle between combatants fighting under hostile banners. (OL 254)

The sheer duration of this doctrine of complementarity in Mill's thought suggests it is one of his deepest beliefs. I want to contend that fundamental conflicts can't really be solved as Mill says, and more particularly that Mill's own thought manifests conflicting attitudes toward private interests—approval on the one hand, censure on the other. To establish that this *is* a conflict and not just a seeming conflict, however, it seems necessary to call into question Mill's notion that discordant "truths" can be made to agree by adding part of one to part of the other (or could be made to agree if not for our narrow-mindedness). Perhaps the best way to do this is to call into doubt his reconciliation of Bentham and Coleridge.

"In every respect," Mill writes, Bentham and Coleridge are "each other's 'completing counterpart': the strong points of each correspond to the weak points of the other" (CW X, 121). In every respect? Is this not a little too good to be true? We know that Mill came to reject sectarianism (having been brought up in the sect of Bentham); here, though, his determination to see both sides leads him to fashion a perfect philosophical fit, a coincidence as dubious as a happy ending. It also leads Mill to assume the congruence of different scientific world-views, a point strongly contested in our own day by the historian of science Thomas Kuhn. In "Coleridge" Mill argues that "ideas which seemed mutually incompatible, have been found only to require mutual limitations"; not to profit from opposition views is

> an error much the same as if Kepler had refused to profit by Ptolemy's or Tycho's observations, because those astronomers believed that the sun

moved round the earth; or as if Priestley and Lavoisier, because they differed on the doctrine of phlogiston, had rejected each other's chemical experiments. (CW X, 122)

As it happens, Kuhn opens *The Structure of Scientific Revolutions* by arguing that competing scientific theories represent "incommensurable ways of seeing the world"; that the great revolutions of modern science have each overthrown "one time-honored scientific theory in favor of another incompatible with it"; and that scientific knowledge doesn't grow in an additive way as by the laying-on of one brick after another to make a house (the sort of fitting of truth to truth Mill often speaks of).[1] Instead of embracing the view that Bentham and Coleridge fit together just so, like puzzle pieces (or like poison and antidote), we would do better to call their visions incompatible. Mill's statement that only a few know how to equilibrate conflicting "truths" isn't a reliable philosophical maxim, but an act of self-advertisement: without question, he numbered himself among the few capacious and impartial minds. I am skeptical of Mill's doctrine of fractional "truths" just as I doubt the ranting Carlyle when he argues that

in all human convictions, much more in all human practices, there [is] a true side, a fraction of truth; which fraction is precisely the thing we want to extract from them, if we want anything at all to do with them.[2]

The difference between Coleridge's and Bentham's ways of seeing can be gauged by the radically different uses to which they put optical imagery itself. In a passage cited by Mill, Coleridge describes a clerisy or learned class standing watch over the culture of the nation, superintending the whole of national life:

A certain smaller number [are] to remain at the fountain-heads of the humanities, in cultivating and enlarging the knowledge already possessed, and in watching over the interests of physical and moral science; being likewise the instructors of such as . . . constitute, the remaining more numerous classes of the order. The members of this latter and far more numerous body [are] to be distributed throughout the country, so as not to leave even the smallest integral part or division without a resident guide, guardian, and instructor. (CW X, 147)

For his part, Bentham's darling project was the Panopticon, a facility so constructed that an inspector could keep all inmates in view from a central vantage point. In *On Liberty*, when Mill alleges that everyone in Victorian England "lives as under the eye of a hostile and dreaded censorship" (OL 264), he envisions society as a great Panopticon. He protests the suffocation of action. (Bentham wanted schools, prisons, factories built on the Panopticon principle.[3] Why not society itself?) By contrast, at the very end of *On Liberty*, Mill recommends the creation of a superintending body with a "comprehensive sphere of observation" over all localities, rather on the model of Coleridge's clerisy, its function being to "watch . . . over" the execution of the laws, spread knowledge, and advise local governments in their political experiments (OL 309). But the supervisory authority that Mill contemplates also happens to be modeled on the Poor Law Board set up on Benthamite principles in the 1830s to keep watch over local officers— the Poor Law itself being a repellent "measure of social police."[4] In this whirl of imagery, this confusion of censors who paralyze and overseers who empower, inspectors who spy and advisers who aid, Mill hasn't so much reconciled anything as he has written his conflicts into the text itself. If the essays on Bentham and Coleridge purport to show that ideological differences can be made to vanish, that purpose wasn't achieved. In the thought of Coleridge, indeed, the reconciliation of opposites serves as "the root-principle of his cosmogony, his epistemology, and his theory of poetic creation alike";[5] but in borrowing this article of Coleridgean doctrine, Mill has, it seems to me, abstracted it from the context where it has its meaning. In its context— in *On the Constitution of the Church and State*, for example, the very work Mill quotes from in "Coleridge"—the reconciliation principle gives the Christian Church the character of "the appointed Opposite" to the kingdom of this world, "*sustaining, correcting, befriending*" the latter.[6] Mill carries over the principle of reconciliation but not the divine appointer without whom such a happy disposition of things wouldn't be possible.

I have thought it necessary to dispute Mill's notion of the consonance of conflicting truths because I mean to argue that he himself is committed to values that can't be reconciled. "Values may easily clash within the breast of a single individual."[7] Mill founds *On Liberty* on the principle that we are each the best judge of our own interests—that no one knows better than we what makes for our well-being; yet he holds in contempt the Victorian who decides that well-being lies in conformity. He defends the legitimacy of private interests and of peaceably looking after them; yet he would have us *dis*interestedly serve the public good, an idea rooted in a republican tradition not so peaceable and distinctly more activist in its conception of virtue. And evidently Mill believed republican values were scanted in Victorian England, for immediately after his discussion in *On Liberty* of the art of balancing conflicting truths, he offers a defense of the republican principle and the active life, as correctives for reigning Victorian values. Because this passage is vital to my argument, indeed because it is the nub of *Mill's* argument with society, I quote it here at some length.

> Christian morality (so called) has all the characters of a reaction; it is, in great part, a protest against Paganism. Its ideal is negative rather than positive; passive rather than active; Innocence rather than Nobleness; Abstinence from Evil, rather than energetic Pursuit of Good: in its precepts (as has been well said) "thou shalt not" predominates unduly over "thou shalt." In its horror of sensuality, it made an idol of asceticism, which has gradually been compromised away into one of legality. It holds out the hope of heaven and the threat of hell, as the appointed and appropriate motives to a virtuous life: in this falling far below the best of the ancients, and doing what lies in it to give to human morality an essentially selfish character, by disconnecting each man's feelings of duty from the interests of his fellow-creatures, except so far as a self-interested inducement is offered to him for consulting them. It is essentially a doctrine of passive obedience. . . . What little recognition the idea of obligation to the public obtains in modern morality, is derived from Greek and Roman sources, not from Christian. (OL 255–56)

This, as I say, is the essence of Mill's accusation in *On Liberty*. The pith of his argument with society is contained in this critique of Christians who no longer bear themselves erect. Quite openly, Mill declares his differences with a Christian morality that makes supine beings of us and conditions us to think in mean "self-interested" terms; a morality that produces what he once called a "morbid feebleness of conscience" (CW XXIV, 866).[8] Apparently Mill feared that, with the energy of the supposedly dynamic middle class restricted to selfish pursuits like money-making, the capacities of bourgeois men and women were depleted, leaving them weakened, without the ability to contribute to the public weal. Mill's condemnatory use of "self-interested" in the passage just cited is the more noteworthy in that *On Liberty* both follows from Adam Smith's defense of self-interest and rests on every individual's interest in his or her own happiness. The author's attachment to the morality of self-interest did not, it seems, keep him from endorsing a more active ideal of citizenship at just that point in his argument when the moment came to state his case—to assert the values his countrymen most needed to recover.

Mill defends private interests, then, at the same time that he protests the morality of self-interest in the name of a high-minded republicanism. He believes individuals must be free to achieve their own happiness and that the public good is nothing but the happinesses of the people making up the public; yet he believes individuals should be citizen-soldiers able to subordinate their own good to the common weal and exercise such non-hedonistic virtues as fortitude. In one respect, we can satisfy Mill simply by leaving others alone—by doing nothing but keeping to our own affairs; in another respect, we can satisfy Mill only by actively exercising our abilities as civic beings. Mill read Tocqueville's *Democracy in America* as a study not so much of a democratic as of a commercial revolution—a revolution enshrining the morality of private interests—and for this reason, as well as because *Democracy in America* deeply influenced *On Liberty*, it may be fitting to pause for a moment on that great work. But note first that Tocqueville doesn't find that the small virtues hallowed by the new order agree in some essential way with the ancestral values of aristocracy. Although he reconciles himself as a nobleman to the displacement of aristocratic by democratic principles, Tocqueville doesn't reconcile the principles themselves; he deems them to be incommensurable. So radically different are the democratic and aristocratic orders that "they cannot be submitted to a just or fair comparison."[9]

Tocqueville anatomizes a social revolution of great depth and scope. It has set in motion the transformation of classes into masses; and for the permanent bonds and brilliant displays of the aristocratic order, it has substituted impermanence and a considerably narrower emotional regimen. It has dignified self-interest, small virtues, mild manners, and strict habits—in all, a discipline suitable to a nation given to commerce and the ownership of small property. At the same time, this revolution has created the risk of a society of "enfeebled" individuals, between whom and the supreme power of the state nothing is left standing. In Tocqueville's dystopia, the citizenry is "reduced to nothing better than a flock of timid and industrious animals, of which the government is the shepherd."[10] Readers of *On Liberty* recognize in that text the same fears of mass conformity and the atrophy of action. But where Tocqueville looks back a little romantically to the aristocratic values of his forebears, Mill looks back to the values of an antique republicanism—to the tradition that finds inspiration in the classical past and understands virtue not as devotion to private interests, but as active commitment to the public good. The republics of antiquity present a vista of greatness, inspire "high conceptions of the capabilities of human nature" (CW XVIII, 195), free the mind from the meanness of the present commercial age; by the same token, the noblest of the modern republicans, men like Armand Carrel, remind us that "a hero of Plutarch may exist amidst all the pettiness of modern civilization" (CW XX, 215). Not that Mill didn't welcome the moderation of manners and the regimen of small virtues—in a word, modern civilization. He did. In his essay on "Coleridge," for example, he takes note of "the softening of manners; the decline of war and personal conflict; the progressive limitation of the tyranny of the strong over the weak" (CW X, 123). Whenever Mill spoke of "improvement" he had such changes as these in view, and indeed he forecast the improvement of mankind.[11] Mill is not a cheering writer, though. In his most enduring work he impresses on our minds not the prospect of human improvement, but the risk of enervation and enslavement—the risk of a loss of what may best be called *virtù* in token of its active character and its kinship with the republican tradition that draws on Machiavelli. A dramatic example of virtù would be tyrannicide, which Mill refers to as "an act of exalted virtue" in a circumspect footnote to the text of *On Liberty* (OL 228n). Milton defended tyrannicide, as republicans before him defended Brutus.[12] In the very work that sets forth the idea of the clerisy, Coleridge himself contrasts the small, mean conceptions of the present with the great conceptions of the heroic republicans of the seventeenth century, including Milton, Harrington, and Algernon Sidney.

I mean to say that Mill possesses two understandings of virtue. He sees virtue as strict moral habits that regulate the pursuit of private interests—such habits as foresight and self-restraint. According to Tocqueville, lesser virtues like these make up the morality of self-interest.[13] But Mill also sees virtue, in accordance with the republican tradition, as active and civic in nature: active, if only in the sense of requiring more than the regular fulfillment of existing routines; civic, in the sense of requiring the subordination of private to public good. His two concepts of virtue differ roughly as the humble virtue of thrift differs from the exalted virtue of courage. Mill might have been happy if the many were virtuous in the humble sense (dutifully attended to their own business) and left virtue in the more hazardous sense of public enterprise to the few. But the many didn't press for political enfranchisement just so that they would be able to defer to a few all over again; nor, in any case, is a rigid distinction between the few and the many consistent with Mill's expressed hatred of the idea of a caste ruling over a society that stands still.[14]

Of course, Mill would say his two concepts of virtue are compatible and mutually correcting. I think they aren't, and it seems to me a fact worth noting that the author of the central text of the liberal tradition was distinctly of two minds about the first principle of that tradition, the legitimacy of private interests.[15] Indeed, *On Liberty* fleetingly advocates training (Mill says "habituating") citizens to subordinate their interest to the common good (OL 305)—a sort of political conditioning a long way from doing as you like.[16] *On Liberty* refers to republicanism under the ashen name of "the idea of obligation to the public" (OL 256); never does Mill explain how the code of obligation to the public can be squared with the freest possible pursuit of one's own good. If the word "obligation" *means* obligation, then these values must conflict. (I don't think that Mill means we are under a general obligation to perform acts of charity, with the details to be filled in as we please. In the very passage where he reminds us of our obligation to the public, he assails Christian morality. Mill was not for moral softness. He thought charity corrupts—reduces to dependence. Besides, enough charity was practiced in Victorian England that people didn't need to be scolded by Mill into performing it.) In all, Mill does what he can to smooth the contradiction between the pursuit of private happiness and dedication to the common good, with the result that the essay stands as a charter of consumer values in many ways the reverse of the values Mill most esteemed and thought it most needful to revive.

A certain scholasticism marks some of the literature on Mill, especially the argument over the clarity of his distinctions. To me it seems that *On Liberty* is a richer and fuller text for a certain lack of clarity. Richard E. Flathman warns us against confusing "freedom with abilities, capacities, powers, and the like,"[17] but Mill did just this—it is this "mistake" that gives *On Liberty* depth and force. As his rhetoric of incapacitation shows, Mill did in fact concern himself with the withering of abilities, capacities, and powers (or, for short, *virtù*, a term rooted in the republican tradition), and not just with infringements on liberty narrowly defined. If Mill had defined liberty narrowly, he never would have used such locutions as "slaves of habit and routine" (CW XVIII, 170), for such slaves are, after all, legally free. Not opportunity but capacity, not formal liberty but the spirit of liberty—the determination to put liberty into effect—is what Victorians lack. They are not up to their own freedom. If personal virtue (or virtù) is "the spirit that animates a republican social structure,"[18] *On Liberty* depicts inanimate people, more like machines than living beings, deficient in public spirit, owners of no powers that could supply a republic with its principle of action. My sense, then, is that the author of the most renowned defense of what is called negative liberty (liberty as noninterference) doesn't employ that concept alone, but enriches and complicates his argument by drawing continually on the tradition of republicanism. He reminds us that freedom is as much a spirit, say the spirit of struggle, as it is a set of constitutional provisions. In the course of *On Liberty*, Mill labors, it seems, to transform the republican ideal of valor into something innocuous by comparison—namely, the pursuit of an exclusively private happiness. He himself takes liberties with the republican principle.

In an article entering the debate on negative liberty, Quentin Skinner notes that many, including Isaiah Berlin, hold it to be "a dangerous error to connect individual liberty with the ideals of virtue and public service"[19]—dangerous because liberty properly so called simply means absence of coercion or restraint, and to obscure this fact distorts political discourse. To this argument Skinner replies that, as a matter of historical fact, Machiavelli forged a connection between virtue and individual liberty. Machiavelli's view, ably explained by Skinner, is that only the virtuous are capable of maintaining their liberty. And this becomes the thesis of republicanism. *On Liberty* too undertakes to connect individual liberty and "the idea of obligation to the public"—to make one "truth" of two—although the argument shows the strain of conflicting values. *On Liberty* isn't supposed to have anything to do with republican principles like citizenly duty and public spirit; it simply does.[20] For John Stuart Mill, author of what is judged the cardinal defense of individual liberty, himself subscribed to republican ideals, risky as they were. Any number of the themes and topics of *On Liberty* figure also in the republican journalism of William James Linton, Mill's contemporary; an unoriginal thinker, Linton seems to have found no difficulty in melding individual liberty and those principles of altruism and duty that give his vision its millennial cast.[21] But Mill too could express something like millennial hopes. In February 1848 he wrote breathlessly that if only "a reasonable republican government" were established in France, "all the rest of Europe, except England and Russia, will be republicanised in ten years, and England itself probably before we die. There was never a time when so great a drama was being played out in one generation" (CW XIII, 732). Such expressions of republican sentiment are standing disproofs of the notion that Mill didn't possess feeling. He felt that devout hatred of tyranny and all that sanctions it, which animated many a modern republican. His republicanism was emotionally charged; it was also intellectually elaborated.

For Mill was not a sloganeer. To him republicanism was no mere battlecry, no codeword signifying democracy and death to kings, but a classically inspired set of values including the abolition of hereditary privilege, the practice of representative government, equality before the law, popular sovereignty in a secular state, freedom of speech and conscience, service in a citizen militia, (limited) political participation, voluntary deference to those of superior virtue and ability, an end to the perversion of public office for private gain, but above all conscious dedication to the public good. This last requirement—that the public good be sought consciously—has particular force, for it cannot be met by Adam Smith's economic man, who promotes the public good without ever intending to, merely by heeding his private interest. While defending the pursuit of one's own good in one's own way, Mill doesn't think much of human beings who see no farther than their own interest and intend nothing more than their own happiness. He would prefer us to promote the public good intentionally, acting with eyes open, rather than leaving it to an Invisible Hand to promote it for us as we busy ourselves with other things. Ideally, we ought to be capable of stepping out of the morality of self-interest and committing ourselves to the venture of republicanism.

And unlike Coleridge's "early republican ardours,"[22] which were quenched, Mill's republican passion endured.[23] The fact is that from an early age Mill was inspired by classical examples, that he rebelled (part-way) against the dogma of self-interest in which he had been schooled, that he spoke of the meanness of self-interest, that in his *Considerations on Representative Government* (1861) he elevates public over private interest, and that his writings resonate with Milton's in countless ways—not, assuredly, because the two shared religious views but because both were committed to the republican principle that only those active in virtue "are capable of assuring their own freedom."[24] If Mill defended the claim of individuals to achieve their own goods in their own ways—defended it more ably and memorably than anyone else—he was also intensely critical of private interests, the term "interest" itself often carrying a negative valence in his writings. What is the constriction of the spirit *On Liberty* complains of, what if not the regimen of self-interest? As Mill remarks in his review of the second volume of *Democracy in America*, the habit of going after an exclusively private happiness makes us "mean and slavish" (CW XVIII, 169). But what specific does *On Liberty* offer for this malady? For one thing, the cultivation of public spirit. But as will be seen, Mill makes this recommendation in a sort of parenthesis, and it has never really caught the eye of readers; chiefly, Mill builds a high wall around the private sphere, thus deepening the very estrangement of the individual "from his fellow-citizens" (169) that troubled him to begin with. Mill would have us act like citizens in a republic: that, I think, is the subtext of *On Liberty*. His more audible message sounds, and is, different.

To Rousseau, the bourgeois was that man who has no will to subordinate his own interest to public duty—"who, when dealing with others, thinks only of himself, and on the other hand, in his understanding of himself, thinks only of others."[25] Clearly, Mill detests this half-man, given over at once to the opinions of others and to selfish motives; this figure of pettiness, preening in front of the mirror of society. Where the great caricaturist Daumier ridicules the bourgeois— Joseph Prudhomme, a personage of "satisfied nullity and authoritative banality"[26]—Mill holds up to scorn the dullness of the conforming Victorian. (Daumier began the Joseph Prudhomme series in 1859, the year of the publication of *On Liberty*.) But while Mill possesses an idiom of disfigurement (terms like "dwarfed" and "clipped" [OL 265]) that uses the tactics of caricature, he never achieves the scurrility of Daumier, a militant republican. Clearly, too, Mill works within the bourgeois language-world itself, founding the argument of *On Liberty* on the validity of personal interests and shaping the bourgeois precept of minding your own business into a philosophical defense of noninterference. If "the bourgeois comes into being when men no longer believe that there is a common good,"[27] Mill labors within the bourgeois language-world to reclaim the concept of a common good. He tells people outright to mind their own business (OL 286), but denies "that human beings have no business with each other's conduct in life, and that they should not concern themselves about the well-doing or well-being of one another, unless their own interest is involved" (OL 276–77). He strenuously defends the pursuit of private happiness while drawing on the republican ideal of citizens who realize themselves in commitment to the public good. He invokes the memory of an earlier and more heroic phase of the middle class, when it was able to challenge authority and tradition and institute ways of being that have since become "merely traditional" (OL 267) themselves.

If Mill has discrepant understandings of virtue—one as a steady attention to one's own affairs and one as the vigorous pursuit of the public good—what distinguishes him from any other middle-class theorist who got into contradictions by representing the particular (the "private") good of his class as the good of all? One answer would be that, unlike a hired agent of the middle class, Mill trained on that class some of his most hostile criticism—for example, *On Liberty*. That is, Mill directed against his own class something like the accusation it leveled against the aristocracy. Always conscientious in his choice of words, Mill was incapable of using terms like "the public good" as a mere rallying cry, and he knew well enough that status-seeking and civic valor aren't the same thing. Benjamin Franklin indeed held two conflicting understandings of virtue without apparent intellectual discomfort—he could extol the saving of pennies and the study of private advantage one moment, and public spirit the next—but his was a facile mind, a mind too on more cordial terms with commonplace than Mill's ever could be. Further, I disagree that talk of the public good was nothing but a veil for the interests of the middle class. Franklin for his part is known for genuine public spirit. Today, in consumer society, the public realm has indeed been left without standing or validity—a theater of fictions. Looking into Mill's *On Liberty* in a spirit of inquiry may help to explain, in some small way, how this has come about.

AT THE TIME Tocqueville was touring America, the ideals of the Founding Fathers had already receded into the past, and with them the model of "an elite leadership and passive citizenry."[28] For his part, John Stuart Mill, while an unashamed elitist, cannot condemn the many to the sleep of passivity; he would prefer to see them tutored into political awareness. In a flourishing society the citizenry would learn from an elite possessed of republican virtue—possessed, that is, of a blend of public spirit, moral courage, clear sight, and superiority to vulgar prejudices. But Mill gives no credible account of how this education is to take place; the prescriptions he offers in *On Liberty* tend rather to confirm us in our dedication to private pursuits than to enliven our sense of an "obligation to the public" (OL 256). While Mill's republican principles are faintly inked in *On Liberty*, his defense of the pursuit of private happiness is written in boldface. "Private good" eclipses "public good." One reason Mill found himself in such an awkward polemical position is that he was committed both to classical ideals and to the revolution that antiquated them once and for all. His attitude toward the admission of the middle and lower classes into political power was something like Tocqueville's. Both sought to fortify society against the risks created by the democratic revolution, in what they took to be the interests of that revolution itself. Moreover, the small, "democratic" virtues Tocqueville observed in America—foresight, self-restraint, strict habits—furnished Mill with much of his moral vocabulary. I consider then that Mill tried to reconcile classical conceptions and contemporary realities; republican virtue (virtù) and virtues antiheroic and nonpolitical; disinterest and private pursuits. Tried and failed. I see Mill not as a mind with a single intention, not as the author of ideas logically at one, but as a man subject to "confused and clashing intentions," as Gordon Wood has said of the Founding Fathers,[29] and unable to reconcile what he misleadingly called partial truths. While Mill deplores the loss of a sense of "obligation to the public," which he specifically equates with a loss of moral courage and of the spirit of freedom, *On Liberty* is read and remembered not as an argument impressing on individuals their obligation to the public, but on the contrary as defending actions that are not answerable to the public at all. (The essay all but fixates readers on the concept of a self-regarding act.) The contradiction is inscribed in the text itself. Whereas in *On Liberty* Mill speaks of halves of the truth as though they had equal weight, in "Utilitarianism" (1861) he claims that in only 1 percent of our actions, if that, are we under obligation to the public (CW X, 219). Nothing more forcibly illustrates the dubious nature of Mill's half-of-the-truth trope than this shift from 50:50 to 99:1.

The idea that Mill's thinking was beset by conflict is not in itself a new one. It was advanced in perhaps its most provocative form in Gertrude Himmelfarb's thesis of two Mills, one good and one bad.[30] It is enough to say that I don't share Himmelfarb's highly colored view, and that I see the two Mills as one person. In a review of Himmelfarb's study of Mill, C. B. Macpherson argues that Mill was pledged to two "inconsistent" sets of values: on the one hand, "the Benthamite concept of man as consumer and appropriator"; on the other, a "concept of man as developer and enjoyer of manifold capacities," or what Macpherson calls Mill's "humanistic developmental vision."[31] For this last cumbrous phrase we might substitute "civic humanism." The very measure against which Mill judges the stunted, incomplete persons of his society—that of the independent personality, a figure of moral vigor and political capacity—derives from civic humanism. If Mill's prime concern (or one of them) was how to achieve the full measure of our being, civic humanism was itself "concerned with how the citizen is to develop his human capacities."[32] "Civic humanism denotes a style of thought . . . in which it is contended that the development of the individual towards self-fulfillment is possible only when the individual acts like a citizen."[33] Notice in this connection

that *On Liberty* complains both that the development of the individual
has been blocked and that people have lost the capacity for the active
life. While Mill's thought comes from no single school, we may discern
in his hostility to bureaucracy and the standing army, to jobbers and
placemen, something of the eighteenth-century civic humanism that
saw these evils as imperilling the integrity of the citizen—integrity lost
to the weak and incomplete selves of *On Liberty*.[34] (Not that Mill
simply inherited that way of thinking; he advanced it and gave it a turn
of his own.) But because republicanism takes in more than civic
humanism, I will speak simply of the former. The term itself throws a
strong light on the conflict between the Benthamite view of the human
being as a self-interested monad, and the energetic ideal, largely shared
by Mill, of the citizen acting for the greater good.

Framing the issue as a conflict between the small virtues of self-
interest and the republican ideal not only foregrounds one of the deeper
problems in Mill's thought, but begins to account for it. For the virtues
of foresight and moderation offer a sort of insurance against the risks
posed by republicanism—the risks signaled by the Machiavellian term
virtù (Mill remarks in his defense of the French republicans of 1848
that it is hard to distinguish "heroic virtue" from "breach of faith, and
criminal aggression" [CW XX, 343]); the risks of tyranny when one is
too firmly possessed of a sense of his own virtue (the light in which
Mill may have seen Milton, also a republican); the risks of obsessive
hatred of a corrupt civilization, a hatred like Robespierre's (CW X,
123); the risks of frothy participation in public business (thus Mill's
call for participation, *but not too much*). Affirming the human capacity
not just to live within the law but to write the law in the first place (as
Mill asks us to think "truths" back to their time of inception),
republicanism naturally poses danger. The force of Mill's republican
feeling was itself, perhaps, a risk to be contained. The measure of it
will I hope become clear in the course of this study. For now it can be
estimated by a statement he made in 1832: "When will it be felt in this
country, that there is more good in the most hot-headed republicans,
than in the coterie of jobbers, tricksters, and low *intrigans* who form
the existing Government of France!" (CW XXIII, 429).

Such a statement opens up a revealing line of sight onto Mill's
republican passions and sympathies. For while Mill inclined to the high
or classical style of republicanism—the tradition more concerned with
the restoration of ancient virtue than with the redress of social
wrongs—the republican movement itself comprised many hues of
thought, from anti-property doctrines to the "conservative" republi-

canism of Armand Carrel (CW XX, 202). In some degree, too, the high republican tradition feeds into the "red" republicanism of the nineteenth century: the sacred name of Milton, a classical republican, is invoked in radical circles in Mill's own London; stilted imagery of Roman virtue gives way to radicals signing themselves "Brutus" and asserting a right to bear arms; traditional talk of corruption (as loss of autonomy, a sense still alive in Mill) turns into radical excoriations of the corrupt regime of the few.[35] I mean to say that Mill's republicanism didn't lead him to embrace social revolution (about which *On Liberty* has nothing to say), but neither did it close his mind to the social question or turn him blindly against those more radical than himself, as we can see in his testimonial to the "hot-headed" republicans of 1832. Almost 40 years later, in 1871, Mill argued eloquently for dedicating land to the common good, and stopped not far short of calling for the nationalization of the holdings of the few. Perhaps Mill was influenced the more by republican thought because it was both rich and various, well suited to his own eclectic turn of mind. Mill's affairs with Saint-Simonism and Comte's Positivism ended as affairs do. His entanglement with republicanism itself only deepened.

A republic signified to Mill an order of law within which human beings can achieve the full measure of their nature. (Thus, for example, Mill's belief that the revolution of 1848 had a chance to make the French the citizens they were capable of being.) But if such an order is to be established, a prior order, traditional or monarchical, may have to be overthrown. At least it happened that republicanism bore a revolutionary hue in seventeenth-century England and later in France.[36] With the very warmth he is often thought to lack, Mill was drawn to the cause of French republicans themselves animated by the desire to make good the original promise of the French Revolution, since betrayed. More commonly recognized is that *On Liberty* stands in some lineal relation to "Areopagitica," which was written by an arch-republican in the heat of the English Revolution. Even Machiavelli, the brilliant republican who has been called the first revolutionary—even he may endow Mill's thought; or so I will argue. (Interestingly, Machiavelli, Milton, and Mill held government positions, all three, as secretaries in charge of political correspondence.) Beneath the famous aridity of Mill's thought, beneath his tireless and too often cheerless prose runs the underground river of the revolutionary tradition. And that river comes above ground in the radical republican discourse of Mill's own day—a current that carried some of the themes Mill is best known for, such as the value of fearless free speech and

indeed the value of accomplishing our own natures. While some have
felt that Mill's counsels of noninterference pose a threat to good order,
no such danger is really to be apprehended from people who seek
private happiness, study their own improvement, seclude themselves
within private concerns, keep within the law, and otherwise live out
the libertarian precepts of *On Liberty*. It is when people step out of
the private sphere to act with one another and possibly challenge the
law itself—when people act, for example, like republicans—that the
keepers of order may have reason to fear.

I can't enter into the opinion that in enjoining people to "mind their
own business" (OL 286), Mill was saying something noble. ("Mind
your own business," the segregationists told Martin Luther King.) If
Francis Place had minded his own business, he would have stuck to
his tailor shop and not gotten mixed up in agitation for reform, all the
more because " 'gentlemen' do not wish to give their custom to a
tailor who has wider interests than tailoring."[37] Trying to quell the
spirit of revolt during the Whiskey Rebellion in Pennsylvania in 1794,
an anti-republican worthy admonished his audience "to be quiet, and
to do your own business."[38] Minding your own business was (and still
is) a counsel of common prudence. As Adam Smith portrays the
prudent man in *The Theory of Moral Sentiments*, that figure minds his
own business. When the young Moll Flanders expresses the wish to be
a gentlewoman, she is advised that the way to gentility is to "mind my
Work."[39] Lewis Carroll's Alice, Mill's contemporary, knows that what
makes the world go around is " 'everybody minding their own business!' ",[40] it is one of the platitudes instilled into her by education.
Mill eulogizes Pericles in *On Liberty* (OL 266); but if we actually
consult the funeral oration of Pericles, we find this statement:

> We do not say that a man who takes no interest in politics is a man who
> minds his own business; we say that he has no business here at all. We
> Athenians, in our own persons, take our decisions on policy or submit
> them to proper discussion.[41]

It is as though Mill reversed Pericles' emphasis, laying great stress on
keeping out of the affairs of others and seasoning his argument with a
little talk about taking part in public concerns and with a parenthetical
reminder (OL 276–77) that citizens really do have business outside
their own sphere. Mill's contention that people ought to be free to
drink (etc.) may have been a little ahead of the times, but it wasn't
specially daring; from the 1880s forward, the English police kept hands

off activities like drinking, gambling, and fair-going when the law
allowed them to, probably because there was little to be gained and
much to be lost by offending sectors of the public with "needless busy-
bodying."[42] The police themselves learned to mind their own business.

We understand *On Liberty* better if we read it not as the assertion of
daring ideals of noninterference, but as a retreat from the politically
charged ideals of republicanism. The retreat is well enough conducted
that we the readers are made to feel that in minding our own business
and pursuing private happiness we are somehow realizing the tradition
of Milton, which is surely a non sequitur. *On Liberty* is underwritten
by the tradition of republicanism; at the same time, Mill neutralizes
the dangers of the republican ideal, and nearly the ideal itself. His
argument is underwritten by republicanism: hence his indictment of
the morality, at once selfish and craven, of "Abstinence from Evil"
(OL 255). He neutralizes the dangers of the republican ideal: hence his
famous thesis that we must be free to do as we like, provided we
"refrain . . . from molesting others in what concerns them" (OL 260)—
provided, that is to say, we Abstain from Evil.

For reasons I believe both of principle and of prudence, Mill mutes
his republicanism in *On Liberty*. His disapprobation of private interests
never comes clearly into view in that text, as it does, say, in *Considerations on Representative Government*. And while it has long been
known that *On Liberty* draws on Milton's "Areopagitica," Mill nowhere acknowledges Milton in the text of *On Liberty* and never quite
announces by name the republican principles he and Milton share. In
this his political testament, Mill has attempted as far as possible to
contain the contradiction between a republican code of moral valor
and public good, and a liberalism that would leave people to the pursuit
of their own goods. My argument is that Mill checked the almost
Miltonic force of his republican convictions and ultimately presented
an improved—which is to say, a laundered—version of republicanism
itself; and that *On Liberty* draws on the republican tradition without,
however, raising the "hostile banner" (OL 254) of republicanism. Mill
managed to "reconcile" his views skillfully enough that his republicanism is barely visible in *On Liberty*. Thus Charles Taylor finds that
Considerations on Representative Government, but not *On Liberty*,
"owe[s] something to the ancient republican tradition."[43] I believe *On
Liberty* does so as well, only less palpably, so that the ideal individual
assumed in the text is a sort of republic in miniature, a human image
of a polity that is self-determining, capable of supporting its own
freedom, and possessed of "individuality."[44] Underneath Mill's re-

spect as a liberal for the choices made by people-as-they-are is a republican preference for the way people would choose if they were more nearly autonomous—more nearly the masters of themselves— and more closely approached the civic ideal of a human life. And undergirding Mill's argument that people have lost the capacity to exert themselves for the public good is the republican ideal of active virtue, an ideal lying just below the threshold of visibility as we read *On Liberty*.

Among the precursors of Mill is perhaps Mary Wollstonecraft, who in *A Vindication of the Rights of Woman* employs more than one idea of virtue, like Mill. Possessed of bold conceptions and a soaring contempt for the great ones of the earth, Wollstonecraft sees virtue, first of all, as the power to do away with privilege and prejudice and erect a new political order. Her ideals happen to be republican: no king, no standing army,[45] an active citizenry,[46] a government of laws and not men.[47] On the other hand, Wollstonecraft inculcates prosaic virtues like moderation and precaution: she would have lovers temper their passions in anticipation of the time, not far off, when ardor cools. Moderation and precaution are not virtues that make revolutions, although they make for good shopkeeping. In *A Vindication of the Rights of Woman* Wollstonecraft draws on and argues with the moral theory of Adam Smith, another underwriter of *On Liberty*,[48] who himself viewed bourgeois morality with decidedly mixed feelings. Smith regarded the rise of trade, and with it wealth and gentler manners, in a dual light. On the one hand, he appreciated the gains of this process, such as stricter moral habits, while on the other hand he lamented the price at which the pacification of society had been purchased: a loss of courage, heroism, virtù.[49] I use the republican term here because at times we find Smith "totally espousing the classical 'republican' view that commerce leads to debilitating luxury and corruption."[50] Indeed, the maimed people of *On Liberty* are unmistakably prefigured in Smith's analysis of the "mental mutilation [and] deformity" inflicted by commercial society.[51] Smith's "ambivalence"[52] toward the pacification of society becomes in Mill a full-blown contradiction.

In many passages throughout his writings, Mill displays his belief that the amenities of a commercial age, such as security of property and mildness of manners, have been paid for with a grievous loss of courage and public spirit (virtù).[53] In the *Political Economy*, for in- stance, Mill cautions us to remember that "security of property and person" aren't everything and that "a great amount of public spirit and patriotism" flourished in the free cities of medieval Europe without these modern advantages (CW III, 881); one such city, the mercantile center of Florence, gave rise to the ideal of civic humanism itself.[54] In "Grote's History of Greece," Mill observes that "there is more humanity, more mildness of manners" in the present improved condition of society, but that the idea of "duties to the public" (the republican watchword) has been all but snuffed out (CW XI, 314). In "Coleridge" Mill states specifically that England gave itself up to "material interests" following the defeat of "Republicanism" (among other things) in the seventeenth century (CW X, 142). Again, in Bentham's ideal society, people enjoy security, but nothing that Mill would care to call liberty;[55] hence Mill's differences with Bentham. Mill's critique of pacification culminates in *On Liberty*, with its portrait of a commercial society so well pacified that all courage to act, all virtù, has been lost.[56] The essay ends on that very note:

A State which dwarfs its men, in order that they may be more docile instruments in its hands even for beneficial purposes—will find that with small men no great thing can really be accomplished; and that the perfection of machinery to which it has sacrificed everything, will in the end avail it nothing, for want of the vital power which, in order that the machine might work more smoothly, it has preferred to banish. (OL 310)[57]

On Liberty tells, then, of individuals possessing security of property but not the spirit of liberty—people like the temperance-advocate quoted in chapter 4, who is haunted with threats to his " 'primary right of security' " (OL 288) and doesn't seem to possess the sort of valor needed to establish such rights in the first place.[58] Implicitly, and with little use of oratorical language like that freely employed by others of republican persuasion, Mill looks back to those heroic or revolutionary moments in which people act with one another in the name of principles over and beyond their private good (as in the 1848 revolution in France) and establish arrangements (like security of property) that later come to be taken for granted. This doesn't mean that Mill had no care for security of property, but that he judged that security of property in itself gives no security for liberty. Only moral courage and the *spirit* of liberty, which *On Liberty* represents as dying out, can do so. Not only does Mill believe that the functioning of modern society debilitates the spirit and produces small-mindedness and (though he rarely uses the word) effeminacy, but he revives the republican principle of the subordination of private to public good. What is more, in *On*

Liberty he defends the very idea of reviving, of bringing back to life, "truths" that have already appeared in the world. Where Carlyle and Ruskin, in their hatred of commercial society, look back to the Middle Ages, John Stuart Mill—the leading political economist of the age—looks back to the antique tradition of republicanism.

Mill believes, then, in the republican principle of the superiority of the public good. He founds *On Liberty*, however, on the principle that people are entitled to seek their own good in their own way because each individual is "the person most interested in his own well-being" (OL 277), hence the best judge of it. And this principle he inherited from Bentham, who left no place in his theorizing for disinterested motives or risk-taking for the public good. In addition, Mill approved of the civilizing effects of commerce, the same commerce responsible for the decline of virtù. Security of property; stricter moral habits; a diminished risk of war; frugality and foresight—these are not gains Mill would have been willing to barter away.[59] He comprehends them all under the term "improvement." In the improved condition, people look after their private interests at once peaceably and diligently. In a rather literal sense, they mind their own business. Instructing people not to meddle in the concerns of others (the most obvious teaching of *On Liberty*), Mill drew on the middle class's own maxims of prudence, for as Adam Smith remarks in his *Theory of Moral Sentiments* (1759), the prudent man

> is not a bustler in business where he has no concern; is not a meddler in other people's affairs. . . . [He] would be much better pleased that the public business were well managed by some other person, than that he himself should have the trouble, and incur the responsibility, of managing it.[60]

This passage brings out tensions in the thought of Mill, who would have people keep out of others' affairs *and* learn the meaning of action and of responsibility to the public. Or rather, as much as Mill wants us to act like citizens, he deems it more prudent for now that we stay indoors and concentrate on our own affairs. And he philosophically bolts the door. No doubt Mill would affirm that self-interest and the public good are two halves of one truth. Again, I think not. At one time, indeed, republican theorists had been able to argue that property (and the private interests going with it) makes citizens; that "a man has to have property to be a free man at all; if he is dependent on another for his bread and butter he will be dependent on him in politics too."[61] In *On Liberty* Mill worries about a different kind of dependence—not the dependence of tenant on landlord, or hireling on patron, or pauper on almsgiver, or indeed worker on employer, but the dependence of one and all on a diffuse agency, society. Moreover, far from guaranteeing independence, the concerns of property ownership seem to consume the independence of the status-conscious Victorians portrayed by Mill—a danger that earlier republican theorists were alive to. In Mill's own terms, the argument that private holdings make free citizens no longer applied,[62] and by fencing off the private sphere in *On Liberty*, Mill does not succeed in turning people into citizens. Since the conflict in Mill's thought that I have in view is crystallized in his different attitudes toward interests,[63] it is to this subject that I now turn.

LET US CONCERN ourselves first with Mill as a liberal who endorsed the legitimacy of private interests, a point won by writers before him. Locke, traditionally considered the author of liberalism, is among these fore-laborers. The story of Locke's politics has recently been told in a full and compellingly documented way by Richard Ashcraft, and it is now clear that Locke was a radical member of a sometimes-underground political movement, one of whose articles of belief was the legitimacy of private interests. In 1669 a fellow dissident argued for "preserv[ing] industrious men in a peaceable way of improving their own interests," knitting together the themes of security of property, private interests, and "improvement."[64] A dozen years later it was the Whig position that people pursue their private interests, that it is legitimate to do so, and that tradesmen in particular should look to their interest and elect men of their own class to Parliament. Not only did Locke's party contend that it is valid "to engage in the honest pursuit of one's private interests (commerce, for example),"[65] but it dressed up this claim in flattering colors by associating trade with constitutional government and the liberties of Englishmen. Early in *On Liberty* Mill looks back to "the establishment of constitutional checks, by which the consent of the community, or a body of some sort, supposed to represent its interests, was made a necessary condition to some of the more important acts of the governing power" (OL 218). In England this point was settled in 1688. Mill has no wish to undo this set of arrangements, but accepts it and goes on from there, and so, we might say, he accepts the legitimacy of private interests—a principle in contention during the constitutional struggle—and goes on from there. He goes on to argue that, individuals being the best judges of their own interest, they themselves are the best managers of their own business.

This principle is ringingly proclaimed in Mill's *Subjection of Women*:

> The modern conviction, the fruit of a thousand years of experience, is, that things in which the individual is the person directly interested, never go right but as they are left to his own discretion; and that any regulation of them by authority, except to protect the rights of others, is sure to be mischievous. (CW XXI, 273)

On Liberty invokes the same principle. The reason society is unjustified in prescribing to the individual in matters pertaining to him- or herself is that individuals are the most competent judges of their own interest:

> Neither one person, nor any number of persons, is warranted in saying to another human creature of ripe years, that he shall not do with his life for his own benefit what he chooses to do with it. He is the person most interested in his own well-being: the interest which any other person, except in cases of strong personal attachment, can have in it, is trifling, compared with that which he himself has; the interest which society has in him individually (except as to his conduct to others) is fractional, and altogether indirect; while, with respect to his own feelings and circumstances, the most ordinary man or woman has means of knowledge immeasurably surpassing those that can be possessed by any one else. (OL 277)

(Note that the term "interested" has no inflection of disapproval here.) Mill holds that we judge most accurately when we judge of our own interests (OL 283) and that we know our interests more intimately than, say, society does. He does not, however, confront the possibility that we may decide that our interests and happiness are best served by conformity.[66]

Not only does Mill believe that the private sphere is not society's business; he maintains that, as a rule, business itself is best conducted by those directly interested. In his *Political Economy* he writes that

> Experience shows, and proverbs, the expression of popular experience, attest, how inferior is the quality of hired servants, compared with the ministration of those personally interested in the work, and how indispensable, when hired service must be employed, is "the master's eye" to watch over it. (CW II, 137)

(This last is one of many images of superintendence in Mill's work—
"the eye of a hostile and dreaded censorship" [OL 264] being another.
Probably all derive from the young Mill's experience of being kept
under the watch and ward of his father.) The same principle dictates
that workers in cooperatives "should be identified in interest with the
prosperity of the undertaking" (CW III, 792).[67] The most nearly
categorical statement of Mill's principle that the persons interested are
the best managers of their affairs occurs near the end of the *Political
Economy*. "The great majority of things," Mill asserts,

> are worse done by the intervention of government, than the individuals
> most interested in the matter would do them, or cause them to be done,
> if left to themselves. The grounds of this truth are expressed with
> tolerable exactness in the popular dictum, that people understand their
> own business and their own interests better, and care for them more, than
> the government does, or can be expected to do. This maxim holds true
> throughout the greatest part of the business of life, and wherever it is true
> we ought to condemn every kind of government intervention that conflicts
> with it. (CW III, 941–42)

This passage anticipates the argument of *On Liberty*, where Mill
affirms that "Speaking generally, there is no one so fit to conduct any
business, or to determine how or by whom it shall be conducted, as
those who are personally interested in it" (OL 305). Curiously, then,
On Liberty denounces the tyranny of public opinion in the name of a
"popular dictum." Private interests are at their most wholesome in the
case of peasants working their own land—peasant proprietorship being
Mill's remedy for the desperate misery of Ireland. Over and over again
during the potato famine, Mill agitates to give the Irish poor their own
land to work, on the theory that having the means and the motive to
support themselves teaches peasants industry, raises them up from the
degradation of serfdom, makes them an inspirational example to others, and creates wealth. What makes self-interest so pure a blessing
for peasant proprietors is, first, that it frees them from dependence on
a landlord; second, that the peasant, unlike the towndweller (the
bourgeois), stands outside the false values of the social world—so far
outside that Mill entertains himself with idyllic visions of an agrarian
republic (CW XXIV, 941). In the case of towndwellers, self-interest is
not such an unmixed blessing, if only because they live in a fetid
atmosphere of money-grubbing and status-seeking. In any case, Mill
didn't commend the Victorians to their own interests like peasants to
their vines.

Mill countenanced serious encroachments on individual liberty. He recommended compulsory service in a citizen army, something Adam Smith maintained could be enforced only "by means of a very rigorous police, and in spite of the whole bent of the interest, genius and inclinations of the people."[68] Mill wanted the "whole people trained and disciplined" to fight (CW XXIX, 413). He believed the state could deny the poor the right to marry (OL 304). He favored "habituating" people to postpone their interests to those of others (OL 305). As this last point suggests, Mill was not in fact easy with the principle of private interests.

Shortly after the "popular dictum" passage cited a moment ago, Mill strikes a markedly different note. He deplores the confinement of human beings within "the narrow sphere of their merely individual interests" (CW III, 943)—the narrow sphere he himself fortifies in *On Liberty*. He deplores the loss of virtù that is the cost of improvement. "The advance of civilization and security removes one after another of the hardships, embarrassments, and dangers against which individuals had formerly no resource but in their own strength, skill, and courage" (CW III, 944). Only on the strength of active virtue and public spirit, he says, can liberty be maintained. This is the idiom of republicanism. (Mill goes on to deprecate the habit of dependence, the hunger for government places, the use of office for private ends—the syndrome that republicans call corruption.) In this language-world, "private interest" is a term of censure, and the greater security of an improved age corrupts the spirit (virtù) that enables a people to keep up its liberty. If the *Political Economy* anticipates *On Liberty* in grounding an appeal for liberty on the principle of private interest— one of Mill's headings in the former work reads, "*Objections to government intervention—superior efficiency of private agency, owing to stronger interest in the work*" (CW III, 941)—it also anticipates the later text in representing the feebleness of public spirit as a threat to liberty and in warning of the dying-out of "agency" altogether.

Many of the references to "interest" in Mill are of the disapproving kind. As we have seen, Mill despises Christianity for calling on "self-interested" motives (OL 255). He finds that self-interest breeds a "mean and slavish" spirit (CW XVIII, 169). He damns both the enlightened timidity of the Victorian and sheer unenlightened self-interest. Often, it seems, the term "interest" figures in Mill's writings as it does in the *Federalist Papers*: interests warp judgment and stand opposed to the common good. The authors of the *Federalist Papers* have little faith in the prospect of Americans attaining to a heroic disinterest, but they envision a polity that can flourish all the same—a republic (they never tire of the word) that doesn't depend on the active virtue of citizens or indeed on their participation at all. "Gone was the assumption that citizens would unite around a common conception of the public good."[69] In a strange and unwilling way, the authors of the *Federalist Papers* are beginning to put the ideal of disinterest behind them, rather as though a living god were to become an abstraction. Mill, by contrast, warns in *On Liberty* of the extinguishing of the active principle itself, and in *Considerations on Representative Government* of the perishing of freedom "if, from indolence, or carelessness, or cowardice, or want of public spirit, [people] are unequal to the exertions necessary for preserving it" (CW XIX, 377). Political machinery, he remarks, "does not act of itself" but needs the "active participation" of citizens (CW XIX, 376). I will argue later that Mill meant not too much action. Here the point is, Mill felt that improvement itself saps the ability to act in defense of freedom—that public spirit has been sacrificed to private interests.

Any number of passages in Mill could be entered into evidence to show a critical attitude toward self-interest—toward the creed in which he was brought up. In "Bentham," for instance, Mill criticizes that strange philanthropist's "idea of the world" as "a collection of persons pursuing each his separate interest or pleasure" (CW X, 97). In his *Autobiography* Mill carries the point further:

> Interest in the common good is at present so weak a motive in the generality, not because it can never be otherwise, but because the mind is not accustomed to dwell on it as it dwells from morning till night on things which tend only to private advantage. When called into activity as only self-interest now is, by the daily course of life, and spurred from behind by the love of distinction and the fear of shame, it is capable of producing, even in common men, the most strenuous exertions as well as the most heroic sacrifices. (CW I, 241)

Here Mill envisions as it were a change in the definition of virtue from "peaceable pursuit of private interest" to "martial dedication to the public good." As dry and dusty as it is, Mill's language nevertheless expresses something of the millennial hopes of those nineteenth-century republicans who dreamed that humanity would finally come into its own. Mill broke with Benthamism in part because that narrow creed allowed no place for the altruism—the active virtue—that ennobles and realizes our nature. Elsewhere, too, Mill manifests a disap-

proval of private interests that we might not have expected in the
author of the cardinal defense of a person's right to pursue his or her
own good. For Mill as for Rousseau (who figures so slightly in *On
Liberty*), citizens "are not meant to bring their private interests, hopes,
and opinions to bear upon public affairs."[70] In 1859, the year in which
On Liberty appeared, Mill wrote:

> As regards interests themselves, whenever not identical with the general
> interest, the less they are represented the better. What is wanted is a
> representation, not of men's differences of interest, but of the differences
> in their intellectual points of view. Shipowners are to be desired in
> Parliament, because they can instruct us about ships, not because they
> are interested in having protecting duties. We want from a lawyer in
> Parliament his legal knowledge, not his professional interest in the expen-
> siveness and unintelligibility of the law. (CW XIX, 358)

While committed to the principle that people should be free (within the
rules of order) to act on their own interests as they themselves
understand them, Mill nevertheless reproaches shipowners and lawyers who do just that. When, acting as a body, they try to get favors
from Parliament, they become what Bentham called sinister interests.
Except that *On Liberty* decries the constricting effects of private
interest, we might almost conclude that in Mill's judgment self-interest
is a valid motive for private, but not public conduct. In any case, true
to his position on the representation of "men's differences of interest,"
Mill stipulated to the electors of Westminster that he would not
represent any local interest in Parliament. The full force of Mill's
detestation of private interests appears in such a statement as, "Did
not the slaveowners of the Southern United States maintain [the
doctrine that there are free natures and slave natures] with all the
fanaticism with which men cling to the theories that justify their
passions and legitimate their personal interests?" (CW XXI, 269).
Language like this may persuade us that the personal interests Mill
censured were naked economic interests. Actually Mill didn't frown
on special interests alone. He frowned on all that contracts our views—
on mental narrowness. The slaveowner passage appears in Mill's
Subjection of Women (1869); one of his condemnations of the existing
sexual order is that women are taught *not* to look beyond things
"solely of private interest" (CW XXI, 327). As we have seen in the
passage from his *Autobiography* cited above, Mill believes the same of
men. In an unavowed way, he has presented the republican argument

that effeminacy deprives men of the virtue (virtù) necessary to maintain their liberty. Women wear corsets; men's minds are corseted. Of this, more presently.

But how is it possible to act politically with disinterest? Mill saw a brilliant example in the French revolution of February 1848. That revolution brought republicans into power,

> unselfish politicians; who did not, like the common run of those who fancy themselves sincere, aim at doing a little for their opinions and much for themselves, but, with a disinterested zeal, strove to make their tenure of power produce as much good as their countrymen were capable of receiving, and more than their countrymen had yet learnt to desire. (CW XX, 320)[71]

The government of Louis Philippe, by contrast, appealed directly "to men's immediate personal interests or interested fears" (CW XX, 325). Mill quotes from a magnificent speech by Tocqueville to the Chamber of Deputies, just four weeks before the revolution, in which he assails the corruption of national life, that is, the raising of private interest into a public principle.[72] Tocqueville feels particular scorn for public men given to "the gross satisfaction of their private interests" (CW XX, 327). Recall too that in his own defense of the democratic way of life, Tocqueville went "against his private preferences,"[73] affording a signal example of what it is to check one's own biases and abstain from gratifying private inclinations. In the *Considerations on Representative Government*, Mill for his part calls for the strict subordination of private interest to the public good. A voter, for example, is "under an absolute moral obligation to consider the interest of the public, not his private advantage" (CW XIX, 490). In a healthy polity, Mill argues, people's civic abilities would be exercised, "if even rarely" (CW XIX, 412); citizens would be led out of the littleness of private life in order to take a more responsible part in government. Politics would become a "school of public spirit" (CW XIX, 412) in which education would have the threefold meaning of a leading-out (the root meaning of the word), an exercising of skills, and a raising of tone. Such are the lengths to which Mill carried his rebellion against the Benthamite model of society, in which individuals need only follow their self-interest for the public good to emerge. In no simple way could Mill accept the proposition that the public good would come about by itself if only people looked to their private interests with diligence and altogether forgot about classical ideals of virtue.

A criticism of self-interest that *On Liberty* doesn't make but that it intimates, and that Adam Smith made with power and ironic point, is that in the scramble for happiness, people make themselves more miserable than before. In his *Theory of Moral Sentiments* Smith tells a wry tale of a "poor man's son, whom heaven in its anger has visited with ambition." Seeking after the happiness of the rich, he "devotes himself for ever to the pursuit of wealth and greatness" but immediately endures "more fatigue of body and more uneasiness of mind than he could have suffered through the whole of his life for want of" the delights he yearns for.[74] And so the life of self-interest turns into the pursuit of an illusory happiness. Contained within the simple word "conformity" in Mill's *On Liberty* (265) is a story about the envious emulation and corrosive worry over illusory goods—the "uneasiness of mind"—afflicting the social actors of Victorian England. Mill does not, as I say, call self-interest a cheat. But he does assert in his *Autobiography* that happiness can't be pursued head-on. He defends self-interest; yet the littleness of soul that he despises—what is it but a fixed concentration on private happiness?

Mill could not, then, uncritically assent to the theory of society that requires people to devote themselves religiously to their interests. Such a model does have something in its favor: it makes for stability. "The by-product of individuals acting predictably in accordance with their economic interests [is] . . . not an uneasy *balance*, but a strong *web* of interdependent relationships."[75] How constraining that web might become we may gauge from Mill's protest, in *On Liberty*, against the fettering of the individual. To judge by *On Liberty*, the project of "civilizing" people by confining their energies to small pursuits and habitual routines was realized only too well. In the "improved" state of society, people channel their energies narrowly, a process Mill contemptuously likens to the waterflow through "a Dutch canal" (OL 268), the Dutch themselves being a byword for the small virtues of diligence and industry. Twenty-five years before *On Liberty*, Mill fulminated against people whose one thought is making money— creatures of routine who are governed by "a blind mechanical impulse," who act out of "mere *habit*," and who worry obsessively about their standing in the eyes of others (CW XXIII, 720–21; Mill's emphasis), exactly like the wooden people of *On Liberty*. In this sense *On Liberty* protests not only the spirit of money-getting but the very theory that people are improved by dedicating themselves to their desire to rise in the world. Mill wasn't far behind Rousseau in his contempt for the debility of civilized people, with their corrupt desire to out-show the others, but he was unable to propose a remedy. At one point in *On Liberty*, indeed, Mill projects a way out of the stultifying routines of private interest; he speaks of

> the political education of a free people, taking them out of the narrow circle of personal and family selfishness, and accustoming them to the comprehension of joint interests, the management of joint concerns— habituating them to act from public or semi-public motives. (OL 305)

But this passage reads like a coda to his real argument, and Mill himself—in striking contrast to Tocqueville's treatment of the same subject—plays it down.

What does Mill mean by joint action from semi-public motives? First of all, I think he envisions individuals recouping the agency that has been given up to an Invisible Hand. At present, an Invisible Hand coordinates people's actions (or behavior) for them, so that, as Adam Smith says, in order to produce shears a great number of workers from the miner to the smith "must all of them join their different arts," and yet they share no common intention to make shears.[76] The same Hand redeems private interest by turning acts undertaken for purely selfish motives, to the service of the general good—"an end which was no part of [the agent's] intention."[77] Thus the economic actor advances the happiness of the greatest number without ever striving or even intending to do so. Committed to the happiness of the greatest number, Mill nevertheless wants us to intend the good of others. Perhaps on the principle that "It really is of importance, not only what men do, but also what manner of men they are that do it" (OL 263), he deems that our motives and intentions matter; even if an act passes the test of utility, the agent can't be called public-spirited (can't earn the highest praise) if he or she just acted in self-interest.

> A foreigner lands in London or Liverpool, and seeing such docks, such warehouses, such manufactories as he never saw before, thinks it vastly fine to belong to a country which has such things; but the merchant, or the manufacturer, does *he* ever think of taking credit to himself for toiling and scraping in order that his country may possess docks and manufactories? The man has no such thought. (CW XXIII, 721–22; Mill's emphasis)

Mill would like us to intend the public good. More generally, he would like us to act as purposive beings rather than as mannikins whose motions are regulated in ways they are not aware of. He seems to want us to learn to coordinate our purposes for ourselves, to act in concert. He asks us to perform, as intentional agents and free citizens, that process of coming-to-agreement which now goes on in an undeliberated way; one name for the process as presently conducted is conformity. By semi-public motives, I think Mill simply means motives halfway between private interest and public spirit. By pooling their private interests, people have already (as Mill sees it) won themselves in some degree away from private life and begun accustoming themselves to broader conceptions, including the conception of themselves as acting beings. An example of this salutary process would be the formation of workers' cooperatives. Since this looks like an attractive solution to the problem of private versus public good, the point bears some further comment. First, however, it seems appropriate to review what we know so far of Mill's attitudes toward private interest.

Those attitudes are acutely contradictory. On the one hand, Mill holds that individuals are the best judges of their own interests and the best managers of their own concerns—a doctrine that makes a principle of the legitimacy of private pursuits. On the other hand, "private interest" is a term of opprobrium in Mill, signifying a kind of selfishness and small-mindedness people must grow out of in order to be considered properly political beings. I speak of a contradiction here; Mill speaks of two parts of the truth. Deep in the middle of his *System of Logic*, in the course of his reflections on the tendency of doctrines "to degenerate rapidly into lifeless dogmas" (CW VIII, 681), Mill contrasts two ideas of virtue. According to the first, virtue "consists in a correct calculation of our own personal interests"; the second, the doctrine that needs to be brought back to life, exalts "disinterestedness" (p. 684). Mill argues that the contradiction between the two doctrines should not be suppressed but on the contrary brought out, in order to spark thought. Asking if the "personal interests" school would be justified in banning all references to the other doctrine, he answers no, precisely because the two doctrines are so sharply inconsistent:

> Need we say that [the] abrogation of the old formulas [defining virtue as disinterest] for the sake of preserving clear ideas and consistency of thought, would have been a great evil? while the very inconsistency incurred by the coexistence of the formulas with philosophical opinions which seemed to condemn them as absurdities, operated as a stimulus to the re-examination of the subject. (CW VIII, 684)

It seems to me that Mill's own thought is marked by fruitful inconsistency. Not that he admits it. Immediately following this passage, indeed, Mill refers to the doctrine of disinterest as "a part of the truth," suddenly implying that the two doctrines fit after all, components of the same edifice. He gives no clue as to how these doctrines are to be accommodated. In his 1865 critique of Auguste Comte (who anathematized private interests), Mill decides that it's enough for us to be *ready* to subordinate our interests to the public good, but that most of the time doing as we wish is all right.[78] One problem with this elegant solution to the problem of interest versus disinterest (a solution resembling Mill's proposal that ordinary citizens exercise public responsibility once in a while) is that, according to Mill's own conceptions, our abilities require real exercise if they are to be developed. How then can I learn active virtue if I exercise it rarely if ever? Perhaps Mill's most serious attempt actually to resolve the conundrum of interest is in his thinking about workers' cooperatives.

Discussing cooperative experiments in his *Autobiography*, Mill remarks that unselfish motives are far less called upon in the modern world "than in the smaller commonwealths of antiquity" (CW I, 241), a phrase stamped with the traditional republican bias toward the ancients. Discussing cooperative experiments in the *Political Economy*, Mill looks to the future. He looks toward cooperative societies that will raise workers above the morality of private interest while still drawing on interested motives. In cooperatives, Mill writes, "it is indispensable that all, and not some only, of those who do the work should be identified in interest with the prosperity of the undertaking" (CW III, 792). Thus would private good and the good of all (all in the cooperative) be reconciled, and this not as the unwilled outcome of economic behavior, but as the result of a free and deliberate political experiment. When in *On Liberty* Mill encourages "voluntary associations" and "varied experiments" (OL 306), we must assume he has in mind such undertakings as these, even if he makes his language vague and exiles the issue to the periphery of his argument. Workers' cooperatives will be a means of educating small and selfish motives and of nurturing public ones. They hold promise of "healing" the worst contradictions of modern life. Mill permits himself to hope for a

> moral revolution in society . . . : the healing of the standing feud between capital and labour; the transformation of human life, from a conflict of classes struggling for opposite interests, to a friendly rivalry in the pursuit of a good common to all; the elevation of the dignity of labour; a new

sense of security and independence in the labouring class; and the
conversion of each human being's daily occupation into a school of the
social sympathies and the practical intelligence. (CW III, 792)

As this wishful language makes clear, the closing of the conflict
between private and public motives belongs to the future, a future as
distant in its way as antiquity itself. Some time hence, a happy ending
may be written to that conflict. Some time hence, all will be reconciled.
But this is "a prophecy of ultimate possibilities," as Mill himself later
wrote of the socialist ideal (CW V, 750). It is no more of a present
likelihood than a republic in which power is wielded neither by a
decadent aristocracy nor a small-minded middle class nor an unready
lower class. For the present, the contradiction between public and
private motives stands.

In his study of *The Philosophy and Politics of Freedom*, Richard E.
Flathman endorses the "Liberal Principle" that "it is, prima facie, a
good thing for individuals to form, to act upon, and more or less
regularly to satisfy their interests and desires, their ends and purposes."[79] The most celebrated of liberals, John Stuart Mill, is really of
two minds about this postulate of liberalism. Mill fears that virtue in
the sense of the calculation of private interests has extinguished virtù
in the sense of mettle and public spirit. But he is not willing to
disaccredit the pursuit of private ends. Besides, virtù is a volatile and
dangerous notion, as the Machiavellian heritage of the term warns us,
and as a check on these dangers, Mill is willing to call on secure
property arrangements and on the stabilization of human manners and
morals that allows people to conduct their lives "more or less regularly" in the first place. Mill's thinking is in tension, cross-woven.
Flathman finds that

> Liberals are torn between two inveterately conflicting impulses: to cele-
> brate the freedom of human beings to be what they are and to do what
> (being what they are) they are disposed to do, and the desire to see
> human beings become more self-conscious and self-critical about what
> they are and do. (p. 220)

For his part, Mill is committed to the conflicting principles of: (1)
leaving people to themselves; and (2) "habituating" people to being
much better than they presently are. He protests the regime of public
opinion, yet would bring the full force of public opinion to bear on
individuals in order to shame them into voting responsibly[80] and shame

them out of their selfishness.[81] While liberalism honors "decisions made by individual men and women as they are in ordinary life,"[82] Mill is not at all satisfied with human beings as they are, viewing them (as he testifies in *On Liberty*) as starved or deformed examples of what human beings could and should be. And I believe it is the republican concept of citizenship, as that form of life in which human nature is fully achieved, that underwrites Mill's notion of a flourishing human life. In itself, Mill's advocacy of public voting (to discourage bad choices) marks him as a kind of republican. In his account of the overthrow of the Second French Republic, Victor Hugo, a devout republican, tells of a soldier aglow with civic virtue and moral courage, casting a public vote against Louis Napoleon.[83] Hugo's republicanism is a compound of real militancy, heroic gestures, and high-flying sentiments, chief among them a mighty scorn for the principle of self-interest; next to this, the republicanism of Mill is like an eagle without talons. But Mill would have honored that soldier, and like Hugo he loathed Louis Napoleon.

Maybe it was Mill's hope that we would gradually advance beyond self-interest and learn to act like citizens. He seems to say that with greater self-consciousness about what we are and do—the self-consciousness that "never was awakened" in Bentham (CW X, 92)—we would be less given to following the routines of self-interest that have been laid out for us, and more committed to active virtue, an idea with "Greek and Roman sources" (OL 256). We would perhaps rediscover republicanism itself, or what Mill calls rather more blandly "the idea of obligation to the public" (OL 256). Waking up classical values of citizenship would be quite consistent with all Mill says in *On Liberty* about breathing life back into doctrines that have passed into commonplaces and suffered a "decline in . . . living power" (OL 247). I believe Mill himself came to republican values in consequence of his break with Benthamism.

In DICKENS's *Great Expectations*, written almost concurrently with *On Liberty*, Herbert Pocket is looking for an entry into the ship-insurance business but has no very clear idea of how to go about it. He is simply "look[ing] about him." Pip, our narrator, reports that "I do not remember that I ever saw him do anything else but look about him. If we all did what we undertake to do, as faithfully as Herbert did, we might live in a Republic of the Virtues."[84] A Republic of the Virtues: here nothing but a trope in a description of idleness. At this point in the novel Herbert is doing nothing much, while Pip is falling into the roles and routines that have been appointed for him, getting into debt, and fondly imagining he is to have Estella. In this deflationary novel, much concerned with the renunciation of romantic ambition and the contenting oneself with simple things, how could so heroic a concept as a Republic of Virtue appear to be anything but ridiculous? In this context, a Republic of Virtue is as unreal as Camelot. The virtues endorsed by the mature Pip aren't heroic but small ones, like fiscal and moral probity and steadiness of purpose. And these values would have been shared by Dickens's readers. While republicanism had popular roots in France, a country favorable to the elevated sentiments that Mill responded to, it was on the margins of political thought in England—a point dramatized at a meeting Mill attended in 1871, when a band of protesters unfurled a flag bearing the forbidden word itself: "republic" (CW XXIX, 415). How then did Mill come to republicanism?

The answer must be sought, I think, in the remarkable story of Mill's education, which constituted "a course of Benthamism" (CW I, 67). Mill tells us in effect that Bentham was a man of one idea, and the idea that possessed him seems to have been to write laws and engineer institutions in such a way that, simply by consulting their self-interest, people couldn't fail to promote the general good—"the greatest happiness." (These themes recur in twentieth-century liberalism—for example, in the belief of Edward Bernays, nephew of Freud and one of the first to "engineer" public opinion, that "private interest and public interest coincide" in the United States.)[85] Under the right conditions, the good would emerge as though of its own accord, independently of the intentions of human agents (as in the marketplace), and in this sense, action would give way to automatism and administration. In the case of the Panopticon—Bentham's pet scheme and fixed idea—human action would wither away indeed. The Panopticon, again, was an inspection-house, a sort of human observatory, in which a supervisor could keep all cells in view from a central vantage point. The theory behind the architecture was that "To be incessantly under the eyes of the inspector is to lose in effect the power to do evil and almost the thought of wanting to do it."[86] Thus deprived of the power of action, the prisoners would automatically reform. In the words of Elie Halévy, the Panopticon was designed "mechanically to transform criminals into honest men" (p. 488). Readers of *On Liberty* discern the eye of the inspector in "the eye of a hostile and dreaded censorship," as Mill describes public opinion (OL 264). Prisoners lacking the power of action become in *On Liberty* people who atrophy "for want of . . . vital power" (OL 310)—who have virtue, perhaps, but no virtù. The mechanical men who are ready for discharge become "automatons in human form" (OL 263). Readers of Mill's *Autobiography*, however, see more than this.

In his *Autobiography* Mill tells of a sort of Panopticon childhood in which he was kept under the close and continual supervision of his father, in a virtual isolation cell ("He kept me, with extreme vigilance, out of the way of . . ." [CW I, 35]), with the aim not indeed of reforming him, but of forming him in the first place and making him a leader in the Cause of Reform. The intensity of the inspection under which Mill grew up is suggested by the passing comment that he wrote abstracts of his readings "subject to my father's censorship" (CW I, 71), and the success of the project of mechanizing a human life can be measured by his "mental crisis," in which, by his own description, he became de-animated and pressed on "mechanically, by the mere force of habit" (CW I, 143). What a mockery it would have been to have spoken to Mill, while he seemed to himself to have lost all spontaneity, of the "spontaneous" way the greater good emerges in a well-ordered society. Such talk would have been no less bitterly ironic than talk in our own century of the spontaneous demonstrations organized on state occasions. Let me suggest that Mill's republicanism signifies the fullest sort of rejection of Bentham's notion that, given the right engineering, human behavior will "spontaneously" tend to the greater good, a rejection grounded at once in political conviction and emotional experience. While carrying forward Bentham's hatred of obscurantist arguments and his father's hatred of unearned privilege, Mill was concerned as they were not with the drying-up of the sources of action— and, by the same token, with the republican ideal of the active life.

As J. G. A. Pocock establishes in his study of the republican tradition, the keynote of the tradition was "every citizen's ability to place the common good before his own"; in other words, "virtue as a principle of active life."[87] Given his history, such ideas as these would have taken on heightened meaning for Mill. They would have been as the sweet air of freedom. Active life would have stood in contrast to life in a Panopticon with the power of action taken away. When the republican populace took to the streets of Paris in July 1830, *that* was active life. (Mill was transported by excitement at the event.) Active life would have meant a life undertaken by a self-directing being and not a machine set in motion by someone else. It would have meant the undertaking of "joint concerns" (OL 305), as opposed to solitary confinement, whether in the psychological cell in which Mill grew up or in the "narrow circle" of private interests (OL 305). One such joint concern, Mill tells us in *On Liberty*, is service on a jury—an institution Bentham liked to mock.[88] And the republican principle of placing the common good before one's own would have stood as a direct repudiation of Benthamism. Bentham had held all representations of disinterest to be lies.[89] He considered the idea of sacrificing self-interest to the greater good as "poetry," that is, moonshine; but Mill discovered for himself the healing properties of poetry.[90] In drawing on a republican discourse that pictured human beings accomplishing their own nature in the practice of active virtue, Mill broke with a Benthamite creed that seemed to deny that he *had* a nature of his own.

Bentham wanted things so ordered that people could have sure expectations.[91] Having himself balked some of the notions of the sect he was brought up in, Mill threw into question just about every sense of "expectations" in *On Liberty*: expectations as pre-judgments, ill-founded opinions, restrictive assumptions, vulgar hopes (as in "great expectations"); above all, perhaps, expectations as safe bets. Pocock has written of the eighteenth-century agon between the man of virtù and the man of expectations.[92] Mill warmed to the man of virtù, and took the republican tenet of virtù seriously enough to favor a citizen militia; thus the clause of *On Liberty* calling for each person to "bear his fair share in the common defence" (OL 225). Such was this martial Victorian's love of civic virtue that he argued in 1871, "Henceforth our army should be our whole people trained and disciplined" (CW XXIX, 413). (Does the safety of the nation require the citizen militia, or is it a character-building measure?) From Machiavelli forward, these ideas were insignia of republicanism. In championing the republican principle of a citizen militia, Mill "represented the views of the defenders of civic virtue from the Florentine thinkers of the Renaissance to the British and American Whigs of the seventeenth and eighteenth centuries."[93]

At a time when it seemed to Mill that he had become machine-like and it seemed to others that he was capable only of reproducing ideas programmed into him, he might have felt the attraction of the republican vision of the active life. An acting being does more than perform tasks that have been set by others and reproduce ideas that have been instilled by others. And an acting being acts in company with fellow agents. (Hannah Arendt overstated this point, as was her way: "Real political action comes out as a group act. . . . [W]hatever you do on your own you are really not an actor—you are an anarchist.")[94] Having been brought up in a sort of solitary confinement, Mill would have found that much more meaning in the republican principle of the common pursuit of good. In Bentham's ideal republic there is one citizen: Bentham himself.[95] In Mill's ideal republic all, or at least many, possess the power and habit of acting with one another for public ends. Bentham seems to have regarded unfree peoples (in Russia, Venezuela, India) as his natural constituency, made for his political experiments; his ideal of an administered society was most nearly realized in India. (A Panopticon was built in Lahore.)[96] Mill, himself a bureaucrat in the India service, preferred to imagine people who are self-governing, both individually and as a body—not subjects but citizens. If republicans rebel against kings, Mill rebelled, albeit partially, against a would-be philosopher-king. While James Mill's circle (with its animus against aristocracy and historically settled institutions) seemed to detractors like "a republican sect," the younger Mill rediscovered the republican *character*, the freedom of an agent who is neither a fly in a web (Bentham's model of society) nor a humble drone (James Mill's model of society).[97] Republicanism spoke to Mill's need for autonomy, his wish to feel common cause, his detestation of aristocrats, his elitism, his generosity of sentiment, his passion for civic virtue, his love of antiquity.

Mill broke with a philosophical creed that possessed a null conception of virtue and that left Mill himself with no power of action. In a sense, though, Mill's very reading as a boy prepared him for his venture into republicanism. If classical republicans dreamed of founding Rome anew,[98] if the vision of antiquity entered not only into their thinking but into their imaginations, Mill was possessed with the love of antiquity (and heroic narrative) at an early age. The idea that imagination and the faculty of delight were killed within Mill at about the age of three is quite untrue. Mill's *Autobiography* leaves no doubt about the delight with which he read of antiquity. He read a translation of Plutarch "with great delight" (CW I, 11). Pope's *Iliad* was "one of the books in which for many years I most delighted: I think I must have read it from twenty to thirty times through" (CW I, 13). Mill was assigned the first five books of Livy—"to which from my love of the subject I voluntarily added, in my hours of leisure, the remainder of the first decad" (CW I, 15). He read history, particularly ancient history, avidly. "Roman history . . . continued to delight me" (CW I, 15), and at the age of 11 he began writing a history of "the struggles between the patricians and plebeians" (CW I, 17), based in part on Livy. Without knowing it, Mill had gone back behind that masterwork of modern republicanism, Machiavelli's *Discourses* on Livy—back to the origins themselves. (Machiavelli saw "the quarrels of the Senate and the people of Rome" as "the very origin of liberty.")[99] Without intending it, Mill's overseer had prepared him to enter that tradition of the imagination in which Machiavelli at the end of the day "put on garments regal and courtly; and reclothed appropriately, . . . enter[ed] the ancient courts of ancient men";[100] in which Milton "fought for the ancient liberty of the Greek and Roman republics";[101] in which Rousseau, a republican, envisioned himself "a Greek or a Roman" as a boy;[102] in which John Adams, "aged 23, declaimed [Cicero] aloud, alone at night in his room";[103] in which Lamartine, temporary hero of the 1848 revolution in France, looked to Cicero as his model.[104] As Mill tells the story in his *Autobiography*, he first thought of composing a volume on liberty "in mounting the steps of the Capitol [in Rome]."[105] Mill detested the upper class, feared the lower class, and turned the argumentative force of *On Liberty* against the middle class. His citizenship was in the imagination, a republic; his exemplars, "the Stoic republicans of ancient Rome."[106]

As I say, Mill went back to the origins. And the return to origins is itself a Machiavellian doctrine. "The means of renewing" political bodies, according to Machiavelli, "is to bring them back to their original principles."[107] This doctrine flowed into nineteenth-century radicalism, as when the radical journal the *Black Dwarf* argued that the "corruption" of the English system could be cleansed only by "bringing back the state to first principles."[108] Perhaps it was Mill's wish to return the middle class to its original principles by rekindling in it some part of the spirit the merchants of the Italian republics of the Middle Ages displayed when they won for themselves the sort of privileges that in later centuries routinely accrued to the bourgeoisie. Such a wish seems to form part of Mill's intent in *On Liberty*, where he speaks of the need to refresh practices that have gone stale, and upbraids the middle class for its lack of courage and civic spirit. *On Liberty* is better known, however, for making the argument that *knowledge* requires to be renewed. In his own way Mill refines, as it were, the Machiavellian doctrine of renewal, urging us not to receive knowledge passively but to contest it and so restore it to the life that "truths" originally have. (In the *Logic* Mill states that it is important to "revive" the "original meaning" of doctrines that have passed into commonplaces [CW VIII, 681–83].) Mill himself didn't receive the republican tradition, a tradition turned radical in England, so much as he inducted himself into it after having gone back to its sources and rediscovered its first principles. If he enrolled himself in an antique tradition, hadn't

Machiavelli and John Adams in some sense enrolled themselves among the dead? But if republicanism was beyond the pale in England, it was not in France. In any case it seemed to Mill that "almost all Frenchmen resemble republicans in their habits and feelings" (CW XXII, 152). (Mill's *Autobiography* records with what delight he breathed the sentiments of the French as a young man.) The cardinal tenets of French republicanism—"civil rights, popular sovereignty and the lay state"[109]—were Mill's tenets as well, although he refined them in a highly individual way.

Republicans in eighteenth-century America entered into a tradition then current, powerful, and embodied in a curriculum of texts. Mill came to republicanism differently. Even so, he knew early on the work of one of the mighty names of the republican curriculum, a name sacralized in the nineteenth century, too: Milton. I will try to show that Mill's writing resonates deeply with Milton; that Mill's republican convictions are Miltonic if only in the sense that he uses Miltonic language, as when he accuses Christians of making an "idol" of their thou-shalt-nots (OL 255). (In Milton's view, Christian liberty emancipates from the old, or Mosaic, law, which doesn't mean that the Christian is lawless.) As Mill went behind Machiavelli to Livy, so it is as though he went behind the ritual invocations of Milton in radical republican discourse[110] to engage with Milton himself. Here, concerned as we are with Mill's early education, it is enough to note that as a boy Mill seems to have been introduced to the poetry of Milton, "for whom [James Mill] had the highest admiration" (CW I, 19). This immediately raises the question of whether the republicanism so powerfully voiced in Milton's prose is also attested in the poetry. I believe so. Milton himself "could not separate the function of the poet from the duties of the citizen; he thought of himself as a complete man,"[111] quite unlike the maimed, incomplete beings Mill speaks of in *On Liberty*. Accordingly, the whole of Milton's work from the militancy of the tracts to the quietism of *Paradise Regained* asserts a belief that by surrendering virtue we surrender freedom. And this I take to be identical with the republican thesis that "only those who behave virtuously are capable of assuring their own freedom."[112] Thus Milton's view that the English nation didn't have the virtue to keep up its freedom, but ignobly gave itself back to a king in 1660. Milton "became disillusioned with the failure of the English people to achieve a free commonwealth, and was finally compelled to find the true revolution within the individual."[113] The romantics whose poetry Mill found curative had to reckon with the failure of the French Revolution, and they too turned within. Mill had to reckon with the failure of Reform to reform the nation, and in *On Liberty*, borrowing something of the romantic language of organic growth, he looks within the individual. As Milton, in the manner of a prophet, denounced those who gave themselves up to enslavement, so in *On Liberty* Mill denounces a society that has given itself up to an oppression "enslaving the soul itself" (OL 220).

The republican tradition elevated the figure of the heroic lawgiver. In view of this fact there is a certain comicality in the pretensions of Jeremy Bentham to being such a figure—Bentham, consultant on prison architecture. A note on this point will conclude these speculations about what republicanism meant to Mill.

A chapter of Machiavelli's *Discourses* is entitled "To Found a New Republic, or To Reform Entirely the Old Institutions of an Existing One, Must Be the Work of One Man Only." Machiavelli's thought, for all of its infamous realism, drives toward the legendary One Man who authors and gives laws to a political society. This notion of a sort of underived Man from whom things take their being seems to have been derived itself from Greek political thought, which "had largely conceived leadership in terms of a political hero whose task it was to fabricate the institutions of society and to leave behind a political order bearing the impress of a single personality."[114] The figure of the Lawgiver survives into Mill's "Vindication of the French Revolution of February 1848" (a stout defense of republicanism), where the author contends that "Laws are never well made but by a few—often best by only one" (CW XX, 337). For this role of Only Begetter, Jeremy Bentham nominated himself.

If James Mill made a determined attempt to author a human being, Bentham entertained the fantasy of authoring a country. He was to be Legislator of Mexico. (Aaron Burr was to be Emperor.) He toyed with the idea of going to Venezuela "to do a little business in the way of my trade—to draw up a body of laws for the people there."[115] Bentham also dreamed of being Legislator of India, and with James Mill highly placed in the East India Company, he considered that "I shall be the dead legislative of British India. Twenty years after I am dead, I shall be a despot."[116] This last self-immortalizing remark conveys something of the boyishness that Mill says was Bentham's to the last. It seems Bentham aspired to overthrow the divinities of the republican tradition and replace them with himself. Jeremy Bentham the Lycurgus of Venezuela: this is indeed a fantastic trope, all the more curious in a man who disapproved of metaphor.

THE REPUBLICAN TRADITION as it comes down from Renaissance Italy comprises a complex of beliefs among which four are important for our purposes and one central. These are a love of ancient models; the idea of a natural aristocracy with a claim to the deference of the many (a belief often held right alongside belief in popular sovereignty); the principle of subordination of private to public good; and—the central point—a closely related emphasis on the active character of virtue. Let us see how these themes figure in Mill, beginning with the love of ancient models.

Milton, we have seen, "fought for the ancient liberty of the Greek and Roman republics against the usurpation of kings and priests"[117] (kings and priests still being objects of execration among radicals in Mill's time). Mill looked to the example of Athens, which appealed to him over the more traditional preference of Sparta,[118] and the Athenian ideal generally informs *On Liberty*. At its height (so Mill writes in his review "Grote's History of Greece"), Athens was distinguished by "freedom from social intolerance" (CW XI, 319); the flourishing of "individual genius" (320); "boundless" free speech (324); a vigorous political life that educated and exercised the political abilities of the citizen; and a natural respect for the better argument—along with superior minds able to "recal" (316) the people to their nature in case they forgot it.[119] So apparent is it that Mill took inspiration and delight from the ancients, and so closely does the doctrine of natural respect mesh with the principle of popular deference to a natural aristocracy, that it seems best to pass at once to the second article of the high or classical style of republicanism.

The doctrine of popular deference may or may not have a place in Benthamite thought, which holds that people know their own interests for themselves.[120] It holds a central place in republican thought. According to J. G. A. Pocock, every republican masterpiece states unequivocally that there exists

> a natural aristocracy—an elite of persons distinguished by natural supe-riority of talent, but also by contingent material advantages such as property, leisure, and learning. . . . It was assumed that a supply of such persons was guaranteed by nature, and part of the case against artificially established aristocracies was that the true elite were naturally recogniza-ble by the Many.[121]

Nor, according to the tradition of civic humanism, do the Many simply delegate their power of action to the Few and content themselves with passivity.[122] In principle, therefore, it is possible to believe both in popular sovereignty and in an elite's claim to deference. And this we know was the position of Mill, who favored the admission of the middle and then the lower classes into political power (the "democratic revolution"), while speaking in the voice of an unashamed elitist; who despised born aristocrats and honored real superiority in the same degree. Mill rigidifies the doctrine of voluntary deference, as in his first review of Tocqueville's *Democracy in America*:

> The people ought to be the masters, but they are masters who must employ servants more skilful than themselves: like a ministry when they employ a military commander, or the military commander when he employs an army-surgeon. When the minister ceases to confide in the commander, he dismisses him, and appoints another; but he does not send him instructions when and where to fight. He holds him responsible only for the results. The people must do the same. . . . The interest of the people is, to choose for their rulers the most instructed and the ablest persons who can be found, and having done so, to allow them to exercise their knowledge and ability for the good of the people freely, or with the least possible control—as long as it *is* the good of the people, and not some private end, that they are aiming at. (CW XVIII, 72; Mill's emphasis)

With a kind of Platonic perfection, Mill's doctrine of voluntary deference poises the many on a dot half-way between participation and quiescence. One push in either direction wrecks the beauty of the arrangement. This is doll-house republicanism. The many, Mill imagines, will choose to defer to an elite with scientifically established knowledge of the laws of progress; but there are no such laws and no such knowledge—it is all sheer fantasy. Apparently Mill hoped to reconcile the practice of deference with a democratic age, so that the many would be able to defer voluntarily where before they had deferred perforce. But surely the notion of voluntary deference—such a perfect solution to the conflict between his democratic and elitist leanings—surely it is one of the least credible aspects of Mill's thought. It is as suspect as (and of a piece with) Mill's "proof" that higher pleasures rank above lower pleasures because the highest-ranking authorities have found them to do so—a sort of question-begging that will not pass in a democratic age that has lost the habit of deference. In ancient Athens the populace might commission a general, might submit to a general's rebuke; that was long ago.

In any case, whether because of the allure of the idea or because no other solution to the problem of the Few versus the Many presented itself, Mill held to the ideal of voluntary deference. That ideal carries into *On Liberty*, where Mill argues that

> No government by a democracy or a numerous aristocracy, either in its political acts or in the opinions, qualities, and tone of mind which it fosters, ever did or could rise above mediocrity, except in so far as the sovereign Many have let themselves be guided (which in their best times they always have done) by the counsels and influence of a more highly gifted and instructed One or Few. (OL 269)

While Mill protests the smallness of our views and courage—our inability to act like citizens—his republicanism nevertheless asks not much more of us than to stay out of politics for our own good. As James Harrington, the seventeenth-century republican, would have a senate or natural aristocracy propose laws to the people's representatives, who alone would have the power of enactment; so Mill argues in his *Considerations on Representative Government* that it should be left to a select Commission of Legislation to draft the laws and to Parliament to pass them.[123] It seems the many can best prove their fitness for political power by more or less abstaining from the exercise of it when it is in their hands. Democrat though he was, Mill thought little of the many, and while he deplored the decline of virtù, he would probably have been content if ordinary people possessed virtue in the sense of strict moral habits and a dutiful attention to their own business, and (at least for now) left virtù in the sense of risk-taking and public enterprise to their betters.[124] His attitude on these points seems to have been that of the republican Lamartine, of whom it has been said that he "believed in the People in principle, but was unhappy with them in the flesh."[125]

Considering that Mill is both a democrat and an elitist, both an enemy of hereditary privilege and a champion of deference; considering that he calls both for unfettered debate and for checks on the people, it is little wonder he should have been attacked from all sides. My own sense is that Mill is to be faulted not for being (say) too democratic or too antidemocratic, but for wanting it both ways: wanting to reconcile participation and passivity, virtù and virtue, citizen and bourgeois, lion and lamb. Mill may well have wished, like Milton, to see heroic virtue and public good established, but he ended up prescribing nonheroic virtues like prudence and diligence, and writing the philosophical charter of the pursuit of private happiness. This takes us to the next tenet of republicanism, the subordination of private to public good.

To Auguste Comte, the proclamation of a republic in France in 1848 signified "that each citizen is to devote all his faculties to the service of Humanity."[126] That is taking the republican principle rather far. Mill for his part ranks the public good over particular interests but is unwilling to sacrifice the happiness of individuals to any political ideal or abstraction, such as Comte's Humanity. This tension characterizes the whole of Mill's political thought. He esteems public over private interests, but credentials the pursuit of an exclusively private happiness. In his *Considerations on Representative Government* Mill asserts that a citizen's vote

> is not a thing in which he has an option; it has no more to do with his personal wishes than the verdict of a juryman. It is strictly a matter of duty; he is bound to give it according to his best and most conscientious opinion of the public good. (CW XIX, 489)

One of Mill's concerns in *On Liberty* is exactly the *debility* of personal wishes—"the deficiency . . . of personal impulses and preferences" (OL 264). Mill's own desires—held in check, as he tells us in *On Liberty* strong desires must be—ran I think to republicanism. So it is that in *On Liberty* Mill revives the republican doctrine of the active character of virtue and warns of the extinguishing of the active principle itself. Implied in his criticism of a social order in which people are copies of one another is the ideal of an order in which people (or at least some people) are animated by the desire to achieve public distinction.

As I have argued, *On Liberty* portrays Victorian England as a society in which security of property and improved manners have been purchased at the price of a terrible loss of public spirit—a loss indeed of the power of action (virtù) itself. As Rousseau alleged that the theater "expelled authenticity and action,"[127] so, we might say, John Stuart Mill feared that the social theater of Victorian England had quenched the power of action. That power Mill honored in Armand Carrel, the republican journalist. In his eulogy to Carrel, Mill repeatedly refers to the Frenchman as a man of action, by which he means specifically that Carrel had the courage to incur risks for his principles and to venture out of the narrow sphere in which we pursue nothing more than our own interest.[128] Mill finds the Victorians to. be without the power of action in this sense. The theme of the asphyxiation of action runs through *On Liberty*. Thus, for example, Mill alleges that churchgoing Victorians utter Christian pieties they would never think of acting on. Instead of action, Victorian society encourages busy-ness. According to Mill, "There is now scarcely any outlet for energy [virtù?] in this country except business" (OL 272)—money-getting. (Bentham talked up the virtues of keeping busy.)[129] That is to say, too little energy goes into public-spirited acts. As Mill puts it, "there is need of a great increase of disinterested exertion to promote the good of others" (OL 277).[130] Grave need, he might have said, for he issues in *On Liberty* a prophetic—a Miltonic—warning of a society where the power of action has dried up and liberty has been forfeited because people lacked the ability to sustain it. In terms evoking the civic humanist theme of corruption, he speaks of a lapsed autonomy, a vitiating dependence, an inability to advance the greater good, a "moral degeneration of the individual."[131] He fears a loss of "vital power" (OL 310). The loss of vital power, the power to act, reminds us of Bentham and his behaviorist fantasy of social relations so restrictive that (in the words of Elie Halévy) the individual "will no longer be able not to act morally,"[132] which means that he or she will no longer be able to act at all.

The concept of action—or, more descriptively, the concept of the active exercise of civic virtue—animates the republican tradition. The "ideal of active citizenship in a republic"; the image of the citizen "constantly involved with his fellows in the making of public decisions"; "virtue as a principle of active life"—these themes, each of them evocative of the others, charged the imaginations of republicans.[133] It was because of his respect for the active life that Mill could not reconcile himself to "Bentham's comparatively passive and literally 'reactionary' picture of man."[134] Mill took up the republican concept of action again—took it up, worked with it, metaphorized it, so that knowledge is pictured in *On Liberty* in active terms. Just as courage not proven in action is not courage at all, so Mill argues that knowledge not tested in the lists of dispute is not knowledge at all. Milton makes the same argument of virtue in "Areopagitica." We might say all of this in a short way: virtù exists in action. And in *On Liberty* Mill indicts a social order in which action and virtù have perished. Earlier Mill had described the decline of Athens in similar terms:

At the time when Philip commenced his career of aggrandisement, the only Grecian state in a condition to meet him with anything like equality of strength was Athens; still free and prosperous, but so lowered in public spirit and moral energy, that she threw away all her opportunities, and only rallied with a vigour worthy of her ancestors, when it was too late to do more than perish honorably. (CW XI, 312)

Like a prophet, like Milton, Mill warns of what awaits the society that cannot support its own freedom.

But why is active citizenship so important? Maybe if Mill had lived in an age when immemorial custom was still in force, he would have deemed it enough to inherit tradition in a passive way. However, Mill believed he was living in an age of disruption, when old truths had lost their force and in effect their truth. He attests this belief as early as "The Spirit of the Age" (1831) and re-asserts it in *On Liberty*. *On Liberty* may seem to, but does not exactly arraign society for believing in all the old traditions; it arraigns what we in the twentieth century would call the bad faith of a society that doesn't necessarily believe its own received truths but can't face up to that fact. In Victorian England "people feel sure, not so much that their opinions are true, as that they should not know what to do without them" (OL 233). In this context, active citizenship is vital because no valid alternative exists. We can't just hold with tradition, because we don't authentically possess tradition.[135] We are in the modern condition, confronting the unfixity of things, having to create what is no longer given, having to rediscover tradition itself. The pretense that we can do without all this bother is untenable (like the pretense that today we could return to an agrarian way of life). I stress this point because the patron saint of republicans, Machiavelli, also found himself living in a time "when men [were] no longer guided by structures of habitual legitimacy."[136] The same is true of Milton. It is in a world of broken tradition—the new prince and the deposed king—that Machiavelli and Milton act. For Mill, too, the world cannot just be received, but must be created. I have argued that *On Liberty* refers back *implicitly* to those moments of creation when people act with one another in the name of principles over and beyond their private welfare. Evidently Mill elected not to speak of these things too openly in *On Liberty*, as he chose to put his emphasis not on our "obligation to the public" (OL 256) but precisely on our freedom from the public, and not on the importance of many individuals coming together to act but on the importance of each and every individual's minding his or her own business.

EARLIER I CITED Pip's ironic reference to a Republic of the Virtues in *Great Expectations*. Dickens himself, though, feared for the death of action. By the 1860s, it has been said, Dickens had come to feel that the socio-economic system was "so all-embracingly powerful, or so complex, that it [made] the possibility of moral action within it nearly impossible."[137] But it was an American, writing a few years before the publication of *On Liberty*, who perhaps most hauntingly evoked a world in which action has withered away. As we close this chapter, let Melville's "Bartleby the Scrivener" serve to illustrate the snuffing out of action and "vital power," an idea admittedly hard to hold in the mind.

Milton writes in "Areopagitica," "I cannot praise a fugitive and cloister'd vertue, unexercis'd & unbreath'd, that never sallies out and sees her adversary, but slinks out of the race, where that immortall garland is to be run for, not without dust and heat."[138] The narrator of "Bartleby the Scrivener" lives a cloistered existence (so he tells us) and feels no need of hard striving. His tale is one of evaded decisions, fizzled arguments, passive choices, non-events. It situates us in a lifeless world where, in Tocqueville's phrase, the springs of action have been unbent[139] and where the very assertion of a rebellious will is somehow like the testament of one already dead. If sentimental fiction permits us to sup on emotions without ever undertaking an action and encourages in its consumers a passive dependence on a constant supply of the commodity, our narrator presents himself as a sentimental soul and seems purged of the power of action, almost like someone whose emotions have been expended on the sentimental illusion.[140]

The lawyer, as I have said, leads a cloistered existence. His life lacks a public dimension. "I am one of those unambitious lawyers who never addresses a jury, or in any way draws down public applause; but, in the cool tranquillity of a snug retreat, do a snug business among rich men's bonds, and mortgages, and title-deeds."[141] The man goes on to describe his office as a virtual tomb. In the office is a bust of Cicero, the renowned republican to whom Mill pays high tribute in *On Liberty* (OL 245); the lawyer himself eschews Ciceronian oratory, and seems in some sense as little animate as the bust itself. Indeed his tale recounts his "mortification" at the hands of Bartleby. Images of death hover over this tale of the death of action, and when Bartleby enters the narrator's life—or rather, office—he is described as ghostly and "cadaverous." The narrator gives him work to do. Bartleby shows himself to be a model of quiet labor, even temper, honesty—a model of virtue, in one understanding of the word. Soon enough, however, Bartleby declines to obey his employer's orders, in the immortal words, "I would prefer not to." The sentence has all the finality of a last will and testament. Bartleby keeps up this polite insubordination until he is carted off to the Manhattan House of Detention ("The Tombs"), where, preferring not to eat, he withers and dies—slinks out of the race. The narrator for his part would prefer not to choose between Bartleby and his reputation for good business sense. He postpones the decision and finally slinks out of it, leaving it to the police to deal with the inarguable scrivener. Both lawyer and clerk find action totally unprofitable. Bartleby never bothers to state his case and never engages in drama, while the narrator makes money without need of courtroom heroics and would prefer to get rid of Bartleby with "no vulgar bullying, no bravado of any sort, no choleric hectoring, and striding to and fro across the apartment, jerking out vehement commands": no action. Both principals do without action, and one dies in a tomb while the other lives in one. Like the respectable Victorians Mill holds up to scorn in *On Liberty*, they are copies of one another.

Jeremy Bentham, fantasist of a world in which the power of action is nil, as in a Panopticon, distinguished between the kind of beneficence that costs nothing and the kind that costs something. By all means engage in beneficence of the first kind, says Bentham. By doing so, you "contribute to a sort of fund, a savings-bank, a depository of general good will."[142] Readers of "Bartleby the Scrivener" will discern this sort of thinking in the cost/benefit language of the narrator, a softhearted lover of hard cash who seems to believe that by putting up with Bartleby he is making a deposit in the bank of good will. "To befriend Bartleby; to humor him in his strange willfulness, will cost me little or nothing, while I lay up in my soul what will eventually prove a sweet morsel for my conscience." When harboring Bartleby does begin to cost the narrator, when it alters the world's good opinion of his prudential character, he takes a different view of the case. (Like the Victorians portrayed in *On Liberty*, this man dreads scandal.) Such is the narrator's utilitarian understanding of virtue. The early Bartleby himself, as I have noted, is a human model of those "habits of regularity, temperance, [etc.]" that, Tocqueville tells us, constitute a commercial society's understanding of virtue. In this tale, virtue in the sense of passivity (Bartleby) and prudent calculation of interests (the lawyer) has displaced virtù in the primary sense of the power to act. Security of property ("I felt my most precious papers perfectly safe in his hands"), the pacification of relations ("no vulgar bullying"), the small virtues (incarnated in the early Bartleby)—all that goes under the name of "improvement"—has been paid for in effect by a loss of "vital power." That is the story told by John Stuart Mill as well—in his own way. Mill feared that improvement had extinguished the virtù, the mettle, necessary to maintain freedom; but to this problem of modern society he was unable to frame an effective response.

NOTES

1. Thomas Kuhn, *The Structure of Scientific Revolutions*, 2nd ed. (Chicago: University of Chicago Press, 1970), pp. 4, 6. On the issue of alternative scientific *descriptions* in distinction to alternative scientific *explanations*, see John C. Rees, *John Stuart Mill's* On Liberty (Oxford, U.K.: Clarendon Press, 1985), p. 124.

2. See Thomas Carlyle's essay on Diderot in *Critical and Miscellaneous Essays*, vol. 3 (New York: Scribner's, 1900), p. 230. At one point in this performance, Carlyle joins the names of Bentham and Diderot (p. 243).

3. Douglas G. Long, *Bentham on Liberty: Jeremy Bentham's Idea of Liberty in Relation to His Utilitarianism* (Toronto: University of Toronto Press, 1977), p. 188.

4. See Asa Briggs, *The Making of Modern England: 1783–1867* (New York: Harper & Row, 1959), p. 280. Also see OL 309; and CW XVIII, xl-xli.

5. M. H. Abrams, *The Mirror and the Lamp: Romantic Theory and the Critical Tradition* (New York: Oxford University Press, 1953), p. 119.

6. *On the Constitution of the Church and State*, vol. 10 of *The Collected Works of Samuel Taylor Coleridge* (Princeton, N.J.: Princeton University Press, 1976), p. 114. Coleridge's emphasis.

7. Isaiah Berlin, "On the Pursuit of the Ideal," *New York Review of Books*, March 17, 1988, p. 15.

8. The phrase comes from a newspaper article, directly relevant to *On Liberty*, co-authored by Harriet Taylor. Date is 1846.

9. Alexis de Tocqueville, *Democracy in America*, tr. Henry Reeve; rev. Francis Bowen and Phillips Bradley (New York: Vintage, 1945), vol. 2, p. 351.

10. Tocqueville, *Democracy in America*, vol. 2, p. 337.

11. See John M. Robson, *The Improvement of Mankind: The Social and Political Thought of John Stuart Mill* (London: Routledge and Kegan Paul, 1968).

12. On the figure of Brutus, see J. G. A. Pocock, *The Machiavellian Moment: Florentine Political Thought and the Atlantic Republican Tradition* (Princeton, N.J.: Princeton University Press, 1975), pp. 52–53.

13. In one of his moods Mill looks forward to an age that will lay up empirically determined knowledge in something of the same steady way that people lay up capital with the aid of this code of virtue. "The things in which mankind chiefly improve, are those which admit of being, either literally or virtually, stored up." See Mill's essay on "Centralisation," CW XIX, 612.

14. Joyce Appleby finds virtue in the sense of self-interest to be "almost

the opposite of" virtue in the classical republican sense. See *Capitalism and a New Social Order: The Republican Vision of the 1790s* (New York: New York University Press, 1984), p. 15.

15. On liberalism and the pursuit of private interests, see E. J. Hobsbawm, *The Age of Revolution: 1789–1848* (New York: New American Library, 1962), pp. 278–79: "For classical liberalism, the human world consisted of self-contained individual atoms with certain built-in passions and drives, each seeking above all to maximize his satisfactions and minimize his dissatisfactions. . . . In the course of pursuing this self-interest, each individual . . . found it advantageous or unavoidable to enter into certain relations with other individuals, and this complex of useful arrangements—which were often expressed in the frankly commercial terminology of 'contract'—constituted society and social or political groups." A more uplifting view of liberalism is that of Irving Howe in "Literature and Liberalism." See Howe, *Celebrations and Attacks: Thirty Years of Literary and Cultural Commentary* (New York: Harcourt Brace Jovanovich, 1979), pp. 239–54.

16. In "Utilitarianism" (1861), again, Mill recommends the conditioning of citizens: "Education and opinion, which have so vast a power over human character, should so use that power as to establish in the mind of every individual an indissoluble association between his own happiness and the good of the whole" (CW X, 218). On Rousseau's notion of a Spartan virtue "that is sustained by the pressure of public opinion," see Judith N. Shklar, *Men & Citizens: A Study of Rousseau's Social Theory* (Cambridge, U.K.: Cambridge University Press, 1985), p. 31.

17. Richard E. Flathman, *The Philosophy and Politics of Freedom* (Chicago: University of Chicago Press, 1987), p. 177.

18. Shklar, *Men & Citizens*, p. 66.

19. Quentin Skinner, "The idea of negative liberty: philosophical and historical perspectives" in *Philosophy in History: Essays on the Historiography of Philosophy*, eds. Richard Rorty, J. B. Schneewind, and Quentin Skinner (New York: Cambridge University Press, 1984), p. 197. On negative liberty and John Stuart Mill, see Isaiah Berlin, *Four Essays on Liberty* (New York: Oxford University Press, 1969).

20. Adam Smith, champion of negative liberty (liberty as noninterference), isn't supposed to have anything to do with the stoic tradition of positive liberty; he simply does. His *Theory of Moral Sentiments* is imbued with stoical values from the tradition of positive liberty. Smith exalts a figure of male autonomy who comes straight from that tradition, a figure who despises, moreover, the driving motives of the capitalist way of life, such as the craving for wealth, status, and "approbation."

21. On Linton, see F. B. Smith, *Radical Artisan: William James Linton, 1812–97* (Manchester, U.K.: Manchester University Press, 1973). In turn, behind Linton (an engraver) was the millennial-minded Blake, whose work encrypts a powerful critique of the morality of submission and obedience.

22. Basil Willey, *Nineteenth Century Studies: Coleridge to Matthew Arnold* (London: Chatto & Windus, 1949), p. 44.

23. Cf. Mill's statement in "Utilitarianism," "especially those who have . . . cultivated a fellow-feeling with the collective interests of mankind, retain as lively an interest in life on the eve of death as in the vigour of youth and health" (CW X, 215).

24. Skinner, "Idea of negative liberty," p. 214.

25. See Allan Bloom's Introduction to his own translation of Jean-Jacques Rousseau, *Emile* (New York: Basic, 1979), p. 5.

26. See Charles F. Ramus, *Daumier: 120 Great Lithographs* (New York: Dover, 1978), p. 133.

27. See Bloom's Introduction, p. 5.

28. Appleby, *Capitalism and New Social Order*, p. 5.

29. Gordon S. Wood, "The Fundamentalists and the Constitution," *New York Review of Books*, February 18, 1988, p. 38.

30. Gertrude Himmelfarb, *On Liberty and Liberalism: The Case of John Stuart Mill* (New York: Knopf, 1974). On two-Mill theses, see Rees, *Mill's On Liberty*, pp. 106–25.

31. C. B. Macpherson, Review of G. Himmelfarb's *On Liberty and Liberalism: The Case of John Stuart Mill* in *Mill News Letter* (Winter 1976), 23.

32. Pocock, *Machiavellian Moment*, p. 329. See also Pocock, *Politics, Language and Time: Essays on Political Thought and History* (New York: Atheneum, 1973). On Mill and civic humanism, see Bernard Semmel, *John Stuart Mill and the Pursuit of Virtue* (New Haven, Conn.: Yale University Press, 1984), particularly p. 7.

33. Pocock, *Politics, Language and Time*, p. 85.

34. On eighteenth-century civic humanism, see Pocock, *Politics, Language and Time*, ch. 3. On the attitude of Bentham and James Mill toward corruption and place-holding, see Joseph Hamburger, *Intellectuals in Politics: John Stuart Mill and the Philosophic Radicals* (New Haven, Conn.: Yale University Press, 1965), ch. 2.

35. See, for example, Joel H. Wiener, *Radicalism and Freethought in Nineteenth-Century Britain: The Life of Richard Carlile* (Westport, Conn.: Greenwood Press, 1983), pp. 16, 42, 102. Pocock finds, too, that Chartist ideology carried forward the opposition republicanism of eighteenth-century England. See *Politics, Language and Time*, p. 145.

36. Also in America at the time of its revolution, although that would seem to be a different case.

37. *The Autobiography of Francis Place (1771–1854)*, ed. Mary Thale (Cambridge, U.K.: Cambridge University Press, 1972), p. xv.

38. Cited in Appleby, *Capitalism and New Social Order*, p. 73.

39. Daniel Defoe, *Moll Flanders* (New York: Crowell, 1970), p. 14.

40. Lewis Carroll, "Alice's Adventures in Wonderland" in *Alice in Wonderland*, ed. Donald J. Gray (New York: Norton, 1971), p. 70.

41. Thucydides, *History of the Peloponnesian War*, tr. Rex Warner (Harmondsworth, Middlesex, U.K.: Penguin, 1978), p. 147. Cf. Cicero, *On Duties*: "Those there are, too, who either because of their deep interest in their own affairs or their utter lack of interest in their fellow men insist that they always mind their own business, and they never seem to themselves to be doing any injury to anybody. Such folk avoid one variety of injustice, only to commit the other; they are, indeed, sinners against human society, to which they contribute neither of their concern nor of their energies nor of their means." See Cicero, *Brutus; On the Nature of the Gods; On Divination; On Duties*, tr. Hubert M. Poteat (Chicago: University of Chicago Press, 1950), pp. 475–76.

42. F. M. L. Thompson, "Social Control in Victorian Britain," *Economic History Review* (May 1981), 199.

43. Charles Taylor, "What's Wrong with Negative Liberty," in *The Idea of Freedom*, ed. Alan Ryan (New York: Oxford University Press, 1979), p. 175.

44. Pocock, *Machiavellian Moment*, p. 53.

45. See Mary Wollstonecraft, *A Vindication of the Rights of Woman*, ed. Carol H. Poston (New York: Norton, 1988), p. 17: "A standing army . . . is incompatible with freedom."

46. See *Vindication*, p. 146: Wollstonecraft hopes "that society will some time or other be so constituted, that man must necessarily fulfil the duties of a citizen, or be despised, and that while he was employed in any of the departments of civil life, his wife, also an active citizen, should be equally intent to manage her family, educate her children, and assist her neighbours."

47. See *Vindication*, p. 178: "Should more noble, or rather, more just principles regulate the laws, which ought to be the government of society, and not those who execute them, duty might become the rule of private conduct."

48. On Adam Smith's influence on Bentham, see Sheldon Wolin, *Politics and Vision: Continuity and Innovation in Western Political Thought* (Boston: Little, Brown, 1960), p. 331; and Elie Halévy, *The Growth of Philosophic Radicalism*, tr. Mary Morris (London: Faber and Faber, 1928), pp. 17, 488.

49. "That in the progress of improvement the practice of military exercises, unless government takes proper pains to support it, goes gradually to decay, and, together with it, the martial spirit of the great body of the people, the example of modern Europe sufficiently demonstrates. But the security of every society must always depend, more or less, upon the martial spirit of the great body of the people. . . . Even though the martial spirit of the people were of no use toward the defence of the society, yet to prevent that sort of mental mutilation, deformity, and wretchedness, which cowardice necessarily involves in it, from spreading themselves through the great body of the people, would still deserve the most serious attention of government." Adam Smith, *The Wealth of Nations* (New York: Modern Library, 1937), pp. 738–39.

50. Albert O. Hirschman, *The Passions and the Interests: Political Arguments for Capitalism before Its Triumph* (Princeton, N.J.: Princeton University

Press, 1977), p. 106. On Adam Smith's political views, see Donald Winch, *Adam Smith's Politics: An Essay in Historiographic Revision* (Cambridge, U.K.: Cambridge University Press, 1978). On the seeming inconsistency between Smith's censure of private interests and his legitimization of private interest as the moving force of commercial society, see Gertrude Himmelfarb, *The Idea of Poverty: England in the Early Industrial Age* (New York: Knopf, 1984), p. 49.

51. Smith, *Wealth of Nations*, p. 739; see also p. 740.

52. Hirschman, *Passions and Interests*, p. 105. On this matter, see also Joseph Cropsey, *Polity and Economy: An Interpretation of the Principles of Adam Smith* (The Hague: Martinus Nijhoff, 1957), p. 95: "It is precisely because of [the] power of commerce to generate civilization that Smith can conscientiously advocate commerce in spite of what he takes to be its radical defects."

53. Cf. Semmel, *Mill and the Pursuit of Virtue*, p. 107: "Mill saw himself countering the tendencies of a weak-willed, commercial, modern democratic society and providing basis for a virtuous one." On the other hand, in his essay on "Centralisation," Mill salutes the public spirit of the English— another mark, it seems to me, of the unreconciled character of his thought.

54. An example of city-spirit: When Florence and Siena went to war in 1260, "one of the chief Sienese merchant-bankers, Salimbene dei Salimbeni, gave the commune 118,000 florins, closed his shops, and himself hurried off to war." Jacques Le Goff, *Medieval Civilization, 400–1500*, tr. Julia Barrow (Oxford, U.K.: Basil Blackwell, 1988), p. 295.

55. See Long, *Bentham on Liberty*, p. 118: "A community rendering undeviating obedience to the dictates of utility would represent at one and the same time the apotheosis of majority tyranny in J.S. Mill's terms and the maximization of the Benthamite values of security, predictability, stability, and physical comfort."

56. England was not, in fact, exempt from turmoil. But the system of controls was tight enough to have withstood the French Revolution, the threat of revolution from the working class, 1848, and the easing of state controls on publication. On mid-Victorian dullness, see for example Asa Briggs, *Victorian People: A Reassessment of Persons and Themes, 1851–1867* (Chicago: University of Chicago Press, 1972), pp. 113–14.

57. "Vital power" was a catch-all term of nineteenth-century American (and British?) medicine, referring somewhat vaguely to the body's internal forces and relations; the view of the body encoded in the use of the term was centuries-old, and ultimately classical. See Charles E. Rosenberg, "The Therapeutic Revolution: Medicine, Meaning, and Social Change in 19th-Century America," in *Sickness and Health in America: Readings in the History of Medicine and Public Health*, eds. Judith Walzer Leavitt and Ronald L. Numbers (Madison: University of Wisconsin Press, 1985), p. 47. In using the phrase "vital power," Mill has perhaps invoked the traditional figure of the *body* politic.

58. On Bentham's obsession with security, see Long, *Bentham on Liberty*.

59. On this point, see Mill's *Political Economy*, CW III, 737–38.

60. Adam Smith, *The Theory of Moral Sentiments*, ed. D. D. Raphael and A. L. Macfie (Indianapolis, Ind.: Liberty Classics, 1982), p. 215.

61. Alan Ryan, "Property, Liberty, and *On Liberty*," in *Of Liberty*, ed. A. Phillips Griffiths (Cambridge, U.K.: Cambridge University Press, 1983), p. 219.

62. Mill did want peasants to hold their own land.

63. On the vagueness-around-the-edges of Mill's concept of interests, see Rees, *Mill's* On Liberty, ch. 5.

64. See Richard Ashcraft, *Revolutionary Politics and Locke's Two Treatises of Government* (Princeton, N.J.: Princeton University Press, 1986), p. 73. Ashcraft cites John Owen.

65. Ashcraft, *Revolutionary Politics and Locke's Treatises*, p. 234.

66. On competent judgment, cf. Antony Flew, "'Freedom Is Slavery': A Slogan for Our New Philosopher Kings," in *Of Liberty*, ed. Griffiths, p. 58.

67. Admittedly, the pooling of interests in a cooperative venture differs from private interests in a significant way. More of this presently.

68. Smith, *Wealth of Nations*, pp. 659–60.

69. Ruth H. Bloch, "The Gendered Meanings of Virtue in Revolutionary America," *Signs* 13 (1987), 55. A differently weighted account is in Robert N. Bellah, Richard Madsen, William M. Sullivan, Ann Swidler, and Steven M. Tipton, *Habits of the Heart: Individualism and Commitment in American Life* (Berkeley: University of California Press, 1985), pp. 284–85.

70. Shklar, *Men & Citizens*, p. 18.

71. An official of the Provisional Government offered this assessment of Lamartine, who headed it: "What seduced him most in the acquisition of power was the faculty it bestowed of pardon, of generosity, of the opportunity to show fine sentiment. Less anxious to found the future than to conquer the past by virtue of disinterestedness and abnegation, he transmogrified politics into a species of chivalry, more poetic than practical: permissible when only personal interests are sacrificed, but blameworthy when the public weal is at stake." Cited in H. Remsen Whitehouse, *The Life of Lamartine* (London: T. Fisher Unwin, 1918), bk. 2, p. 324.

72. On the notorious corruption of France under Louis Philippe, see Ramus, *Daumier*, p. xv.

73. Raymond Aron, "Tocqueville and Marx," in *History, Truth, Liberty: Selected Writings of Raymond Aron*, ed. Franciszek Draus (Chicago: University of Chicago Press, 1985), p. 183.

74. Smith, *Theory of Moral Sentiments*, p. 181. Cf. Tocqueville's analysis of the "secret disquietude" and blighted happiness of the Americans in vol. 2, bk. 2, ch. 13 of *Democracy in America*.

75. Hirschman, *Passions and Interests*, pp. 51–52. His emphasis.

76. Smith, *Wealth of Nations*, p. 12.

77. Smith, *Wealth of Nations*, p. 423.

78. See CW X, 336.

79. Flathman, *Philosophy and Politics of Freedom*, p. 229.

80. See ch. 10 of *Considerations on Representative Government* (CW XIX).

81. See Mill's thoughts on the uses of public opinion in "Utilitarianism," CW X, 218.

82. Jeremy Waldron, "Theoretical Foundations of Liberalism," *Philosophical Quarterly* 37 (1987), 133.

83. See Victor Hugo, *History of a Crime* (New York: A. L. Burt, n.d.), p. 277.

84. Charles Dickens, *Great Expectations* (New York: Penguin, 1965), p. 294.

85. Edward L. Bernays, *Biography of an Idea: Memoirs of Public Relations Counsel Edward L. Bernays* (New York: Simon and Schuster, 1965), p. 679.

86. Bentham cited by Halévy, *Growth of Philosophic Radicalism*, p. 83.

87. Pocock, *Machiavellian Moment*, pp. 184–85.

88. On this point, see Halévy, *Growth of Philosophic Radicalism*, p. 400. Particularly informative on Mill's differences with Bentham are Robson, *Improvement of Mankind* and Long, *Bentham on Liberty*. The latter volume reveals that Bentham did in fact affirm the right of free political association (p. 145).

89. See Halévy, *Growth of Philosophic Radicalism*, p. 405.

90. See Halévy, *Growth of Philosophic Radicalism*, p. 500.

91. See Wolin, *Politics and Vision*, p. 329; and Long, *Bentham on Liberty*, throughout.

92. J. G. A. Pocock, *Virtue, Commerce, and History: Essays on Political Thought and History, Chiefly in the Eighteenth Century* (Cambridge, U.K.: Cambridge University Press, 1985), ch. 6.

93. Semmel, *Mill and the Pursuit of Virtue*, p. 110.

94. See the interview with Arendt in *Hannah Arendt: The Recovery of the Public World*, ed. Melvyn A. Hill (New York: St. Martin's, 1979) p. 310.

95. William Thomas, *The Philosophical Radicals: Nine Studies in Theory and Practice, 1817–1841* (Oxford, U.K.: Oxford University Press, 1979), p. 25.

96. Eric Stokes, *The English Utilitarians and India* (Oxford, U.K.: Clarendon Press, 1959), pp. 281, 247.

97. Thomas Macaulay, the sometimes-nemesis of James Mill, called the utilitarians "a republican sect." See Thomas, *The Philosophical Radicals*, p. 135. The spider-web analogy is Thomas's (p. 143), and his analysis of James Mill's thought turns up a Platonic vision of a society divided into guardians and drones.

98. See Hannah Arendt, *Willing* (New York: Harcourt Brace Jovanovich, 1978), p. 207. *Willing* is volume 2 of *The Life of the Mind*.

99. See ch. 4 of the first book of Machiavelli's *Discourses*. I quote from the Modern Library edition of the *Discourses*, tr. Christian E. Detmold (New York, 1950), p. 119. The same volume contains a translation of *The Prince*.

100. Letter of Machiavelli cited by Hanna Fenichel Pitkin, *Fortune Is a Woman: Gender and Politics in the Thought of Niccolò Machiavelli* (Berkeley: University of California Press, 1984), p. 45.

101. Northrop Frye, *The Return of Eden: Five Essays on Milton's Epics* (Toronto: University of Toronto Press, 1965), p. 113.

102. See *The Confessions of Jean-Jacques Rousseau*, tr. J. M. Cohen (New York: Penguin, 1953), p. 20.

103. Bernard Bailyn, *The Ideological Origins of the American Revolution* (Cambridge, Mass.: Harvard University Press, 1967), p. 26.

104. Whitehouse, *Life of Lamartine*, bk. 2, p. 341.

105. See CW I, 249. Cf. Mill's letter to Harriet Taylor Mill from Rome, January 15, 1855, in CW XIV, 291–94.

106. Semmel, *Mill and the Pursuit of Virtue*, p. 181. See also p. 100: Mill came to adopt "Montesquieu's and Cicero's view that the secret ballot in the last years of the Roman republic had been responsible in part for its fall."

107. Machiavelli, *Discourses*, p. 397 (ch. 1, 3rd book).

108. Cited in James Epstein, "Understanding the Cap of Liberty: Symbolic Practice and Social Conflict in Early Nineteenth-Century England," *Past and Present* 122 (1989), 94.

109. John A. Scott, *Republican Ideas and the Liberal Tradition in France, 1870–1914* (New York: Columbia University Press, 1951), p. 31.

110. Note Linton's use of the sacred name of Milton in Smith, *Radical Artisan*.

111. *Complete Prose Works of John Milton*, vol. 4, ed. Don M. Wolfe (New Haven, Conn.: Yale University Press, 1966), p. 1.

112. Skinner, "Idea of negative liberty," p. 214.

113. Frye, *Return of Eden*, p. 112.

114. Wolin, *Politics and Vision*, p. 84.

115. Cited in Halévy, *Growth of Philosophic Radicalism*, p. 297:

116. Cited in Halévy, *Growth of Philosophic Radicalism*, p. 510.

117. Frye, *Return of Eden*, p. 113.

118. Pocock, *Machiavellian Moment*, p. 500.

119. A process that required art. See Mill's *Autobiography*, CW I, 23.

120. On this point see Hamburger, *Intellectuals in Politics*, p. 84; Halévy, *Growth of Philosophic Radicalism*, p. 491. Also see Thomas, *The Philosophical Radicals*, p. 128. (See also p. 103, however.) As Thomas reveals, James Mill did figure on popular deference. He was a pedagogue who envisioned the many deferring to a "paternalistic" elite (p. 137); it's hard to call the deference voluntary, however.

121. Pocock, *Machiavellian Moment*, p. 515.

122. See Pocock, *Machiavellian Moment*, for example pp. 203, 485, 515.

See also Bloch, "Gendered Meanings of Virtue," 41: In classical republican theory, "the people were to rise against threats of foreign invasion and political corruption." Mill was particularly impressed with the example of the Parisians who took to the streets in July 1830 but still seemed "willing . . . to leave their interests in the hands of their natural leaders, the educated men" (CW XXII, xlvii).

123. In making this recommendation, Mill may have had in mind "the work of the Indian Law Commission and Legislative Council." Stokes, *English Utilitarians and India*, p. 177.

124. See, for example, Mill's statement in "Utilitarianism," "Those alone the influence of whose actions extends to society in general, need concern themselves habitually about so large an object" (CW X, 220). Elsewhere Mill complained of people's selfishness and small views.

125. Richard Sennett, *The Fall of Public Man* (New York: Vintage, 1978), p. 231.

126. Auguste Comte, *A General View of Positivism*, tr. J. H. Bridges (New York: Robert Speller, 1957), p. 420.

127. Benjamin R. Barber, "Rousseau and the Paradoxes of the Dramatic Imagination," *Daedalus* (Summer 1978), 84.

128. Mill's homage to Carrel (1837) appears in CW XX, 167–215. On the civic humanist conception of the common good, see Sebastian de Grazia, *Machiavelli in Hell* (Princeton, N.J.: Princeton University Press, 1989), pp. 175–77. That conception reverberates in the language of Mill.

129. See Long, *Bentham on Liberty*, p. 188.

130. By this Mill doesn't mean charity or do-goodism, for in *The Subjection of Women* he notes with disapproval "The great and continually increasing mass of unenlightened and shortsighted benevolence, which, taking the care of people's lives out of their own hands, and relieving them from the disagreeable consequences of their own acts, saps the very foundations of . . . self-respect, self-help, and self-control" (CW XXI, 330).

131. Pocock, *Politics, Language and Time*, p. 88.

132. Halévy, *Growth of Philosophic Radicalism*, p. 471.

133. See Pocock, *Machiavellian Moment*, pp. 4, 49, 185.

134. Long, *Bentham on Liberty*, p. 118.

135. Cf. Lamartine's statement, "Opinions are a scramble; parties are a jumble; the language of new ideas has not been created; nothing is more difficult than to give a good definition of oneself in religion, in philosophy, in politics. One feels, one knows, one lives, and at need, one dies for one's cause, but one cannot name it. . . . The world has jumbled its catalogue." Cited by Terence Ball, "When Words Lose Their Meaning," *Ethics* 96 (1986), 621. Lamartine, who for a time headed the Provisional Government following the February 1848 revolution, figures in Mill's "Vindication."

136. Pocock, *Machiavellian Moment*, p. 165.

137. Wilfred P. Dvorak, "Dickens's Ambivalence as a Social Critic in the

1860's: Attitudes to Money in *All the Year Round* and *The Uncommercial Traveller*," *Dickensian* 80 (1984), 98.

138. *Complete Prose Works of John Milton*, vol. 3 (New Haven, Conn.: Yale University Press, 1959), p. 515.

139. Tocqueville, *Democracy in America*, vol. 2, p. 141.

140. On this point, see Ann Douglas, *The Feminization of American Culture* (New York: Avon, 1977).

141. Herman Melville, *Selected Tales and Poems* (New York: Holt, Rinehart and Winston, 1950), pp. 92–93.

142. Cited in Halévy, *Growth of Philosophic Radicalism*, p. 476.

2

Mill and Milton

I BEGAN THIS study by questioning Mill's claim that conflicting schools of thought can be reconciled by expertly adjusting the one to the other. Mill's own thought, like that of all other human beings, contains unreconciled elements—for example, his commitment on the one hand to the common good and on the other to the pursuit of one's own good in one's own way. Nowhere is the unreconciled character of Mill's thought more sharply in evidence than in the bond between his political ideas and those of Milton, *whom Mill said he detested.* "It is not agreeable to me," he wrote to a correspondent, "to be praised in the words of a man whom I so wholly disrespect as Milton, who with all his republicanism had the soul of a fanatic a despot & a tyrant" (CW XIV, 91; see the Introduction to this book, note 17). It has long been recognized, of course, that Milton's "Areopagitica" stands behind *On Liberty* in some way (although that in itself doesn't exhaust the bond I refer to). Mill keeps Milton behind him, too, rather like a family secret. It would embarrass Mill's critique of puritanism to record a debt to a famous puritan;[1] it would embarrass his critique of intellectual dependence, to acknowledge Milton's authority. What is more, invoking Milton might well associate Mill with republicans in his own time for whom Milton was a sacred name. But above all, Mill shouldn't by rights owe anything to a poet who believes that the freedom to do as you like is itself bondage.[2] He shouldn't, but he does. For any or all of these reasons, Mill nowhere confesses or brings into view his relation to Milton, despite the fact that the similarities in their political thought

75

aren't incidental but deep and grounded, for both men drew on the republican ideal. Gertrude Himmelfarb notes that "No discussion of *On Liberty* is complete without a tribute to *Areopagitica*. Yet Mill himself did not mention that work, and perhaps for good reason."[3]

The reason Himmelfarb advances is that the Mill of *On Liberty* was in philosophical terms a bomb-throwing radical who removed virtually all checks on the individual, while the Milton of "Areopagitica" argued for a much more restricted, that is, sensible, liberty. I contend that on any fair reading of the evidence it was Milton who was the revolutionary, it was Milton who was the visionary. I contend that Mill himself asserted (in *On Liberty*, too) exactly what Himmelfarb charges him with denying, namely "that self-control and self-restraint would have to make up for the want of external constraints, that free men more than others required a strong sense of discipline."[4] Mill: The individual is to "judg[e] himself all the more rigidly, [when] the case does not admit of his being made accountable to the judgment of his fellow-creatures" (OL 225). Mill doesn't abolish self-control; he redoubles it. "The same strong susceptibilities which make the personal impulses vivid and powerful, are also the source from whence are generated the most passionate love of virtue, and the sternest self-control" (OL 263–64). It seems to me Mill's love of virtue (or virtù) was itself sternly checked, and I imagine that Milton illustrated for Mill the risks of too passionate a love of virtue (virtù), too intense and unqualified a commitment to the republican principle. By contrast, Himmelfarb claims that Mill argues in *On Liberty* for an all-but-unchecked liberty (a claim that caricatures the text itself) and that Mill didn't care to cite an argument for liberty that is so much more intelligently qualified than his own. In the eyes of Himmelfarb, one proof of Milton's sensible attitude toward liberty is that he would outlaw popery.[5]

For both Mill and Milton, active virtue stands in contrast to an unthinking reliance on tradition and customary usage. Active virtue breaks out of the ordinary round of things, whether the brutal routine Milton's Samson suffers under as he labors at a mill with slaves; or the "mill-horse round" (OL 308) of bureaucratic life.[6] Both of our principals refuse to be custom-bound. Taking part in the first of the great revolutions, Milton must have felt it was impossible to pretend that pre-existing relations still held good or that one had any morally valid course but to decide disputed questions in the tribunal of conscience, without regard to custom.[7] For his part, Mill came early to the belief that old traditions were crumbling and new ones hadn't yet been settled, and he felt common cause with the French republicans struggling against clerical and monarchical traditions, which continued to exist even though the French Revolution had happened. Mill seems to have believed that to engage in political creation, people must finally depend on their own active virtue, their civic abilities. But it is hard to determine from *On Liberty*, famous for its defense of noninterference with the individual, that its author shares with Milton the belief that government ought to cultivate those abilities.

In "The Readie and Easie Way to Establish a Free Commonwealth" (1660), a last vain appeal to England not to return to monarchy, Milton asserts as an argument for republican government that "of all governments a Commonwealth aims most to make the people flourishing, vertuous, noble and high spirited."[8] Today, when we are apt to read *On Liberty* as though it asked nothing of us but not to meddle, as though it echoed back and in no way challenged our own notions, it comes as a surprise to find that Mill held to the same republican principle.[9] He sets it forth quite plainly in his *Considerations on Representative Government*:

> The first element of good government, therefore, being the virtue and intelligence of the human beings composing the community, the most important point of excellence which any government can possess is to promote the virtue and intelligence of the people themselves. (CW XIX, 390)

At the end of *On Liberty*, as it were at the very margin of the text, Mill makes the same point a little less explicitly. Government should dedicate itself, he says, to "calling forth the activity and powers of individuals and bodies" (OL 310). In his *Autobiography* Mill uses virtually the same language in respect of his own education: it was calculated, he says, "to call forth the activity of my faculties," and in some sense did so (CW I, 33). But what choice had he? If, in *On Liberty*, Mill had given full voice to the argument that the first responsibility of government is to raise up a strong citizenry, might it not have jarred with his argument that the first maxim of good policy is to leave people to themselves? (As it is, Mill refers disdainfully at one point to "misplaced notions of liberty" [OL 304].) What if people don't want to learn to subordinate their interests to the common good, don't want to be made strong?

Logically, the principle that the state has an interest in the character of its citizens pulls against the principle of noninterference; historically, it has given rise to forms of brainwashing and political "education'' that are about as far as may be imagined from the respect for the individual Mill is known for.[10] Mill himself looked to political education; after the 1848 revolution in France, for example, he hoped the new government would be able ''to republicanize the public mind'' (CW XX, 335). His ''idea of popular government was, a government in which [thinkers] . . . strove with all their might to impress their [principles] on the public mind'' (CW XXIX, 395). To be sure, Mill strictly distinguished between impressing ideas and imposing them, the latter being a tyrant's method (and one Milton might not have stopped short of); still, the policy of impressing ideas on the public mind seems a far cry from the official liberal position of neutrality. I don't think Mill reconciled his views so much as he attempted to manage the contradiction between a strongly felt republicanism and a liberalism at once less militant, more prudential, and friendlier to private interests. In any case, the ideal of a robust political life educating and exercising the abilities of citizens is written into Milton's criticism of book-licensing for ''disexercising and blunting our abilities,'' and ''hindring and cropping'' the discovery of truth;[11] and into Mill's attack on a socialized censorship that leaves us ''cramped and dwarfed'' (OL 265), and ''dulls and blunts'' our nature (OL 266). How strongly felt Mill's republicanism was, we can estimate from his use of Miltonic metaphors and idioms like these.

Immediately after the statement quoted a moment ago from ''The Readie and Easie Way,'' Milton works up an animal husbandry metaphor the point of which is that monarchy reduces the people to sheep. The aim of monarchs, Milton alleges, is not to raise up a strong citizenry, but

> to make the people, wealthy indeed perhaps and wel-fleec't for thir own shearing, and for the supply of regal prodigalitie; but otherwise softest, basest, vitiousest, servilest, easiest to be kept under; and not only in fleece, but in minde also sheepishest.

Mill: Without public spirit, the people become ''a flock of sheep innocently nibbling the grass side by side'' (CW XIX, 412). (The splendid modifier ''innocently'' recalls Milton's argument in ''Areopagitica'' against keeping the people in a state of spiritual childhood.) In the *Political Economy* Mill deplores the sort of despotism modeled on ''the government of sheep by their shepherd, without anything like so strong an interest as the shepherd has in the thriving condition of the flock" (CW III, 943). And in *On Liberty* itself Mill declares, "Human beings are not like sheep; and even sheep are not undistinguishably alike" (OL 270). In the first instance Mill's sheep imagery may derive from Tocqueville; in spirit it is Miltonic. Both in Mill and in Milton the sheep betoken not just a passive conformity, but an entire loss of political capacity—a loss of the virtù necessary to maintain liberty, according to the republican vision. Like Tocqueville, both Mill and Milton believe that liberty is an arduous thing and that it comes more naturally to human beings to give up their liberty than to exercise and cherish it. What could be more natural than the lovely pastoral imagery of sheep and shepherd? Again, in "The Readie and Easie Way" Milton condemns the backsliders who willingly "run thir necks again into the yoke which they have broken," that is, who welcome back monarchy (p. 363). In *On Liberty* Mill argues that Englishmen freed themselves from "the tyranny of the political rulers" (OL 217) only to make themselves slaves all over again, slaves of commonplace. "Thus the mind itself is bowed to the yoke" (OL 265). The story shadowed forth in Mill's language curiously resembles one that held deep meaning for Milton: the Exodus narrative of a freed people yearning for the sweets of slavery.[12] But all these are pale resemblances next to that between Mill's statement of September 1830, "if the French people had not valued something else more highly than tranquillity, they would now have been the abject slaves of a priest-ridden despot" (CW XXII, 129), and the invective of Milton's tracts.

Mill's hatred of the tyrant enslaved to his own passions (there is something of this in Milton's Satan) and of the slave tyrannizing over others, appears as early as a speech he gave on the vices of Catiline to the London Debating Society in 1826. In it the young Mill brands Catiline a "slave" to his own "ungovernable passions," a man unable to "resist temptation."[13] If language like this allies Mill with Milton, so does his scorn of priests and despots, and this he shared, knowingly or not, with Shelley (favorite poet of Harriet Taylor), who in turn had honored Milton as a great republican. It's ironic that Shelley confessed an admiration for the "majesty" of Milton's Satan,[14] for the very word smells of royalty, and indeed in Satan we observe a Monarch, an Emperor (so Milton calls him), jealous of his high rank, fond of the prerogatives and regalia of power, consumed with a resentful hatred of what is really a republican moral order where all must stand on their own merits and all equally possess the ability to stand.[15] ("Sufficient to have stood, though free to fall.")[16] Satan speaks with all the corrupt opulence of kingship. In *Paradise Lost*, raised to the highest degree of poetic power, is the hatred of hereditary distinctions that John Stuart

Mill, too, must have felt. To be sure, James Mill hated hereditary distinctions (and admired *Paradise Lost*); it was his conviction that once men swept away privilege and broadened the franchise, the rest would, with a kind of mathematical certainty, take care of itself. By contrast, *On Liberty* starts from the premise that even a broadly enfranchised society may corrupt and that in no sense can we rely on electoral arrangements to supply our own lack of active virtue (virtù); we must stand on our own. Similarly, while James Mill embraced "the morality of a cautious, prudent, commercial civilization,"[17] *On Liberty* makes the all-but-explicit argument that this morality itself has incapacitated people for action. The son's republicanism begins where the father's ends. It is the depth of Mill's feeling for the republican principle that accounts for his bond with Milton.

ON LIBERTY OPENS with a survey of "the struggle between Liberty and Authority" over the centuries (OL 217), a struggle that Mill clearly implies has been concluded in the pacified society of his own day. When the struggle was alive, "patriots" (OL 217) contended against kings, and in some cases (as in England), royal authority was at length forced to wait upon the consent of a representative body. Militant of virtue, defender of regicide, servant of the Commonwealth: Milton was a party to the struggle between liberty and royal authority.[18] And he knew quite as well as Mill that liberty could be threatened not only by royal authority but by the community itself, or its agents, for in "Areopagitica" he remonstrates with a Parliament that has made over to itself those formidable powers of censorship that had been possessed and exercised by the Crown. Mill scans this era from a great distance, and while he has no wish to bargain away secure property arrangements, parliamentary government, comparative religious tolerance, or the other happy results of the closing of the conflict between Liberty and Authority, he fears these gains have proved hollow, for the pacification of society has produced an effete individual without the capacity to support liberty. There has been a "sacrifice of the entire moral courage of the human mind" (OL 242). As Mill traced oligarchical rule back to the constitutional settlement of 1688, so it seems that he saw in the settlement the expiration of the energy of the Commonwealth, for in "Coleridge" he writes,

> The repose which followed the great struggles of the Reformation and the Commonwealth; the final victory over Popery and Puritanism, Jacobitism and Republicanism, and the lulling of the controversies which kept

speculation and spiritual consciousness alive; the lethargy which came upon all governors and teachers, after their position in society became fixed; and the growing absorption of all classes in material interests—caused a character of mind to diffuse itself, with less of deep inward workings, and less capable of interpreting those it had, than had existed for centuries. (CW X, 142)

A torpor, a sleep set in not long after the defeat of Milton's cause.

(In his "Vindication of the French Revolution of February 1848," a defense of French republicanism, Mill advances an explanation for the defeat of the Commonwealth that is quite Machiavellian in spirit. The founders of the Commonwealth failed, he says, because "their republicanism offended the taste for kingship and old institutions, their religious freedom and equality shocked the attachment to prelacy or presbyterianism, which then were pervading principles in the majority of the nation" [CW XX, 357]. Custom is not sacrosanct, but for reasons of policy new laws must not be too far in advance of the many. They "should not violently shock the pre-existing habits and sentiments of the people" [CW XX, 356]. It seems to me Mill tempered his own republicanism for reasons both of policy and principle. For his part, the prince of the republicans, Machiavelli, advises that "He who desires or attempts to reform the government of a state [as Milton desired to see the work of the Reformation completed] and wishes to have it accepted and capable of maintaining itself to the satisfaction of everybody, must at least retain the semblance of the old forms."[19] Milton was not for preserving the forms of monarchy and didn't care to satisfy everybody, but he did quote widely from Machiavelli's *Discourses* in his Commonplace Book. It is said that "Milton's faith in a republican form of government was strengthened by his reading of Machiavelli."[20])

Both Mill and Milton opposed the despotism of custom and hereditary privilege on the one hand, and anxiously regarded the lower orders on the other.[21] Of the two, it was Milton who stood for the Rational as opposed to the reasonable man—the man who will go as far as his conclusions take him, and no reconciliations.[22] Milton's martial prose and fierce invective find only rare parallels in Mill, who wrote with suppressed passion and observed the "studied moderation of language" that he says in *On Liberty* anyone arguing against the grain of opinion *must* observe (OL 259). Moreover, Mill's intellectual way was that of compromise. When he branded Milton "a fanatic a despot & a tyrant," among other things he may have been objecting to

Milton's contempt for in-between positions. Yet Mill himself is responsible for the most trenchant critique in the English language of the reasonable person, that is, the person who adjusts his or her opinions to those of others. I refer to *On Liberty* and its attack on the socially regulated individual. There remains in Mill something of the Rational as opposed to the reasonable man—something of the man whose reason is his passion. As Milton goes as far as his conclusions require, so Mill scorns those reasonable Christians who "look round for Mr. A and B to direct them how far to go in obeying Christ" (OL 249). Some reject the God of *Paradise Lost* as totally unreasonable,[23] but just this has been said of the Athenian ideal that stirred Mill: that in its demands on human nature, it is totally unreasonable (and the framers of the American Constitution were wise to give up on it).[24] Milton is more grandly unreasonable than Mill, but the bond is there. In the figure of Milton the "despot," Mill might see the risks of all that lay under the "studied moderation" of his language.

Mill has more in common with Milton than he cares to acknowledge, beginning with the belief that only through the exercise of active virtue (virtù) is it possible to sustain political liberty.[25] In the words of Bernard Semmel, Mill "perceived that liberty and a good society could survive only if men were ready to prefer a virtue that could yield the highest and most meaningful happiness over a shortsighted sensual and material pleasure"[26]—as could be said verbatim of Milton. *On Liberty* deplores the atrophy of active virtue and the loss of the very power of action; equally, it deplores a social tyranny "enslaving the soul itself" (OL 220), a Miltonic phrase. Like Milton, the author scourges his countrymen for failing to live up to their own freedom. As we have seen, Mill seems to have dated the decline of virtù in England more or less to the generation after Milton. And in accordance with a practice he recommends in *On Liberty*, that of reviving doctrines that have suffered a "decline in . . . living power" (OL 247), Mill revives the spirit of resistance alive in Milton's day, and in Milton himself, before the decline set in. Mill asserts and justifies the right of rebellion. Not the right of political subjects to rebel (the right sacred to seventeenth-century men like Milton and Locke), which he judges to be moot, but an analogous case: the right of women to rebel. Mill believed that to plead the cause of women's emancipation in his day was to be thrown into the same position as those (like Milton) who had once boldly asserted the right of political rebellion. "The case of women is now the only case in which to rebel against established rules is still looked upon with the same eyes as was formerly a subject's claim to the right of rebelling against his king" (CW XXI, 322). Thus Mill's argument against the subjection of women revives, in a new form, a political doctrine no longer possessing any "living power." In effect, Mill calls on the spirit of opposition that originally established the right of rebellion, a right that now, with the struggle between subjects and rulers concluded, has lost its force. Mill must have perceived Milton as an antifeminist bigot (of this, more as we go), but the fact is that many times in *The Subjection of Women* he sounds such Miltonic themes as the legitimacy of rebelling against kings.

Milton wrote with a sense of election and vocation that can only have offended Mill. But Milton's doctrine of merit, his belief that one must earn one's standing through trial, was itself not uncongenial to Mill. Defending the merit principle in *The Subjection of Women*, Mill writes:

> The principle of the modern movement in morals and politics, is that conduct, and conduct alone, entitles to respect: that not what men are, but what they do, constitutes their claim to deference; that, above all, merit, and not birth, is the only rightful claim to power and authority. (CW XXI, 325)

So completely did Milton believe this that in book 3 of *Paradise Lost* God declares that the Son holds his place by merit more than birth (l. 309). Again, Milton claimed freedom of conscience as a sacred right and held that freedom in the polity follows. from and depends on the inward freedom of men ruling over themselves. In the opinion of Douglas Bush this doctrine of merit constitutes the "one central and unchanging principle . . . in Milton's prose and verse."[27] Arguing that women have been deprived of rule over themselves, John Stuart Mill invokes the same principle, namely that political freedom flourishes where, and only where, conscience rules the individual:

> When [people] have learnt to understand the meaning of duty and the value of reason, they incline more and more to be guided and restrained by these in the exercise of their freedom; but they do not therefore desire freedom less; they do not become disposed to accept the will of other people as the representative and interpreter of those guiding principles. On the contrary, the communities in which the reason has been most cultivated, and in which the idea of social duty has been most powerful, are those which have most strongly asserted the freedom of action of the individual—the liberty of each to govern his conduct by his own feelings

of duty, and by such laws and social restraints as his own conscience can subscribe to. (CW XXI, 336)

Does it follow that the way to nurture "feelings of duty" is not to interfere?

Our liberty to govern ourselves according to our own sense of duty Mill calls "rational freedom" (336), a term that brings to mind Milton's postulate of "the free, rational individual,"[28] just as the former's insistence on interpreting for oneself unavoidably recalls the latter's belief in a sacred right to interpret scripture. If active self-governance constitutes merit and is the virtue that supports liberty, lack of self-governance destroys liberty, in the opinion of both Mill and Milton. Noting the poisonous effects of the heteronomy of women, Mill says that a strong mind "refused the command of itself, . . . will assert its personality by attempting to control others" (CW XXI, 338). Milton's Satan is of course the great controller of others, and while he hasn't been refused command of his own being so much as he has himself refused it, still he confirms the principle that lack of self-rule is baneful to liberty. At the opening of "The Tenure of Kings and Magistrates," his defense of the right of rebellion, Milton states quite plainly that unfrecdom prevails where individuals lack the virtue to rule themselves:

If men within themselves would be govern'd by reason, and not generally give up thir understanding to a double tyrannie, of Custom from without, and blind affections within, they would discerne better, what it is to favour and uphold the Tyrant of a Nation. But being slaves within doors, no wonder that they strive so much to have the public State conformably govern'd to the inward vitious rule, by which they govern themselves.[29]

Milton's Samson, himself enslaved, considers this condition of vice effeminacy, a term of contempt also used by Milton in his own person and by Machiavelli. (And by the Commonwealthmen of the eighteenth century, some of whom, however, located true merit in the middle class Mill finds corrupted.)[30] In the course of a discussion of the decline of virtù in his essay on Coleridge, Mill himself goes so far as to refer to the "effeminate shrinking from even the shadow of pain" (CW X, 123); in a bitter newspaper article of 1846, he and Harriet Taylor railed against the "maudlin weakness" and "feebleness of conscience" of womanish men (CW XXIV, 865–66); in Parliament he denounced the proposed abolition of the death penalty as the triumph of "effeminacy"

(CW XXVIII, 269). Strikingly, too, Mill ends *The Subjection of Women* by condemning men's "jealous" restrictions, "vain" fears, and "idl[e]" apprehensions (CW XXI, 340), terms that might almost be taken for a description of a spoiled woman, queen of the realm of vanity and idleness. Perhaps Mill wants to condemn the effeminacy of men.

In fact, *On Liberty* represents men as the heteronomous beings that, according to *The Subjection of Women*, women are. If the essence of Mill's case in *On Liberty* is that people have given in to a morality of timidity and inoffensiveness, have lost the capacity for public life, what does this mean but that in the author's opinion men have become like women? When Mill wrote in the later text that "social institutions do not admit the same free development of originality in women which is possible to men" (CW XXI, 280), did he simply forget how forcefully he had argued in *On Liberty* that men—far from enjoying the free unfolding of their abilities—have their powers "withered and starved," "cramped and dwarfed" (OL 265)? That men—far from possessing originality—have lost the desire for it, even the understanding of it? The fit between *On Liberty* and *The Subjection of Women* doesn't invalidate Mill's argument against the oppression of women, but it does throw a different light on the earlier volume. In *On Liberty* it is as though Mill found a way to satisfy the republican conviction that virtù has declined—a decline chargeable to the effeminacy of men (*virtù* deriving from *vir*, man)—without giving over to the prejudice against women sometimes alleged against Milton. So it is that *On Liberty* represents men as languishing in the littleness of private life ("the narrow circle of personal and family selfishness" [OL 305]), precisely like women in *The Subjection of Women*. So it is that men in *On Liberty* are cowed by the morality of thou shalt not, the same "principally negative morality" that is impressed on women (CW XXI, 329). So it is that men in *On Liberty* partake of the celebrated feebleness of the Victorian woman. The "yoke" of subjection is "tightly riveted on the necks" of women (CW XXI, 268), while in *On Liberty* the mind of everyone including men is "bowed to the yoke" (OL 265). In effect, Mill has accused men of effeminacy without buying into antifeminism itself. As Mill commits himself to republican principles but relaxes them to encourage the pursuit of private interests; as he is drawn to the idea of armed virtue, as in the form of a citizen militia, but doesn't give in to the Virtue Militant tradition of Machiavelli and Milton; so he decries the loss of active virtue without calling on the notion of male supremacy in which virtù was always rooted.

WE KNOW THAT Mill knew *Paradise Lost*. His father, who had "the highest admiration" for the poetry of Milton (CW I, 19), surely introduced him to the great poem, which Mill quotes from here and there. But did Mill know "Areopagitica"?

He did. If Mill had encountered "Areopagitica" nowhere else, he would have seen two excerpts from it in Coleridge's *The Friend*, which was in his library; one of these is the great passage on the trial and testing of virtue. ("I cannot praise a fugitive and cloistered virtue.")[31] Probably too he had seen Macaulay's tribute to Milton in the *Edinburgh Review* in 1825, which refers to "Areopagitica" as "that sublime treatise which every statesman should wear as a sign upon his hand and as frontlets between his eyes."[32] But the evidence goes beyond hearsay. Near the end of his review of Carlyle's *French Revolution* (1837), Mill notes acidly that

> if even Milton's *Areopagitica*, of which now, it would seem, no one dares speak with only moderate praise, were now first to issue from the press, it would be turned from with contempt by everyone who will think or speak disparagingly of this work of Mr. Carlyle. (CW XX, 165)

Mill wasn't one to bluff about his reading. We may take it as a fact that he knew "Areopagitica," and that the resemblances between his arguments and those of "Areopagitica" are not coincidental—not so many uncanny events. This having been said, we must at once discount for the great differences between the "studied moderation" of *On Liberty* and the sarcasm, the displays of virtuosity, and the prophetic passion of Milton's text, which in its very plea for liberty savors of the spirit of intolerance.

If, as I argue, Milton influenced Mill, it isn't that he projected the power of his mind over the centuries (action at a distance), but that Mill entered so largely into his republicanism. Mill did not enter into his religion, his absolute belief in revealed Truth.[33] Such textual similarities as will now concern us express a shared ideal of active virtue, or more particularly an ideal of citizens who realize their individual nature in choosing the public good.[34] A diversity of citizens pursuing a good common to them all: this idea Milton works into "God does not intend all people for one thing"[35] and Mill into "There is no reason that all human existence should be constructed on some one or some small number of patterns" (OL 270).

When the Council of State called on Milton to defend the republic against the calumnies of Salmasius, Milton took on this assignment knowing it would cost him his sight. Although "the doctors were making learned predictions that if I should undertake this task, I would shortly lose both eyes, I was not in the least deterred by the warning. I seemed to hear, not the voice of the doctor . . . but the sound of a certain more divine monitor within."[36] Don M. Wolfe refers to this as a "fateful moment of conscious choice."[37] Here then is an example of choosing the public good. More highly than his own eyes, Milton valued those garlands awarded for "the greatest service to the public good."[38] (Some fight with arms, some with pens: God does not intend all for one thing.) The garland of glory also appears in "Areopagitica"—a pamphlet presented, Milton says at the beginning, to "advance the publick good" (p. 486)—as does the theme of the sovereign importance of choice. "Reason is but choosing" (p. 527). Only if we are free to encounter different opinions can we realize our natures as choosing beings; otherwise, so Milton argues, we remain in spiritual nonage. Virtue is the act of a self-governing being. For his part, Mill too subscribes to the ideal of active choice. "The human faculties of perception, judgment, discriminative feeling, mental activity, and even moral preference, are exercised only in making a choice. He who does anything because it is the custom, makes no choice" (OL 262). Mill looks back to the republican ideal of virtuous choice, although he also prepares the ground for the consumer ideal of free choice, in which virtue of whatever sort simply doesn't figure.

Curiously, Milton conceived abstention itself in strongly active terms.

> He that can apprehend and consider vice with all her baits and seeming pleasures, and yet abstain, and yet distinguish, and yet prefer that which is truly better, he is the true warfaring Christian. I cannot praise a fugitive and cloister'd vertue, unexercis'd & unbreath'd, that never sallies out and sees her adversary, but slinks out of the race, where that immortall garland is to be run for, not without dust and heat. (pp. 514–15)

Here abstention is presented as an action of the most athletic kind. While Mill alleges that Victorian society has sacrificed the half of morality called "energetic Pursuit of Good" to the half called "Abstinence from Evil" (OL 255), Milton is actually able to picture each of these ideals as the other; at this moment they have no separate existence for him, but form a single dialectical whole to be comprehended in the imagination. In Milton's parlance, "to stand" (that is, not to fall) suggests this kind of active abstinence—a holding fast, a dynamic stillness. In the universe of Milton, where hereditary status (standing) has been abolished, to stand is to strive. When we ourselves strive to make sense of the strain of heroic quietism in Milton—Abdiel standing "unmov'd, / Unshak'n, unseduc'd, unterrifi'd" (*Paradise Lost* v.898–99); those serving "who only stand and wait" ("When I Consider . . ."); Christ abstaining from acts of power in *Paradise Regained*; Samson exerting himself with "quiet passivity"[39] in the destruction of the temple—we might recall the abstinence passage in "Areopagitica." Clearly Milton believed that true obedience is of an active and not a passive nature, as he himself did more than passively carry out the commission of the Council of State, but threw himself into the task and sacrificed his sight.[40] It is in obedience to divine inspiration that Samson shatters the tablets of precedent and performs an action that a moment before, he himself would not have been able to compass: he destroys at one blow the priests and lords of the Philistines.

In the concept of active obedience, Milton fuses two ideals that Mill implies have come apart, the Christian concept of a service that is freedom[41] and the Aristotelian concept of the citizen who both rules and is ruled. Obedience is required of the citizen living under the rule of law—law as opposed to the arbitrary will of a despot—but not a passive obedience, if only because the citizen himself actively exercises his liberty in public life. Public liberty is his own liberty. Ruler and ruled combine in the Miltonic image of the free man subject to God, the Christian citizen. Certainly Mill for his part draws on the tradition of the citizen who realizes his nature in political participation. (Thus Mill's recommendation of participation in *Considerations on Representative Government*—guarded recommendation.) He too cherishes the active principle.[42] He too believes virtue asks more of us than obedience to custom, passive conformity, and a careful regard for our worldly interests. He too has an elevated—in fact, a republican—conception of the general good.

In *Samson Agonistes* Milton allows Dalila to pirate the republican argument. Gold didn't persuade her to betray Samson, she alleges (laden with jewels at the moment she makes this claim), but rather the high principle of duty to the public:

> [A]t length that grounded maxim
> So rife and celebrated in the mouths
> Of wisest men; that to the public good

> Private respects must yield, with grave authority
> Took full possession of me and prevail'd;
> Virtue, as I thought, truth, duty so enjoyning.[43]

Samson rejects these noble protestations. Now that he has had trial of
Dalila, he has a better sense of how to take her words. It is a little hard
to believe that Dalila yielded only reluctantly, and against her own
inclinations, to the idea of betraying Samson—that she didn't really
want to do it and (as she alleges) never meant to bring on him all this
grief. It is in fact impossible to credit her statement that she has no
excuses for what she did (l. 734), because she proceeds to offer one
excuse after another and at length drops the penitential pose entirely.
So in the terms of the poem, Dalila's presentation of herself is simply
a fraud; she is still weaving word-nets to ensnare Samson. In "Areopagitica" Milton argues that there are "cunning resemblances" (p. 514)
between good and evil, and that only by trial and testing can we learn
to judge well; he dramatizes the point in Dalila's cunning forgery of his
own republican principles, the same principles that define the mission
of Christ in *Paradise Regained*: "to do / What might be public good."[44]
How fiercely Milton himself held to the doctrine of the public good we
can judge from the "Second Defense of the English People," in which
he swears he has not been "influenced by ambition, gain, or glory, but
solely by considerations of duty, honor, and devotion to my country,"[45] a statement characteristic of Milton's sense of rectitude. And
this avowal brings up another resemblance between our two principals.

While both Mill and Milton are certainly middle-class in the sense of
rejecting hereditary privilege, asserting the merit principle, and regard-
ing the lower orders warily, neither can affirm the bourgeois principle
of the legitimacy of private gain; or rather, Milton cannot do so at all,
and Mill only conflictedly. Both men go so far as to deprecate trade
itself. In "The Readie and Easie Way," a tract displaying precious
little of the bourgeois virtue of prudence, Milton thunders against
those who would bring back monarchy to restore trade, then in
depression:

> If the people be so affected, as to prostitute religion and libertie to the
> vain and groundless apprehension, that nothing but kingship can restore
> trade . . . if trade be grown so craving and importunate through the
> profuse living of tradsmen that nothing can support it, but the luxurious
> expences of a nation upon trifles or superfluities, so as if the people

generally should betake themselves to frugalitie, it might prove a dangerous matter, least tradesmen should mutinie for want of trading, and that
therefor we must forgoe and set to sale religion, libertie, honour, safetie,
all concernments divine or human to keep up trading . . . [then] our
condition is not sound but rotten, both in religion and all civil prudence.[46]

Here is a remarkable bourgeois, filled with contempt for trade. "Areopagitica" itself reviles the stationers in whose economic interest it
was to petition Parliament to restrict printing. Moreover, Milton uses
metaphors of trading in polemic, a sign that his feeling on the subject
ran deep. He condemns, for example, "the great Marchants of this
world" (meaning prelates) and vindicates those (Puritans) who will
give away but not market spiritual gifts; in the same work he charges
that prelacy prostitutes the gospel and "makes merchandize of the
bodies and souls of men."[47] When Samson revives at the end of
Samson Agonistes, he casts cost reckoning and prudential forethought
to the winds; or rather, a gust of divine inspiration rouses him to
perform a heroic action that he cannot foreknow, an action that in the
event costs his life. Such is the regard of Milton (blind and inspired
like Samson himself) for mere self-interest. Contemptuous as he is of
mental narrowness, Mill too despises the single-minded pursuit of gain
(his hatred of the spirit of money-getting sometimes rising to a passion
[CW XXIII, 720–21]), and in his defense of the French revolution of
February 1848, there appears a more temperate version of Milton's
attack on trade. "The one inducement," Mill says, "by which Louis
Philippe's government recommended itself to the middle classes, was
that revolutions and riots are bad for trade. They are so, but that is a
very small part of the considerations which ought to determine our
estimate of them" (CW XX, 325). Mill pours scorn on "the worship of
the cash-box and of the ledger" (325). Such passages stand in the way
of those who would view Mill as a paid agent of the middle class,
representing its interest as the public interest; they also serve as
indices of the power of his republican convictions and revolutionary
sympathies, power studiously suppressed for the most part, as Mill
suppressed reference to Milton in *On Liberty*. But to return to "Areopagitica," which funds that text.

"I fear yet [the] iron yoke of outward conformity hath left a slavish
print upon our necks," writes Milton (pp. 563–64), attacking those
who would dictate the last petty points of religious observance. According to Milton, this sort of coercion destroys the mental freedom
required to rescue truth "out of the gripe of custom" (564). It produces

"a grosse conforming stupidity" (564). Custom, conformity, the yoke of subjection: Mill preserves and transforms this argument in *On Liberty*. Under the social tyranny of his day, he says, it doesn't occur to people "to have any inclination, except for what is customary. Thus the mind itself is bowed to the yoke: even in what people do for pleasure, conformity is the first thing thought of" (OL 264–65). Mill's prose lacks the loft of Milton's winged words, but all the same it is striking how closely his terms correspond with those of a man he detested—doubly so, considering that at this moment in his argument Mill is protesting against "the theory of Calvinism" (OL 265), and Milton, Presbyterianism. The root of the similarity is both men's love of active virtue (virtù) as opposed to passive conformity, mindless observances, and sheer custom,[48] although Mill tempers that passion with an endorsement of antiheroic virtues like thrift and foresight.[49]

Both, too, celebrate vigorous, enlivening debate. Mill protests the stifling of opposition voices, while Milton's Satan makes a practice of asking rhetorical questions, attempting by that means to pre-empt other voices and cut off the possibility of an unpredetermined answer.[50] Such, to Mill, is the virtue of debate that he would keep argument alive even after knowledge has become so settled that there isn't much to argue about—thus he fought off the deathly implications of his theory that positive knowledge would advance to the point where disagreements would cease and a kind of steady state would set in (OL 250–51).[51] Such, to Milton, is the fallacy of unanimity that he wrote into *Paradise Lost* his differences with those reformers of knowledge who thought to cleanse the human intellect, restore it to its unfallen state, and make all minds see as one.[52] Where Milton argues that free debate "betok'ns us not degenerated, nor drooping to a fatall decay, but casting off the old and wrincl'd skin of corruption to outlive these pangs and wax young again" (p. 557), Mill warns,

> There is only too great a tendency in the best beliefs and practices to degenerate into the mechanical; and unless there were a succession of persons whose ever-recurring originality prevents the grounds of those beliefs and practices from becoming merely traditional, such dead matter would not resist the smallest shock from anything really alive, and there would be no reason why civilization should not die out, as in the Byzantine Empire. (OL 267)

By such a decline, perhaps, had Milton's beliefs turned into the evangelical dogmas of Mill's contemporaries, who extolled "true self-government, the power of resting on one's own centre and consciously choosing the course of life instead of remaining a slave to outward circumstance and custom."[53] Externally, this resembles the Miltonic ideal closely enough; and only externally. Mill wrests ideas like "slavery to custom" from the evangelicals, breaking their straight and narrow meaning—in a sense, an act of virtù. Both Mill and Milton, it seems, look to the regenerating effects of virtù, in the absence of which the polity corrupts. As the means of regeneration, Mill exhorts men "to reassume the ill deputed care of their Religion into their own hands again" (p. 554). While Mill despises those Christians who "look round for Mr. A and B to direct them how far to go in obeying Christ" (OL 249), he is not eager for a revival of religion, and might prefer that citizens reclaim the power of forming common intentions and concerting their actions, a power given up at present to the engines of conformity; at the same time, he is cautious of inciting to action.

The Miltonic cast of the language of *On Liberty*, of which more examples could be cited, is prefigured as early as Mill's essay "Coleridge." There Mill discusses, with sympathy, Coleridge's idea that the orthodox themselves can be considered heretics if they hold their faith with a wrong disposition of the heart. It is the manner in which beliefs are held that is decisive. Coleridge judges (says Mill) "that there may be orthodox heretics, since indifference to truth may as well be shown on the right side of the question as on the wrong" (CW X, 161). "A man may be a heretick in the truth," says Milton in "Areopagitica" (p. 543). In *On Liberty* Mill contends that our beliefs may be true (or true in part) but if we don't know the basis of them and don't try them against other beliefs, we might as well be in bondage to error. This argument, a Miltonic one, had long been in Mill's mind and was deeply grounded in his experience. Mill would deny it, but the rigorous questioning that he advocates is a secular analogue of the puritan practice of interrogating the self—searching the conscience—rooting out falsehood.

BUT LET US pass from the inspection of textual resemblances to a more general consideration of the spirit in which our principals argue. It would be idle to say who challenged public opinion more: Milton in his writings on divorce and regicide, or Mill in his position on the emancipation of women and his insults to public opinion as such. Neither the author of "Areopagitica" nor the author of *On Liberty* can accept that these advanced arguments will not carry. As stringently qualified as it is,[54] Milton's position on freedom of expression was an advanced one in his own day. The abolition of prior restraint on publication, what he pleads for in "Areopagitica," came about a half century later, in 1695. Yet the legal apparatus of censorship didn't pass into disuse until the Victorian era, by which time an efficient moral police had taken over, making Liberty's victory a hollow one. Rather similarly, *On Liberty*'s plea for free private consumption didn't really triumph until the advent of consumer society, which has made museum pieces of the language, the literacy, and the republicanism of John Stuart Mill.[55]

The loft and power of Milton's prose in "Areopagitica" may mislead us into believing that such an argument cannot have failed. Actually it is hard to see how it could have succeeded. After all, Milton was petitioning Parliament to set aside its own act in deference to "the voice of reason" (p. 490), that is, *his* voice. "Areopagitica" is "an appeal to the supposedly reasoned good sense of a Parliament which has nevertheless somehow mistakenly instituted a savage censorship."[56] If the men of Parliament were really endowed with the "undaunted Wisdome" (p. 487) Milton would like to credit them with, they would never have enacted such a benighted policy. And if, having enacted it, they were to revoke it at the urging of one man, they would have to be quite unlike the bondservants of error that Milton himself so often pictures fallen men as being. "Areopagitica" seems to suppose the men of Parliament cherish their rational freedom, in the sense that they are not at all bound to their errors but are willing to renounce them "speedily" (p. 487) once rationally persuaded. But the poetry and prose of Milton abound with images of human beings in bondage to their errors—actors having surrendered their freedom. In Milton's view it seems to be the nature of human beings to enter into bondage, as it is the responsibility of the prophet (Milton) to denounce this betrayal and to point the way to freedom. (Probably it is because of the prophet's insight into our human penchant for enthralling ourselves that Christ rejects Athenian wisdom in *Paradise Regained* as far inferior to the prophetic kind.)[57] Some few may cherish their rational freedom, but more commonly people rid themselves of it, which is unsurprising in view of Milton's belief that freedom "is not something man naturally wants for himself, but something that God is determined he shall have."[58] "Areopagitica" soars clear above these problems, as though by sheer heroism of language it could triumph over them all. It can't for a moment accept the fact that in real terms, it is an exercise in failure; its "vital power" is such that we ourselves can hardly imagine it either. "Areopagitica" conveys a sense of victory over all impossibilities. Elsewhere in his poetry and prose, as I have noted, Milton depicts actors who do not conduct themselves like the rational free agents he imagines the audience of "Areopagitica" as being; who swear away their freedom because they lack the virtue (virtù) to cherish it. Of this Milton is intolerant. His "sense of his own rationality and rectitude drives him to harsher and harsher attacks on almost all his contemporaries,"[59] and in time he is strongly drawn to the idea of the rule of the virtuous over the unvirtuous, a position at some distance from the comparative tolerance of "Areopagitica."

"Areopagitica" is based on the improbable hope that Parliament will submit to Milton's correction. *On Liberty* practically stipulates its own failure. It is as it were self-doomed. "I insist thus emphatically," Mill writes,

> on the importance of genius, and the necessity of allowing it to unfold itself freely both in thought and in practice, being well aware that no one will deny the position in theory, but knowing also that almost every one, in reality, is totally indifferent to it. (OL 268)

It would seem prodigiously unlikely that the Victorian public would revoke its enactments at the urging of one man, and that a man who views it with open contempt. The Victorian public was not going to voluntarily defer to John Stuart Mill. Indeed on Mill's terms it is simply impossible for the many to assent to his argument. "Originality is the one thing which unoriginal minds cannot feel the use of" (OL 268). How then should unoriginal minds be moved by Mill's plea for the free unfolding of genius? (Interestingly, however, Mill himself disclaimed originality—an issue still to be looked into.) Mill presses on with his argument regardless. Defeated as he is, he keeps an even temper and allows himself no bursts of resentment. He specifically rejects "the sort of 'hero-worship' which applauds the strong man of genius for forcibly seizing on the government of the world and making it do his bidding in spite of itself" (OL 269)—which rules out Carlyle's Abbot Samson, if not the Samson of Milton. Remarkably, then, in the same essay where Mill asserts that the many lack the virtù necessary to support freedom, he also, and with equal conviction, asserts that the title of the many to freedom is *not* thereby forfeited.[60] But there was that in Mill which was drawn to the idea of the rule of the instructed over the uninstructed. The early essay "The Spirit of the Age" (1831) gives evidence of this, and it seems to me significant that the essay ends with an allusion to Milton: "But 'fit audience,' even 'though few,' cannot be found for such discussions" (CW XXII, 316). Milton went further with the idea of the rule of the few than Mill would permit himself to, and was willing to make deference involuntary; this, I think, helps to explain why Mill called him "a fanatic a despot & a tyrant."

Milton also made freer use than Mill of vituperation and shabby tactics. In fact he could write gutter prose. Milton liked to slang opponents, and in his regicide tracts he "hides behind the vehemence of his own rhetoric, spitting out phrases that are the Renaissance equivalent of 'capitalist lackey,' 'jack-booted tyranny,' and 'making the world safe for democracy.' "[61] Writing an "improved" prose, Mill more or less abstains from the use of thought-drugging epithets and only on occasion serves up the liquor of metaphor. His prose isn't entirely dry, though: where Milton likes to speak of hermaphrodites and unmanned men, Mill likes to speak about dwarves.

Milton, then, "used flimsy evidence, hearsay, rumor, ridicule, and abuse; yet he believed that his writings stood free of moral blame."[62] Even "Areopagitica," for all of its magnificence, is marred. This speech is as fierce in its anti-Catholic invective as it is eloquent in its vision of liberty; quite falsely, it represents censorship as a South European invention unknown in England until introduced there by crypto-Catholics. One of Milton's aims seems to be to draw all red-blooded Protestants together against a common foe, and to this end he plays on a holy-war mentality and a sense of apocalyptic crisis that don't usually make for tolerance. Passages like this convey some idea of Milton's really venomous hatred of Catholicism, some sense of how fully he entered into the common opinion that the Roman Church was a conspiracy against liberty:

> Sometimes 5 *Imprimaturs* are seen together dialogue-wise in the Piatza of one Title page, complementing and ducking each to other with their shav'n reverences, whether the Author, who stands by in perplexity at the foot of his Epistle, shall to the Presse or to the spunge. These are the prety responsories, these are the deare Antiphonies that so bewitcht of late our Prelats, and thir Chaplaines with the goodly Eccho they made. (p. 504)

Such are the heights of hatred Milton reaches. Mill was not given to such expression, although, true to that principle of secret sharing which I have been discussing, he does stigmatize the Roman Catholic

Church as the "most intolerant of churches" (OL 232) and specifically
criticizes the indexing of books (OL 246). Mill abhorred Comte's
scheme for a secular religion on the model of the Catholic Church; like
Milton, his principles were "of an extreme Protestant type."[63]

IN ONE OF the "Applications" that conclude *On Liberty*, Mill touches
on the question of why we aren't legally free to enter into slavery; why
"in this and most other civilized countries . . . an engagement by
which a person should sell himself, or allow himself to be sold, as a
slave, would be null and void" (OL 299). Mill's answer is (in short)
that "the principle of freedom cannot require that [one] should be free
not to be free. It is not freedom, to be allowed to alienate his freedom"
(OL 300). This legal point isn't a highly charged issue in *On Liberty*;
consenting slavery figures in the text less in its literal than its meta-
phorical aspect, and less as a legal than a moral question. That is, the
contention of *On Liberty* isn't so much that it is legally invalid to enter
into slavery as that it is morally invalid to give over to a conformity
"enslaving the soul itself" (OL 220). In the seventeenth century the
distinction between legal and moral slavery seems to have been less
clear, and the issue of consenting slavery was taken up, in the context
of resistance to popery and tyrannical rule, by Locke's party and,
before that, by Milton. Locke states his position in the *Second Treatise
of Government*: "A man not having the power of his own life cannot
by compact or his own consent enslave himself to any one, nor put
himself under the absolute arbitrary power of another to take away his
life when he pleases."[64] One twist to give this argument is that where
tyranny exists it cannot have been consented to, therefore cannot be
legitimate. Thus the first Whigs contended that "because no one can
legitimately consent to slavery, and hence to absolute monarchy, the
latter must be viewed as a government by 'conquest,' in which the
subjects have only the status of 'slaves.' "[65] Such an argument appeals
to the principle of consent, a principle enshrined in the *Second Treatise*. Yet Locke's formulation also seems to imply that, in the event
people should consent to tyranny (contract to be slaves), their decision
would be null and void; in this sense the rule that no man can enslave
himself serves as an appeal against the principle of consent. It was in
this latter sense that Milton invoked the rule against consenting slavery
in "The Readie and Easie Way," written at a moment when the English
people were about to subject themselves to a king, in defiance (so it
seemed to Milton) of reason and virtue. "Nevertheless the people

refused to obey the voice of Samuel; and they said, Nay; but we will
have a king over us" (1 Samuel 8:19). Milton argues that

> to fall back, or rather to creep back so poorly as it seems the multitude
> would, to thir once abjur'd and detested thraldom of kingship, not only
> argues a strange degenerate corruption suddenly spread among us, fitted
> and prepar'd for new slaverie, but will render us a scorn and derision to
> all our neighbours. (pp. 356–57)

Milton himself pours scorn and derision on those "running headlong
again with full stream wilfully and obstinately into the same bondage"
(p. 358) from which England had only recently freed itself. (Mill once
claimed that "the French people surrendered themselves willing
slaves" to Napoleon [CW XXII, 144].)[66] Emphatically, Milton does
not believe that no one willingly enters into slavery, or that where
tyranny exists it cannot have been consented to. He finds human
beings quite capable of betraying their liberty.

Adam does so in *Paradise Lost*. In Mill's terms, Adam alienates his
freedom; as Northrop Frye puts it, Adam uses his freedom "to lose
freedom."[67] Specifically, he subjects himself to Eve, making as it were
an idol of her. After confessing to God, "Shee gave me of the Tree,
and I did eat," Adam is reproved in these terms:

> Was shee thy God, that her thou didst obey
> Before his voice, or was shee made thy guide,
> Superior, or but equal, that to her
> Thou didst resign thy Manhood, and the Place
> Wherein God set thee above her made of thee,
> And for thee, whose perfection far excell'd
> Hers in all real dignity: Adorn'd
> She was indeed, and lovely to attract
> Thy Love, not thy Subjection. (X.145–53)

Thus an unmanly Adam lacks the virtue to sustain his freedom. Later
in the poem, commenting on Adam's forfeiture of freedom, Michael
says,

> Since thy original lapse, true Liberty
> Is lost, which always with right Reason dwells
> Twinn'd, and from her hath no dividual being:
> Reason in man obscur'd, or not obey'd,
> Immediately inordinate desires

> And upstart Passions catch the Government
> From Reason, and to servitude reduce
> Man till then free. (XII.83–90)

Adam failed his own freedom. On his side, John Stuart Mill would cut the inheritance of privilege and prejudice (and land), which ideally would put all individuals on a par with Adam, the first man, compelled to stand on their own merits. Neither of our authors has great faith, though, in the human ability to stand up to such hard testing. In Milton's opinion, not only can and do we enslave ourselves, but all too often we are slaves *to* ourselves, given up to our passions and lusts. Perhaps Samson enslaved himself to a passion for Dalila, that sensual queen. If he had given in to her entreaties at the mill in Gaza and put himself into her custody, he would have entered into slavery yet again. Like the Israelites, like Samson, we are in the habit of betraying our liberty. Milton follows this line of reasoning straight through to the conclusion that neither of the consenting slaves—neither the man who subjects himself to a tyrant nor the man subjected to his own vicious passions—has a claim to the privileges of freedom. They have forfeited them. "Man is free to lose his freedom, and there, obviously, his freedom stops."[68] If a majority should consent to tyranny, it has simply proven its unfitness for the making of political choices, its lack of virtue (virtù). Milton states this principle with reckless candor in the second edition of "The Readie and Easie Way":

> They who past reason and recoverie are devoted to kingship, perhaps will answer, that a greater part by far of the Nation will have it so; the rest therfor must yield. Not so much to convince these, which I little hope, as to confirm them who yield not, I reply; that this greatest part have both in reason and the trial of just battel, lost the right of their election what the government shall be.[69]

In Milton's view, no earthly hero—not Cromwell, not Milton himself, not "a whole nation of Brutuses"[70]—can make people free who are determined to be slaves, but this moral fact does not commit Milton to a program of inaction. It doubles his sense of urgency and mission. The nation must be warned before it swears away its own freedom irreversibly. Rather than doing nothing (because the really free man can't be enslaved and the enslaved can't be freed), Milton argues, with a Machiavellian sense of the moment and a prophetic sense of the need not to spurn God's grace, that the time is *right now* for putting English liberties on a secure foundation.

If that task should require that the many—the idolaters and backsliders—be deprived of a political voice, then so be it. Those who lack the virtù necessary to support freedom, those who would consent to tyranny—even if they are a majority—must be ruled against their will. Judgment is not according to "number," in which there is "little vertue," but according to "weight and measure."[71] Milton ends "The Readie and Easie Way" with a grieving elegy to "the language of the good old cause." Mill for his part protested the tyranny of numbers, proposed weighted votes, put aside the simplicity of Benthamite calculation, weighted the kinds of pleasure, celebrated the opposition to the Bourbons as "incorruptible adherents of the good old cause" (CW XXII, 136), and in his eulogy to Armand Carrel explicitly called attention to the "close . . . parallel" between the last Bourbons and the last Stuarts (CW XX, 186).

It is striking how fully the author of *On Liberty* shares Milton's contempt for a self-enslaved majority and how firmly he dissents from Milton's illiberal conclusions. Victorian society as Mill describes it has indeed surrendered to tyranny, "a social tyranny more formidable than many kinds of political oppression" (OL 220). Mill envisions this tyranny as "enslaving the soul itself" (OL 220), and he sees the majority, also in Miltonic terms, as both despotic and weak-willed, as both the enslaver and the enslaved. Yet he doesn't go on to argue that the many are politically incompetent, fit only to be ruled against their will. Indeed he forbids any such despotic arrogation. He wants virtue to be "voluntarily accepted as a guide to life in the Stoic manner, not . . . imposed by a Savonarola, a Cromwell, or a Robespierre"[72]—or a Milton. Rather than declaring that the majority has forfeited its right to make decisions for itself, Mill exhorts people to do just this and bars the moral police from interfering in the realm of private decision; he fervently hopes, of course, that people will make the right use of their liberty and defer to the wise few. In his tribute to Armand Carrel, Mill specifically repudiates the idea of taking the freedom of the many into political trusteeship; he praises Carrel for having nothing to do with

> the notion of governing by an active minority, for the good of the majority, but if necessary in opposition to its will, and by a provisional despotism that was to terminate some day in a free government. (CW XX, 206)

I imagine that if Milton read *On Liberty* he might judge Mill to be a backslider, a man who betrayed his premises and failed, for lack of courage, to draw the rational conclusion. That is, he might condemn

Mill for barring an elite from taking charge of a majority without political capacity or virtue. (And to Milton a "self-regarding" act might be Eve falling in love with her own image in the pool.) Milton's will to take over the freedom of the many follows directly from his conviction that people "resist and oppose their own true happinesse,"[73] whereas Mill is officially committed to the principle that no one knows better than the individual where happiness lies and how to achieve it. And yet if people know best what makes them happy, then Mill has no warrant to criticize Victorians for their conformism, their meanness of soul—perhaps that's what makes them happy. While not as openly contemptuous as Milton of people's right to make the wrong decisions, Mill nevertheless goes only so far with the principle that no one but the person concerned can say what makes for his or her well-being. Otherwise he would never have written *On Liberty* at all.

IN HIS CONTEMPT for legality and custom,[74] in his rationality that drove to extreme conclusions, in his determination not to shrink from those conclusions, Milton was a revolutionary. His very quietism can be understood as an extreme statement or limiting case of the republican thesis: here virtue is not only necessary for liberty, but in and of itself *is* liberty. But revolution for Milton is less a thrust into the future than a return to original principles. Northrop Frye has put the matter well in a passage, part of which we have met before:

> The Protestant in Milton fought for the restoration of the primitive church of the gospels, against the usurpation of tradition, or custom and error. The humanist in him fought for the ancient liberty of the Greek and Roman republics against the usurpation of kings and priests. The Parliamentarian in him fought for the liberties of the lords and commons against the usurpations of Star Chamber and royal prerogative. All these causes are rooted in history, models of the past to be recreated in the future.[75]

This theme of return and renewal finds striking expression in "Areopagitica," where Milton prophesies "the reforming of Reformation it self" (p. 553), that is, a renewal of the Reformation through a return to the principles of Wyclif. (In 1823 Mill had sent letters to the *Morning Chronicle* under the name of Wickliff.) According to Machiavelli, cited as the ancestor of modern revolutions,[76] such bodies as republics "or religious sects" require now and then to be brought "back to their original principles" and cleansed of the corruption that comes with time.

And those are the best-constituted bodies, and have the longest existence, which possess the intrinsic means of frequently renewing themselves, or such as obtain this renovation in consequence of some extrinsic accidents. And it is a truth clearer than light that, without such renovation, these bodies cannot continue to exist; and the means of renewing them is to bring them back to their original principles.[77]

Milton was a revolutionary in this Machiavellian sense, a turner-back. In his Commonplace Book appears this entry:

To return a republic to the very source of government, either by enacting good laws or by reducing magistrates to the ranks of ordinary citizens or by restoring the control of things to the decision of the people, is often beneficial. see Machiavel.[78]

To return, to restore: here is the language of revolution. Milton's aim, we might say, was to roll back time, or alternatively to re-establish truths that had dimmed with time, as he re-awakened the story of Adam and Eve. Mill was not in point of fact a revolutionary—he *did* have revolutionary sympathies and leanings—but he deeply believed that truths dim with time and require to be revived, as he himself wanted to revive the concept of active virtue: if not the "fierie vertue" of Milton's Samson (l. 1690) as his spirits revive, not the passive virtue of the conforming Victorian either.

Milton's causes, writes Northrop Frye, were rooted in history. To glance back to the beginning of this study, Mill esteems Coleridge over Bentham just because of the former's respect for history, and from Coleridge (a close reader of Milton) he learned to look for the original meaning of doctrines now received, "to discover by what apparent facts [they were] *at first* suggested" (CW X, 119; my emphasis). Thus in his *Logic* Mill argues that meaning itself needs to be brought back to its original principles. "It is natural and inevitable," he writes,

that in every age a certain portion of our recorded and traditional knowledge, not being continually suggested by the pursuits and inquiries with which mankind are at that time engrossed, should fall asleep, as it were, and fade from memory. It would be in danger of being totally lost, if the propositions or formulas, the results of the previous experience, did not remain, as forms of words it may be, but of words that once really conveyed, and are still supposed to convey, a meaning: which meaning, though suspended, may be historically traced, and when suggested, may

be recognised by minds of the necessary endowments as being still matter
of fact, or truth. While the formulas remain, the meaning may at any time
revive. (CW VIII, 681–82)

At this point Mill's discussion fills with the language of re-awakening.
"Revive . . . rediscover . . . recovered . . . words in their original
acceptation . . . revived . . . recover . . . rediscovering the lost
signification . . . original meaning . . . rediscovered . . . revival." In
effect, Mill has rarified Machiavelli's concept of renovation into an
intellectual exercise. Meaning itself tends to corrupt and stands in need
of renovation, and the only means of renovation is the challenging of
received truths (what Mary Wollstonecraft calls "moss-covered
opinions"[79]). This argument is elaborated in *On Liberty*. There Mill
contends, for example, that "religious creeds . . . are full of meaning
and vitality to those who originate them, and to the direct disciples of
the originators" (OL 247), but settle into dogma—a charge that Milton,
with his contempt for dogma and his zeal to revive the spirit of Wyclif,
would second. Mill calls on his readers to enter into original meanings,
meanings that were alive at some point in the past when men possessed
the power to originate, or what Machiavelli calls *virtù*.

> When [a doctrine] has come to be an hereditary creed, and to be received
> passively, not actively—when the mind is no longer compelled, in the
> same degree as at first, to exercise its vital powers on the questions which
> its belief presents to it, there is a progressive tendency to forget all of the
> belief except the formularies, or to give it a dull and torpid assent. (OL
> 248)

As much as Machiavelli (the premier republican), Mill feels it necessary to reverse the decline of things through time. Both in *On Liberty*
and in *The Subjection of Women* he seeks to revive the spirit of
resistance that originally established liberty and has since expired, but
he purges resistance of its more violent properties. Just so, Mill takes
over the concept of virtù but "reconciles" it somehow with the steady
prosecution of private interests. And like Machiavelli, who credited
the contention between the Senate and the people of Rome with
maintaining public liberty; like Milton, who quoted Machiavelli to this
effect in his Commonplace Book and whose Samson is "in struggle,"
contending; so Mill believed in strong contention—of the intellectual
sort. Mill did celebrate the February 1848 revolution in France, but *On
Liberty* does not call for revolution, nor does it recognize any debt to
the revolutionary Milton. And as though his doctrine of intellectual

struggle and rediscovery (as "improved" as it is) were still too dangerous, Mill later mocked the idea that "at the moment when some man
feels tempted to meddle with the property or life of another, he ha[s]
to begin considering for the first time whether murder and theft are
injurious to human happiness" (CW X, 224).

In reading *On Liberty* we encounter a man who is temperate, tolerant
(if at times opinionated), and liberal. But as this drawing-out of the
resemblances between Mill and Milton may suggest, there is that in
Mill which is intemperate, disdainful, and passionately republican. It
was Mill's own "most passionate love of virtue" that required to be
checked by "the sternest self-control" (OL 264), for Mill was committed to not being the despot of virtue he saw Milton as being. In his
effort to manage the risks of his own position, Mill had, as I will argue,
mixed success. To his credit, Mill didn't let his admiration for heroic
virtue draw him into the kind of reactionary claptrap espoused by
Carlyle—or the cult of the archaic later taken up by Eliot, Yeats, and
Pound. Mill rejected, too, the lethal fantasy of a dictatorship of virtue;
it is well that he did so. However, he himself was an apologist for
despotism—despotism over what he considered to be the lower races,
in their own interest. As for Mill's republican principles, they are
diluted perhaps too well in the text of *On Liberty*, making that essay a
rather watery wine. While decrying the pacification of society—the
sleep that has fallen over it, the loss of heroic spirit, the waning of the
power to act—Mill himself pacifies the republican ideal. He so defends
against the dangers of republicanism that *On Liberty* serves as a
philosophical license for the very preoccupation with private interests,
the very neglect of the "obligation to the public" (OL 256), that Mill
wanted to discountenance. Mill's thought, I find, isn't the solid and
well-balanced structure that it presents itself as being, but an uncertain
structure subject to strains and faults. His very belief that "truths" fit
rests on no more solid foundation than Milton's vision of piecing
together the dismembered body of Truth.[80]

MILTON IS AN absent presence in *On Liberty*, haunting the text. Early
in his life, Mill himself might have felt in the presence of Milton: this
would have been in 1810, when the Mills briefly lived in Milton's own
dwelling. (The house bore the inscription, "Sacred to Milton, Prince
of Poets.")[81] At this time Mill was under the tutelage/censorship of his
father, learning Greek. Milton too was destined for great things by his
father, and his education, like Mill's, seems to have been closely
watched. Perhaps it will be fitting to end this consideration of the way

Mill stands to Milton—and in this case Mill was neither pupil nor intellectual ward—with a note on education.

Douglas Bush has said of Milton that he "was concerned with education, with individual cultivation and growth and public responsibility."[82] All this is strictly true of John Stuart Mill. Mill's strong sense of the public weal is attested in too many ways to number. His passionate concern with individual cultivation and growth is inscribed in the organic metaphors of *On Liberty*, such as:

> Human nature is not a machine to be built after a model, and set to do exactly the work prescribed for it, but a tree, which requires to grow and develope itself on all sides, according to the tendency of the inward forces which make it a living thing. (OL 263)

Neither is this a dead metaphor. Where Milton evinces a love of the sheer profusion of being in the Garden of Eden, Mill pleads (in the *Political Economy*, of all places) for preserves in which plants and animals are left alone, even though this extension of liberty to nature should serve no narrowly utilitarian purpose. Again, a deep concern with education—not surprising in an individual who was himself the subject of a Frankensteinian educational experiment—is plainly stamped on Mill's writings. In a discussion of taverns in *On Liberty*, for example, Mill calls for every effort to be made "to educate [the laboring classes] for freedom" (OL 299), education meaning the right cultivation of the inward forces of the human being. Mill did not propose that freedom be withheld pending the conclusion of this educational experiment—he favored the admission of the middle and then the lower classes into political power—but that the working class should be given freedom and educated for freedom at once. As a pedagogical aid, Mill was willing to bring intense moral pressure to bear on the individual, for example by public voting; like Milton, who esteemed "honourable shame,"[83] he was alive to the uses of public opinion. Here, in any case, in the idea of educating a people for freedom, Mill's democratic sympathies and intellectual snobbery meet. Education is the answer to the riddle of how the masses, with all their "ignorance and . . . selfishness and brutality" (CW I, 239), can possibly be trusted with freedom. If they learn their lessons well (a mighty if, as Mill must have been aware), the conflict between the democratic and the elitist principles will be brought to a happy close. The masses will learn to voluntarily defer. Having gained political power, they will more or less abstain from using it. Those who were hardly ready for capitalism will be ready for co-operation.

Milton confronted the same riddle as Mill: "the problem of how to establish liberty before all men were educated up to it."[84] By 1660, when a "misguided and abus'd multitude"[85] showed itself willing to embrace monarchy once again, Milton had evidently determined that liberty could only be established by a virtuous few, against the will of the many. If they were misguided, they must now be guided rightly. Christopher Hill reminds us, in the same paragraph from which I have just quoted, that Milton was "a revolutionary, not a nineteenth-century liberal." The textbook example of the nineteenth-century liberal is John Stuart Mill. Less widely recognized is the fact that Mill, like Milton, enlisted in the tradition of republicanism. Like Milton but under different historical circumstances, Mill contended with country-men who possessed (as it seemed to him) small capacity for freedom. Rather than calling for the unvirtuous to be made wards of the state, Mill chose to defend their right and educate their capacity to make political choices.

It would appear that in his relation to his father, Mill had seen enough of wardship. In his attack on "the system of despotic, or what is called paternal, government" in *On Liberty* (OL 299), we perhaps detect the protest of a son held in subjection by his father. Milton on his side records that "My father destined me in early childhood for the study of literature. . . . [M]y father took care that I should be instructed daily both in school and under other masters at home."[86] According to E. M. W. Tillyard,

> The effect of this concentrated care and unremitted pressure on Milton's powerful, sensitive nature was to make him believe from a very early age, to make him assume indeed axiomatically, that he was no ordinary person, but destined to some high achievement in one of the fields of learning.[87]

The mature Milton is filled with a sense of vocation and merit.

Milton's childhood "seems to have been somewhat of the kind which led John Stuart Mill to nervous collapse through the excessive intellectual pressure of his father." But Milton emerged from this hard tutelage with a strong "sense of his own capacity."[88] With Mill it was otherwise, as his *Autobiography* records. Mill came to know too well what it is to be "captivat[ed] under a . . . childhood of prescription."[89] Only in his bureaucratic capacity would he feel a calling to play the paternal despot, ruling over those deemed unfit to rule themselves.

NOTES

1. On the puritanism of James Mill, see William Thomas, *The Philosophical Radicals: Nine Studies in Theory and Practice, 1817–1841* (Oxford, U.K.: Oxford University Press, 1979).

2. See Stanley Fish, *Surprised by Sin: The Reader in Paradise Lost* (London: Macmillan, 1967), p. 337.

3. Gertrude Himmelfarb, *On Liberty and Liberalism: The Case of John Stuart Mill* (New York: Knopf, 1974), p. 280.

4. Himmelfarb, *On Liberty and Liberalism*, p. 283.

5. Himmelfarb, *On Liberty and Liberalism*, p. 280.

6. Bentham intended his Panopticon as "a mill for grinding rogues honest." Cited among other places in Thomas, *Philosophical Radicals*, p. 18.

7. See Robert M. Adams, *Ikon: John Milton and the Modern Critics* (Ithaca, N.Y.: Cornell University Press, 1955), pp. 149–50: "For Milton, the proper judge of what, to be technical, are controversies in faith and religion was the inward conscience of the individual Christian, as enlightened by heavenly grace and guided by right reason." In appealing to conscience, Milton invalidates the argument that classical republicanism did not allow for the right of conscience. On this last, see David A. J. Richards, "Autonomy in Law," in *The Inner Citadel: Essays on Individual Autonomy*, ed. John Christman (New York: Oxford University Press, 1989).

8. In *Complete Prose Works of John Milton*, vol. 7 (New Haven, Conn.: Yale University Press, 1980), p. 384. Mill looked back to the "high-spirited people" of the free medieval cities (CW III, 881).

9. Cf. Jean-Jacques Rousseau, *Confessions*, tr. J. M. Cohen (Harmondsworth, Middlesex, U.K.: Penguin, 1953), p. 377: "So the question of the best possible government seemed to me to reduce itself to this: 'What is the nature of the government best fitted to create the most virtuous, the most enlightened, the wisest, and, in fact, the best people, taking the word "best" in its highest sense?' "

10. On this point, see Paul Johnson's attack on Rousseau in *Intellectuals* (New York: Harper & Row, 1988), especially p. 25.

11. "Areopagitica" in *Complete Prose Works of John Milton*, vol. 2 (New Haven, Conn.: Yale University Press, 1959), pp. 491–92.

12. On the Exodus story, see Michael Walzer, *Exodus and Revolution* (New York: Basic, 1985).

13. The speech appears in the *Mill News Letter* of Spring 1972; I quote from p. 6.

14. Preface to "Prometheus Unbound" in *Shelley's Poetry and Prose*, eds. Donald H. Reiman and Sharon B. Powers (New York: Norton, 1977), p. 133.

15. Cf. Northrop Frye, *The Return of Eden: Five Essays on Milton's Epics* (Toronto: University of Toronto Press, 1965), p. 64: Satan "can only understand ruling and serving, and prefers reigning in hell to serving in heaven." In a republican order these are false categories; they have been abolished.

16. *Paradise Lost*, III.99. I use the Merrit Y. Hughes edition of Milton's *Complete Poems and Major Prose* (Indianapolis: Odyssey Press, 1957). Of the rebels and the loyalists God says: "Equal in thir Creation they were form'd" (VI.690).

17. Thomas, *Philosophical Radicals*, p. 102.

18. So indeed was Locke, a member of a radical underground who, like Milton, asserted the right to take up arms against a king.

19. I quote from the Modern Library edition of Machiavelli's *Discourses*, tr. Christian Detmold (New York, 1950), p. 182. The same volume contains a translation of *The Prince*.

20. *Complete Prose Works of John Milton*, vol. 1 (New Haven, Conn.: Yale University Press, 1953), p. 415n.

21. On this last point, see Andrew Milner, *John Milton and the English Revolution: A Study in the Sociology of Literature* (Totowa, N.J.: Barnes and Noble, 1981) and Christopher Hill, *Milton and the English Revolution* (New York: Viking, 1977).

22. Cf. Milner, *Milton and the English Revolution*, p. 123.

23. On this point, see for example Frye, *Return of Eden*, p. 101.

24. See Richards, "Autonomy in Law," p. 249.

25. Cf. Milner, *Milton and the English Revolution*, p. 189, on "active virtue, the virtue that challenges tyranny."

26. Bernard Semmel, *John Stuart Mill and the Pursuit of Virtue* (New Haven, Conn.: Yale University Press, 1984), p. 185.

27. Douglas Bush, *John Milton: A Sketch of His Life and Writings* (New York: Macmillan, 1964), p. 126. Bush classifies Milton, accurately in my opinion, as an aristocratic republican.

28. Milner, *Milton and the English Revolution*, p. 105.

29. *Complete Prose Works of John Milton*, vol. 3 (New Haven, Conn.: Yale University Press, 1962), p. 190.

30. See G. J. Barker-Benfield, "Mary Wollstonecraft: Eighteenth-Century Commonwealthwoman," *Journal of the History of Ideas* 50 (1989), 95–115.

31. See *The Friend* in *The Collected Works of Samuel Taylor Coleridge*, vol. 4, ed. Barbara E. Rooke (London: Routledge and Kegan Paul, 1969), p. 80.

32. Thomas Babington Macaulay, *Critical and Historical Essays*, vol. 1 (New York: Dutton, 1966), p. 191.

33. Milton contends that the ancients did not practice licensing because they didn't approve of it, not because they didn't know of it ("Areopagitica," p. 522); Mill argues that "a large portion of the noblest and most valuable moral teaching has been the work, not only of men who did not know, but of men who knew and rejected, the Christian faith" (OL 257). Nevertheless, in "Utilitarianism" Mill holds that that doctrine, rightly understood, is consonant with the best Christian morality.

34. Cf. Fish, *Surprised by Sin*, p. 207: With the "decision to subordinate the self to a higher ideal" comes "the discovery of the true self."

35. *Complete Prose of Milton*, vol. 1, p. 405 and vol. 2, p. 413n.

36. *Complete Prose Works of John Milton*, vol. 4, ed. Don M. Wolfe (New Haven, Conn.: Yale University Press, 1966), p. 588.

37. *Complete Prose of Milton*, vol. 4, p. 6.

38. *Complete Prose of Milton*, vol. 4, p. 550n.

39. Darryl Tippens, "The Kenotic Experience of *Samson Agonistes*," *Milton Studies* 22 (1986), 184.

40. In his chronicle of Louis Napoleon's coup d'état in 1851, Victor Hugo contrasts the infamous passive obedience of soldiers to the valor of citizens whose obedience to the Constitution drives them to the barricades. See Victor Hugo, *History of a Crime* (New York: A. L. Burt, n.d.).

41. See for example Fish, *Surprised by Sin*, p. 332: "Paradoxically, freedom (liberty) is obedience because true freedom is the freedom to follow the best, while freedom from God is servitude." Mill would find language like this scandalous, although he too, after all, would teach people to overcome their own selfishness, error, thralldom.

42. On Milton's idea of an act, see Frye, *Return of Eden*, p. 21.

43. Lines 865–70. My text is the Hughes edition of Milton's *Complete Poems and Major Prose*. Critical controversy swirls around the figure of Dalila.

44. *Paradise Regained*, I.203–4. Hughes edition.

45. *Complete Prose of Milton*, vol. 4, p. 587. Cf. Sebastian de Grazia, *Machiavelli in Hell* (Princeton, N.J.: Princeton University Press, 1989), p. 176: "Any single man who wishes to reform his republic must wish to benefit 'not himself but the common good, not his own succession but the country. . . .' The common good is part of Niccolò's own profession of faith. . . . ; it is part of why he considers himself a good man and of why he can be an impartial counselor, of why he is willing to face the 'envious nature of men' and the attendant 'troubles and difficulties' of taking a path 'not yet trod on by others.' He is 'driven' . . . by that natural desire to work, come what may, for those things that he believes bring the common benefit 'to each one.' "

46. *Complete Prose of Milton*, vol. 7, pp. 385–87. Cf. Milton's derisive sketch of a hypocrite "in the shop trading all day without his religion" in "Areopagitica," pp. 544–45.

47. See "The Reason of Church-Government" in *Complete Prose Works of Milton*, vol. 1, pp. 802, 849.

48. Milton cites "the Apostle to the Thessalonians, Prove all things, hold fast that which is good" ("Areopagitica," pp. 511–12). Mill: "We must regard as an evil, all restraint put upon the spirit which never yet since society existed has been in excess—that which bids us 'try all things' as the only means by which with knowledge and assurance we can 'hold fast to that which is good' " (CW V, 457).

49. In overpopulated places (such as Europe) Mill would accord the right to marry to those only who could show that they were able to provide for

children; thrift and planning would be necessary to achieve such financial competence. See OL 304.

50. Stanley Fish, however, finds that Milton himself bullies the reader into submission by drumming on the same "truths" and presenting illusory arguments. See his analysis of "The Reason of Church-Government" in *Self-Consuming Artifacts: The Experience of Seventeenth-Century Literature* (Berkeley: University of California Press, 1972). There is a lot to be said for Fish's argument.

51. Implicitly, Bentham "call[ed] for an end to political debate as such." See Douglas G. Long, *Bentham on Liberty: Jeremy Bentham's Idea of Liberty in Relation to His Utilitarianism* (Toronto: University of Toronto Press, 1977), p. 209.

52. See Fish, *Surprised by Sin*, pp. 107–30, esp. p. 125.

53. Eric Stokes, *The English Utilitarians and India* (Oxford, U.K.: Clarendon Press, 1959), p. 30.

54. Stringently qualified in that Milton would not extend toleration to impiety, popery, or immorality.

55. The hope for a republican revival is voiced in Robert N. Bellah, Richard Madsen, William M. Sullivan, Ann Swidler, and Steven M. Tipton, *Habits of the Heart: Individualism and Commitment in American Life* (Berkeley: University of California Press, 1985).

56. Hugh Richmond, *The Christian Revolutionary: John Milton* (Berkeley: University of California Press, 1974), p. 109.

57. On the attractions of slavery, see Walzer, *Exodus and Revolution*.

58. Frye, *Return of Eden*, p. 85.

59. Richmond, *Christian Revolutionary*, p. 116.

60. The other side was taken by the French republican Emile Faguet (1847–1916): "Since the masses in his view distrusted and even hated really aristocratic and talented people, they chose only mediocrities to rule them, men who were as petty and inept as themselves. He concluded, therefore, that the people were not fit to choose responsible rulers." See John A. Scott, *Republican Ideas and the Liberal Tradition in France* (New York: Columbia University Press, 1951), p. 112.

61. Bruce Boehrer, "Elementary Structures of Kingship: Milton, Regicide, and the Family," *Milton Studies* 23 (1987), 114.

62. Note by Don M. Wolfe in *Complete Prose of Milton*, vol. 4, p. 587. Cf. Adams, *Ikon*, p. 175: "To gain a point Milton . . . makes use, on occasion, of the glib, abstract distinction; what his opponents want is 'license,' what he wants is 'liberty.' "

63. John M. Robson, *The Improvement of Mankind: The Social and Political Thought of John Stuart Mill* (London: Routledge and Kegan Paul, 1968), p. 138.

64. John Locke, *Second Treatise of Government* (Indianapolis: Library of Liberal Arts, 1952), p. 15.

65. Richard Ashcraft, *Revolutionary Politics and Locke's Two Treatises of Government* (Princeton, N.J.: Princeton University Press, 1986), p. 206.

66. Cf. Mill's letter to Henry Samuel Chapman of May 28, 1849: "France having had the rare good fortune of finding two men in succession of perfectly upright intentions, enlightened principles & good sense, Lamartine & Cavaignac, has chosen to reject both & be governed by a stupid, ignorant adventurer [Louis Napoleon]" (CW XIV, 33).

67. Northrop Frye, *Anatomy of Criticism: Four Essays* (New York: Atheneum, 1967), p. 212. See also Frye, *Return of Eden*, pp. 21–22.

68. Frye, *Return of Eden*, p. 21.

69. *Complete Prose of Milton*, vol. 7, p. 455.

70. Arnold Stein, *Heroic Knowledge: An Interpretation of* Paradise Regained *and* Samson Agonistes (Minneapolis: University of Minnesota Press, 1957), p. 70.

71. *Complete Prose of Milton*, vol. 7, pp. 415–16.

72. Semmel, *Mill and the Pursuit of Virtue*, p. 14.

73. *Complete Prose of Milton*, vol. 1, p. 803.

74. On this point, see Milner, *Milton and the English Revolution*, p. 55.

75. Frye, *Return to Eden*, p. 113.

76. Hannah Arendt, "What Is Authority?" in *Between Past and Future: Eight Exercises in Political Thought* (New York: Penguin, 1978), p. 139.

77. Machiavelli, *Discourses*, p. 397.

78. *Complete Prose of Milton*, vol. 1, p. 477.

79. Mary Wollstonecraft, *A Vindication of the Rights of Woman*, ed. Carol H. Poston (New York: Norton, 1988), p. 113.

80. "Areopagitica," pp. 550–51.

81. Michael St. John Packe, *The Life of John Stuart Mill* (London: Secker and Warburg, 1954), p. 21.

82. Bush, *John Milton*, p. 93.

83. *Complete Prose of Milton*, vol. 1, p. 841.

84. Hill, *Milton and English Revolution*, p. 157.

85. "The Readie and Easie Way," in *Complete Prose of Milton*, vol. 7, p. 388.

86. *Complete Prose of Milton*, vol. 4, p. 612.

87. Cited in Richmond, *Christian Revolutionary*, p. 33.

88. Richmond, p. 34.

89. "Areopagitica," p. 514.

3

Checks and Balances

ON LIBERTY AUTHORIZES the pursuit of one's own good in one's own way and bars government and society from interference in the private realm. And yet we know Mill ranked the public good over selfish pursuits and charged government with the responsibility of promoting the virtue of citizens. He prized active pursuit of the public good—civic virtue. He dreaded the drying-up of the active principle. He was convinced that "the great danger in modern society was that citizens would give their attention to commercial interests or to amusement . . . and would withdraw from an active participation in government."[1] He believed that security of property, strict moral habits, and the other tokens of "improvement" had been gained at the price of a grave loss of courage and public spirit, which he hoped to revive. He hoped to revive virtù. But as the Machiavellian provenance of this term suggests, virtù poses moral risks, as do other republican values. When Mill wrote that Milton "with all his republicanism had the soul of a fanatic a despot & a tyrant" (CW XIV, 91; see the Introduction of this book, note 17), he may have meant that Milton was all those things *in spite of* being a republican; but the sentence equally says that Milton was a fanatic, a despot, and a tyrant *in virtue of* being a republican. Republicanism is a hazardous ideal, affirming as it does, not merely the human ability to keep within the law, but the ability to challenge the law (as Milton did in his contempt for legalities) and institute a new political order (as Mill remarks in *On Liberty* that ordinary Americans are able to invent government itself in a pinch). Indeed, the watchword of republicanism—"the public good"—is at once a high ideal and a slogan used to beautify treachery and assassination, as when leaders lie "for the public good"[2] or murder "for reasons of state." Such are the dangers of Mill's own sentiments that he himself once said that an obsession with the lifelessness of civilized people, their nonindividuality, their enervation, their petty routines (the very burden of his complaint in *On Liberty*) leads straight to Robespierre (CW X, 123). Robespierre, a republican.

Mill laments that his age has leveled people who once inhabited "different ranks, different neighbourhoods, different trades and professions" (OL 274), but *level* is exactly what the citizens of a republic are. Stirred by the republican ideal of a capable citizenry, Mill is also on guard against the ideal itself. He plays down political participation by the many. On the other hand, he resists the despot's temptation—he denies a republican elite the right to rule the many in spite of themselves. (For "barbarians," however, he makes an exception.) It seems republicanism poses risks on all sides. People ought to be equal, but not with the equality of sheep. They ought to be spirited, but not unruly. Leaders need to have virtù, but are not to be Miltons, possessed by a tyrannical conviction of duty. Both leaders and people should emulate the Athenians, but not to the point of bringing back slavery. They should honor the manly virtues, but without prejudice to women.[3]

The head of the Provisional Government brought in by the 1848 revolution in France, Lamartine, converted reluctantly to republicanism "because he believed his compatriots insufficiently prepared to understand its fundamental principles, and feared the 'red madness' which had led them before to the 'bottomless pit of anarchy.' "[4] Of course the French, unlike the English, had little experience of constitutional government and had a bloody revolution fresh in their memory. But for their part, the English of Mill's day had little experience of thinking of themselves (much less acting) as citizens, that is, members of a republic, rather than as members of classes. Mill found them unprepared for political participation, which must be one reason why his call for "active participation in government"[5] is scarcely audible in *On Liberty*, his political testament; why *On Liberty* so little encourages people out of the private sphere and into their role as citizens, and this in spite of the fact that Mill feared the imprisonment of the individual within private life as "the great danger"[6] of modern society. Edmund Burke held a belief in free speech and free trade as part of a profound conservatism; indeed, in a strategy loosely corresponding to Mill's approach in *On Liberty*, he drew a line between what government is entitled to do and what it is not. (It is not to establish granaries or set the price of bread, for example.) Mill's defense of noninterference acted as a brake on republican principles whose dangers were dramatized by Burke and felt long after.

From an essay by Macaulay in the *Edinburgh Review* of 1825, an essay Mill probably read, we learn that it wasn't the regicides like Milton but Charles who enjoyed "popularity with the present generation." Those polemicizing against the rebels made sure to call up images of

> upstarts, enriched by the public plunder, taking possession of the hospitable firesides and hereditary trees of the old gentry; boys smashing the beautiful windows of cathedrals; Quakers riding naked through the marketplace; Fifth-monarchy-men shouting for King Jesus; [and so on].[7]

If Mill had been reckless in espousing republican principles, what images of alarm would have been raised? Freethinkers shouting from the rooftops? Armed mobs? Attacks on the royal person? As it is, Matthew Arnold spoke of him as a Jacobin in *Culture and Anarchy*,[8] and the *Times* kicked his carcass in its obituary, pronouncing him an advocate of "revolutionary" change (CW XXIX, lx). But as strongly as he felt, Mill didn't speak unguardedly, or at least not often. For reasons I think both of policy and of principle, Mill used care in his republican expressions. (In *On Liberty* he discusses tyrannicide not in the text itself but in a carefully ambiguous and highly guarded footnote that would seem to vindicate the act but make incitement to it a crime.) I believe Mill's thought is elaborately, but not perfectly, fortified against the risks of republicanism. Like a system of constitutional checks on power, Mill's thought contains checks against his own powerful, one might say Miltonic love of virtue (or virtù).[9] Strong natures, Mill writes in *On Liberty*, are distinguished by "the most passionate love of virtue, and the sternest self-control" (OL 264); I have suggested that Mill governed his passion for virtue (virtù) itself. Affirming the peaceable pursuit of one's own good in one's own way, Mill gives up any ambition to establish a rule of virtue and counteracts his own more heroic, militant, and archaic leanings. Mill's tolerance can be considered as one of a system of checks on republican ambitions and pretenses, a system imperfect like all human works.

Before we proceed, it is best to establish that at times Mill *was* drawn to such high-risk ideas as a revolution instituting a rule of the few. In "The Spirit of the Age" (1831) Mill looks forward to "a moral and social revolution" that will restore society to its "natural" condition, in which an elite holds "the office of thinking for the people" (CW XXII, 252–53). This youthful essay advances views we wouldn't have expected of the author of *On Liberty*, issuing a dire caution, for example, against encouraging the ignorant individual "to assert his liberty of thought" or even to judge "according to his own views of the evidence" (244). (In an 1834 piece on "The English National Character," Mill lays it down that "The most immoral periods in a nation's history are always . . . periods . . . when . . . each person 'does what is right in his own eyes' " [CW XXIII, 727].) It would take a skillful pleader to "reconcile" such views with the argument of *On Liberty*. To be sure, Mill stipulates in "The Spirit of the Age" that the revolution-to-come will "take away no men's lives or property" (245). Later in the same year, however, he expressed himself privately without such nicety. In a letter to John Sterling of October 1831, he avowed that

> If there were but a few dozens of persons safe (whom you & I could select) to be missionaries of the great truths in which alone there is any well-being for mankind individually or collectively, I should not care though a revolution were to exterminate every person in Great Britain & Ireland who has £500 a year. Many very amiable persons would perish, but what is the world the better for such amiable persons. (CW XII, 84)

Systematic extermination; the rebuilding of the world by a virtuous saving remnant surely this is equal to anything proposed by the "fanatical" Milton. This expression of an unwise moment gives us some notion of the force of Mill's "most passionate love of virtue," and adds meaning to that temperate expression which is his intellectual signature. By the time he wrote *On Liberty*, Mill no longer entertained fantasies of making England virtuous by force; he put his hope in that cure-all, education. Moreover, he reprobated the idea of thinking for the people and denied any elite the right to hold the people morally in subjection. When it came to dealings with "uncivilized" peoples, Mill made an exception to his liberal principles, and here, as I will contend, he was indeed possessed by an overweening sense of duty. But his racism, which comports so poorly with his intellectual decency, is mostly out of sight in *On Liberty*.

As TO THE dangers of virtù—a compound of political fortitude, "vital power" (OL 310), and public spirit that contrasts sharply with the

Christian morality of passivity and obedience. (In *On Liberty* we read, "What little recognition the idea of obligation to the public obtains in modern morality, is derived from Greek and Roman sources, not from Christian" [OL 256].) Virtù is what Machiavelli's political hero possesses; that in itself announces danger. In his "Vindication of the French Revolution of February 1848," which celebrates the French republicans for seizing the political moment, Mill comments that "the most delicate [questions] in political ethics" are

> concerned with that nice question, the line which separates the highest right from the commencement of wrong; where one person regards as heroic virtue, what another looks upon as breach of faith, and criminal aggression. (CW XX, 343)

Probably this is as close as Mill came to Machiavellism.[10] In the same essay, however, Mill praises the French republicans for forbidding themselves the use of "coercion or deception" (335). "The democratic principles of these men forbade them to impose despotically, even if they had the power, their political opinions upon an unwilling majority" (335). These self-denying republicans have forsworn the ambition of ruling over a people in spite of themselves. The rigor of their restraint makes them exemplary for Mill. In *On Liberty* as well, Mill plays virtù against propriety, defending virtù at the same time that he blacklists traits like "rashness, obstinacy [and] self-conceit" (OL 278) that give virtù the character of a moral gamble. It has been said of Milton that he was "profoundly stirred by the two ideals . . . of heroic individual energy and complete moral responsibility," and, moreover, that these ideals are "slightly divergent."[11] Mill too was stirred by the ideals of heroic virtù and complete moral responsibility, and it was by moralizing the former that he attempted to square the two.

Virtù—heroic individual energy—contains an element of hazard. Just so, Mill held that the free cities of medieval Europe, where property and person were at hazard, achieved high virtù. Conditions made the citizens "a brave, energetic, and high-spirited people, and fostered a great amount of public spirit and patriotism" (CW III, 881). Those were not sheep. Elsewhere Mill refers to the "high-spirited and numerous *armed* population" of the medieval towns, thus sounding the republican theme of the citizen militia (CW XXII, 186; my emphasis). Adam Smith indeed conceives the free towns to have been something like independent republics. Reliant on their own combined strength, the burghers imposed on themselves "a sort of military

discipline''; necessarily they enjoyed less liberty to dedicate themselves to their own interests than the modern bourgeoisie, but they
participated more fully and more actively in the freedom of the polity
itself.[12] It must have seemed to Mill that in establishing their political
privileges and asserting their economic claims, the merchants of the
free cities of medieval Italy displayed a courage and a civic spirit that
the modern bourgeoisie (who inherit privilege without having to establish it in the first place) cannot come up to.

On Liberty finds Victorian England lacking in just those civic virtues
that distinguished the free cities, depicting as it does a pacified society
where property and person enjoy a high degree of security, and where
virtù is practically nil. Evidently Mill, like many others, connected the
rise of the modern commercial order with the decline of moral autonomy and heroic values. But Mill is unwilling to forgo those protections
of property and person that are such a bar to virtù; or we might say,
he retains them precisely as a check on virtù and its dangers, just as
he inculcates strict moral habits and the bourgeois regimen of "regularity, temperance, moderation, foresight, self-command"[13] as a check
on the more volatile and "high-spirited" nature of virtù. Similarly,
Mill's ideal of the person who is undefeated when "fate and fortune
do their worst" (CW X, 218) might almost be classed with Machiavelli's ideal of a Prince invulnerable to Fortune—if it weren't so moralized. Again, Mill fears that virtue in the sense of quiet attention to
private interests has extinguished virtù in the sense of bravery, mettle,
public spirit, but he gives private pursuits every protection, and all the
emphasis, in his essay On Liberty.

As to the risks incurred by the appeal to Athens and Sparta as
political models: In Athens in particular, Mill thought he saw a happy
combination of thriving public spirit and tolerance of private conduct.
He was aware that slaves didn't partake of these blessings; indeed he
characterizes slavery as "the greatest blot" on Athenian institutions
(CW XI, 314). Surprisingly, however, he tried to bleach out this blot,
and even opined that slavery in that time and place "may have been
. . . a great accelerator of progress" (315). In Considerations on
Representative Government he repeats the point:

> Personal slavery, by giving a commencement to industrial life, and
> enforcing it as the exclusive occupation of the most numerous portion of
> the community, may accelerate the transition to a better freedom than
> that of fighting and rapine. It is almost needless to say that this excuse
> for slavery is only available in a very early state of society. (CW XIX,
> 394–95)

In his own time Mill found slavery indefensible, although he did defend despotic rule over "savages" for their own good. The enlightened slavery of Mill's Athenian model helps to legitimize latter-day despotisms over those judged to be ineligible as yet for liberty. One risk of the Athenian model is actually using it.

On the issue of the status of women, Mill broke with the Athenians. The subjection of women he calls "another great blot" on the Athenian record (CW XI, 314). Where Aristotle's citizen "qualified for public power by his capacity for exercising private power within his household,"[14] Mill might have said that one qualifies for political participation first of all by *not* acting the despot in private relations, and he seems to have regarded the household as a redoubt of arbitrary male power. I have argued, too, that Mill contrived a way to accuse men of effeminacy (as other republicans, notably Machiavelli and Milton, had done before him), without tapping into the antifeminism that ran deep in the republican tradition and in the political models to which it referred. If Mill finds men lacking in the virtù necessary to maintain liberty, if he pities the man who—like a woman—can't raise himself above private concerns, he also argues (and with force) for the emancipation of women. He corrects against the decided antifeminist bias of classical republicanism. He corrects, too, against the life-denying austerity of the Spartan style of public spirit. Sparta seems to have represented for Mill not only the extreme case of the subjection of individual to state, but the grotesque result of an experiment in character-formation a little like the experiment that had been performed on him by James Mill. Lycurgus, man-god of republican lore, succeeded very largely "in making the whole body of Spartan citizens . . . exactly what he had intended to make them" (CW XI, 302). Such is Mill's respect for public spirit and political fortitude that even in the Spartans he finds something to admire. Their "habitual abnegation of ordinary personal interests, and merging of self in an idea, were not compatible with pettiness of mind" (302). If Mill had let his scorn of private interests go unchecked, he might conceivably have arrived at a Spartan position. (Or a Positivist one, for Comte too discredited personal interests.) As it is, he counters any inclination of that kind, philosophically chartering personal interests and encouraging the unfolding, rather than the Spartan repression, of human manyness. Mill speaks for a liberalized—Milton might have said a neutered—republicanism. His very ranking of Athens above Sparta bespeaks a liberalization, for among republicans, "Sparta, where the appetites had been repressed, had traditionally been preferred to Athens, where they had been transcended."[15]

Deriving as it does from *vir* (man), virtù is of masculine polarity, and in drawing on the notion of virtù, along with such associated concepts as the citizen militia and the corrupting effects of softness,[16] Mill risks giving in to the antifeminism he abominates. When in *On Liberty* he lectures his readers that "it was men of another stamp than [men of the present] that made England what it has been" (272), he comes close indeed to sounding like a votary of a male cult. The poet of republicans, Machiavelli, looked back to the *virtus* of the citizens of Rome, who served with courage and spirit in a citizen militia

> sufficiently disciplined and effective to protect their collective autonomy. Here was an uncorrupted community of real men, competent to take care of themselves without being dependent on anyone else, sharing in a fraternal, participatory civic life that made them self-governing.[17]

The ideal of participatory civic life survives into *On Liberty*, where Mill proposes (in passing) a citizen army as well as a political education that will train citizens "to act from public or semi-public motives, and guide their conduct by aims which unite instead of isolating them from one another" (OL 305). Mill reduces this last issue to a sort of footnote, though, claiming it isn't properly a question of liberty—this in spite of the fact that, unless citizens possess such political abilities, "a free constitution can neither be worked nor preserved" (305). It may be that Mill was wise to hush the matter as he does, for in truth it isn't clear how one can reconcile free choice with any scheme for conditioning, or as Mill says "habituating" (305) the minds of citizens as a body. With his imagery of organized volunteerism and mental conditioning, it might almost seem Mill was describing an army. ("Something has been lost as well as gained by no longer giving to every citizen the training necessary for a soldier," Mill once wrote [CW X, 339].) Commenting on the political vision of Rousseau, Judith N. Shklar observes that "Heavy doses of civic education and manipulation by a great legislator and by censors are needed to keep the civic self alive. Rousseau's medicine may well have been worse than the disease."[18] Mill's medicine was more like a placebo. In his concern to contain the risks posed by republican values, he practically effaced the republican tradition itself. (Note what a minor character Rousseau himself is in *On Liberty* [OL 253].) Nevertheless, republicanism still figures in Mill, like those forms overpainted on an artist's canvas. Not only the ideal of civic-military participation but the quality of *virtus* itself survives into Mill's prose, revealing itself as gravity and fearlessness. If *virtus* was "that quality of stern, serious, strong-minded, courageous manliness that despises pleasure and playfulness, cleaving to duty and strenuous effort,"[19] Mill's very prose seems imbued with *virtus*, and this raises the question of how Mill guards against the retrograde tendencies of the republican cult of manliness.

He does so not only by committing himself to the emancipation of women, but also, and still more decisively, by making over to a woman the essence of male power: the power to generate. I am referring to Mill's claims that Harriet Taylor, later Harriet Mill, was the real begetter of his work; that she was the oracle, he the mere interpreter. (This issue is explored more discursively in Chapter 4.) The republican tradition immortalizes the figure of the Sole Begetter, the male who gives birth to a political order, for example Romulus or Theseus; Mill immortalizes Harriet Taylor, whose potent mind we are to believe gave birth to *On Liberty*. Now in one sense of the word, virtù refers to the political abilities required to maintain freedom; thus, immediately following his reference to a training regimen for citizens, Mill comments that unless citizens have practice acting for public ends, freedom can't live. In another sense, virtù refers to the ability to establish freedom in the first place, to originate it. The Machiavellian actor is called on not to preserve old forms, which in any case are in disarray, but to act and establish new ones. This sense of virtù survives in Hannah Arendt's commemorations of the founding of freedom and her insistence that action is of its nature a break with what is, a beginning. Mill credits Harriet Taylor with being the source of what is original in his work and, what is more, with being able to see and to lay the foundations in theory for the freedom that is not yet. The powers of political creation that tradition ascribes to a Lycurgus, Mill awards to Harriet Taylor. He attacks the male bias of the republican tradition at its source.

From time to time one sees in the United States a bumpersticker asserting the right to keep and bear arms, a blood-brother of the idea of the citizen militia. The tradition of armed virtue descends at last to survivalist fantasies, incantatory slogans, and primitive emotions—to know-nothingism. In the arguments of the make-believe militiamen of today, it is as though republicanism were denuded of all that ever ennobled it as a political ideal, so that nothing remains but hatred of political society and sheer male force. Mill accepts that people are born for membership in political society, and he counters the antifeminist bias of the republican tradition by agitating for sexual equality and indeed by elevating Harriet Taylor as absolutely as women had been debased by Machiavelli. As we have seen, he also takes precautions against the hazards of virtù. Mill guards less well against the risks of despotic presumption. Under certain circumstances, he does believe in a despotism of those fit to rule over those unfit to rule, a distinction that Milton made too and that was built into the ancient republics both men used as reference points for the imagination.

ON LIBERTY IS addressed to an enfeebled people that needs to be reminded of those political abilities without which "a free constitution can neither be worked nor preserved" (OL 305). Mill accuses his countrymen of yielding themselves up to a tyranny "enslaving the soul itself" (OL 220). He finds them lacking the virtù necessary to maintain freedom. This is very close to finding England unfit for freedom. Mill doesn't scruple to declare "backward" (OL 224) societies unfit for freedom, but England is in another class, and rather than calling for an elite of the politically competent to take over the freedom that the English seem so little able to support, Mill does the opposite. He forbids any such thing. *On Liberty* stands, therefore, as a defense of the individual, the same individual who has as it were sold him- or herself into slavery. It marks off, and fences round with protections, a sphere within which each individual can act as he or she sees fit. Let no one suppose, however, that Mill was never drawn to the idea of denying the individual this freedom. Some 30 years before *On Liberty*, in the same letter to John Sterling cited earlier in this chapter, Mill abused the principles of liberalism that he was later to defend. Liberalism, he writes,

> is for making every man his own guide & sovereign master, & letting him think for himself & do exactly as he judges best for himself, giving other men leave to persuade him if they can by evidence, but forbidding him to give way to authority; and still less allowing them to constrain him more than the existence & tolerable security of every man's person and property renders indispensably necessary. It is difficult to conceive a more thorough ignorance of man's nature, & of what is necessary for his happiness or what degree of happiness & virtue he is capable of attaining than this system implies. (CW XII, 84)

Mill agrees rather with those who know that "it is good for man to be ruled" (84). Nor did he altogether abandon the idea of the authority of the few over the many. Even after writing *On Liberty*, Mill was willing to say aloud, in vindication of the American North, that

> a man who has nothing which he is willing to fight for, nothing which he cares more about than he does about his personal safety, is a miserable creature who has no chance of being free, unless made and kept so by the exertions of better men than himself. (CW XXI, 142)

Here the premise that only those with virtù are worthy of liberty is taken almost to a Miltonic conclusion. (Note too the implied contrast between virtù as martial spirit and risk-taking for the greater good, and, on the other side, virtue as care for one's private welfare.) Of this passage Stefan Collini has remarked that it reads more like "the language of Machiavelli and civic *virtù* than that of . . . the age of pacific commercialism."[20] My sense is that both languages are inscribed in *On Liberty*, which sounds with the concept of virtù while at the same time asking little more of us than to look after our own interests and leave others alone. In fact, *On Liberty* carefully averts the more perilous implications of republican principles like martial spirit, the subordination of private good, and the superior political fitness of the few.

These principles were Milton's also, and in his last pamphlet before the Restoration, Milton drew the last conclusion from them. He called for the rule of those fit for freedom over the unfit. In a passage I have already cited, Milton contends that the majority have forfeited their right of political choice. Yearning for a king again, they have shown they care nothing for freedom, which is

> one main end of government: which if the greater part value not, but will degeneratly forgo, is it just or reasonable, that most voices against the main end of government should enslave the less number that would be free? More just it is doubtless, if it com to force, that a less number compell a greater to retain, which can be no wrong to them, thir libertie, then that a greater number for the pleasure of thir baseness, compell a less most injuriously to be thir fellow slaves.[21]

The few are to compel the many to be free: an argument that has since become infamous. This was not an aberrant conclusion to which Milton was blown by an evil wind, but a direct consequence of his deeply held belief that only the virtuous can support their own freedom. Six years earlier, in his "Second Defense of the English People," Milton hadn't shrunk from the conclusion that the liberty of the unvirtuous is to be held in trust by a political guardian:

> Such is the decree of law and of nature herself, that he who cannot control himself, who through poverty of intellect or madness cannot properly administer his own affairs, should not be his own master, but like a ward be given over to the power of another. . . . Then indeed, like a nation in wardship, you would . . . be in need of some tutor, some brave and faithful guardian of your affairs.[22]

John Stuart Mill frowned on loose terms like "decree of nature," and, as we know, he considered Milton a tyrant in his own right. Having been brought up under the strict censorship of an overpowering father, Mill had the more reason to protest against what is called paternalistic despotism. And he did protest, but only in a partial way, for the fact is that he urged that the liberty of the (to him) lower races be held in trust until they should be readied for it. Mill was a racist. In *On Liberty*, which in passing criticizes the "sincere bigot" (222), he keeps this issue as a rule off-stage. However, he does explicitly stipulate that "Despotism is a legitimate mode of government in dealing with barbarians, provided the end be their improvement, and the means justified by actually effecting that end" (OL 224). Indeed Milton the "despot" underlies *On Liberty*.

It wouldn't have served Mill's purpose to discourse on the duties of the master race in the same text that represents the English themselves as slaves. (And if Mill had tried to rescue his argument by revising it to say that backward peoples are to be ruled not by the English nation but by a corps of competent administrators like himself, he might then have been asked what his plans were for the politically backward English.) Nor would it have spoken well of Mill's consistency in argument to stand on the right to despotic rule over barbarians in the same text that says point-blank, "I am not aware that any community has a right to force another to be civilized" (OL 291).[23] Here too it would require skillful pleading to reconcile Mill's positions. In *On Liberty* Mill makes a republican argument while insuring against the risks of the tradition—insuring too against the implications of his own affiliation with Milton. It is in *Considerations on Representative Government* that Mill asserts the sacred duty of the free (whites) to rule over those not yet fit for freedom (nonwhites). To that extreme the heroic imperative carried him. However carefully Mill guarded against the risks of republicanism, he could not in the end subdue the risks of his own high-mindedness. "It was no doubt the magnificent opportunity which [enlightened despotism] permitted to the philosophic reformer that was allowed to outweigh, in the minds of both the Mills, the tradition of political liberty in which they had been trained."[24] The task of ruling India was therefore, as the task of inventing atomic weapons was said to be, "technically sweet."

Mill's most succinct statement of the white-man's-burden position is perhaps this passage in the *Considerations*:

> Under a native despotism, a good despot is a rare and transitory accident: but when the dominion [the native population] are under is that of a more civilized people, that people ought to be able to supply it constantly. The ruling country ought to be able to do for its subjects all that could be done by a succession of absolute monarchs, guaranteed by irresistible force against the precariousness of tenure attendant on barbarous despotisms, and qualified by their genius to anticipate all that experience has taught to the more advanced nation. Such is the ideal rule of a free people over a barbarous or semibarbarous one. We need not expect to see that ideal realized; but unless some approach to it is, the rulers are guilty of a dereliction of the highest moral trust which can devolve upon a nation: and if they do not even aim at it, they are selfish usurpers, on a par in criminality with any of those whose ambition and rapacity have sported from age to age with the destiny of masses of mankind. (CW XIX, 567–68)

Mill didn't mean to say that the "ideal" of political tutelage is a pretense; that everything is permitted, provided only that the civilizers "aim at" higher things; that if the civilizers bring a grandiose sense of mission with them, they may then proceed to debauch themselves as Joseph Conrad's Kurtz did. Mill didn't mean to say these things,[25] but he bears almost the same responsibility as if he did say them, for in the world as we know it, it is the very sense of being under a sacred imperative, such as a "moral trust" from on high, that makes for the worst crimes against liberty and life. There is a faintly odious quality in these last pages of the *Considerations*, with their elegy to the East India Company in which Mill had held a comfortable position for his entire working life. In claiming that the "utmost" England can do is to "give some of their best men a commission to look after" the interests of subject peoples (569), Mill undoubtedly counted himself among that number. He may have been repelled by Milton's "fanatical" sense of merit, but he too could think of himself as one of the elect. Here as at other moments in Mill's writings, high-mindedness seems to be another name for frigid arrogance and special pleading. As a rule, though, Mill didn't practice hypocrisy. He was a most sincere bigot.

Charles Taylor finds that *Considerations on Representative Government* "owe[s] something to the ancient republican tradition, according to which men's ruling themselves is seen as an activity valuable in itself."[26] But the very text that posits the value of self-rule also defends (actually enjoins) despotic rule over other peoples. How can this be? The answer, I think, is that the same high sense of disinterest that is supposed to drive people to subordinate their own good to the general good also drives the virtuous nation to civilize others. The same "exalted patriotism and . . . obligation of public duty" (CW XIX, 489) that are to fill the heart of every voter also fill the heart of the colonial administrator. Yet everywhere in his writings Mill alleges that the English do *not* at present have a sense of the public good, being mired in ignorance and selfishness; one wonders, therefore, how high-mindedness at home can carry over to high-mindedness abroad. More than this, however, Mill is to be blamed for a lack of moral imagination, a blindness to the dangers that impend when men fight for "pure" motives, that is, for ideas. There were those on the left who claimed the United States fought in Vietnam to acquire markets, natural resources, military bases, or whatnot, but surely the point is that the war in Vietnam not only did not serve American interests in any material sense, but cost the United States vastly more than it could ever have gained us. The war was fought to deal a defeat to communism, and later to avoid defeat ourselves. And I contend it was the very "purity" (that is, ideological nature) of these goals that enabled us both to sacrifice blood and treasure for Vietnam and to sacrifice many thousands of Vietnamese civilians in the process. We were never sure what we were doing in Vietnam, winning over a people (a people deemed unready for freedom) or taking an insensate revenge on them and the entire land. Somehow our willingness to shed our blood for the Vietnamese became our warrant to shed their blood. Neo-conservatives like to attack the liberal society in which everything is permitted (as, in the opinion of Gertrude Himmelfarb, *On Liberty* leads to moral anarchy), but it was in the free-fire zones of Vietnam that everything was *really* permitted. The racial imperative of the *Considerations on Representative Government* finally comes down to that. From the point of view of twentieth-century experience, Mill's dream of coercing a people to defer until it learns to defer voluntarily is a bit like those courses of "re-education" in which captives are abused and humiliated until they voluntarily sign a confession.

Presumably Mill saw in Milton a man whose titanic sense of righteousness made him a despot "with all his republicanism." If so, then he saw Robespierre and Saint-Just, also republicans, as outdoers of Milton, men whose fanatical high-mindedness and demonic sense of duty made them executioners. According to Mill, Robespierre and Saint-Just weren't men of low motives; on the contrary, it was their sense of the public good that drove them. Mill writes in his review of the "Writings of Alfred de Vigny":

> [M. de Vigny] shows us these men as they were, as such men could not but have been; men distinguished, morally, chiefly by two qualities, entire hardness of heart, and the most overweening and bloated self-conceit: for nothing less, assuredly, could lead any man to believe that his individual judgment respecting the public good is a warrant to him for exterminating all who are suspected of forming any other judgment, and for setting up a machine for cutting off heads, sixty or seventy every day, till some unknown futurity be accomplished, some Utopia realized. (CW I, 495)

Against this kind of righteousness Mill was on guard. Nor was it entirely an idle danger, for he—like Milton, Robespierre, and Saint-Just—could have made a religion of the public good. Indeed, according to Mill himself, an undue emphasis on the enervation of the modern individual (the very position he would later take in *On Liberty*) leads right to Robespierre (CW X, 123). Mill guarded less well, as I have said, against racial arrogance and heroic pretension. His overweening sense of duty made him an exponent not of the guillotine, but of the white man's burden. He condemns the notion of cutting off heads "till some unknown futurity be accomplished," but not the notion of colonial rule in the interest of what he himself concedes is an unrealizable ideal. ("We need not expect to see that ideal realized.") Peoples not yet ready for liberty, backward peoples, are to be civilized for their own good. But as Mill himself wrote in *The Subjection of Women*, "In the present day . . . whomsoever [power] oppresses, [it] always pretends to do so for their own good" (CW XXI, 299). It is a mark of the unreconciled character of Mill's thought that he can be quoted thus; that from time to time he seems to rebut himself.

To THIS POINT I have argued that Mill tried to exercise "the sternest self-control" in framing his political argument, guarding against some of the highly charged implications of republican principles; and that for all of his checks and defenses, he still permitted himself a sense of heroic entitlement, something comparable to the sense of election he seems to have detested in Milton. But Mill did not only try to keep his own "passionate love of virtue" under control. He also set controls on the multitude. While he held to the republican principle that a citizen both rules and is ruled and that active participation in political life is a requirement of our very natures,[27] he so hedged his position that it almost reads as though he were fortifying the polity *against* the dangers of popular participation. Here again Mill's *Considerations on Representative Government* will be our source.

Only by exercise, Mill believes, can our civic abilities be educated. In that sense, actual political participation is necessary if we are to achieve our full measure. One reason Mill set importance on local liberties and small political experiments may be that these things are ways of bringing the scale and the political intensity of the city-state to a mass society. Where the people are kept passive,

> their moral capacities are . . . stunted. Wherever the sphere of action of human beings is artificially circumscribed, their sentiments are narrowed and dwarfed in the same proportion. The food of feeling is action: even domestic affection lives upon voluntary good offices. Let a person have nothing to do for his country, and he will not care for it. (CW XIX, 400–1)

This language recalls *On Liberty*, with its protest against the dying-out of action and against a social tyranny that produces "cramped and dwarfed" human beings (OL 265). Our capacities thrive on action— but to give action too free a field is a dangerous thing. In particular, to call the uninstructed into action is a dangerous thing. Accordingly, Mill qualifies his position by calling for a *little* participation. Where we expected Mill to give generous encouragement, we find instead that he makes a meager allowance. Under the "ideally best form of government," he maintains, each citizen is called on "at least occasionally" to take part in government (CW XIX, 404). An "occasional demand" is to be made on the citizens "to exercise, for a time and in their turn, some social function" (411). It is salutary that citizens participate, "if even rarely" (412), in the processes of government. Any participation, "even in the smallest public function" (412), is beneficial. The entire public should be "to a certain extent" (436) a participant in government. It would almost seem that rather than favoring participation (as an opportunity for the unfolding of our abilities as political beings), Mill were concerned to hold it to a minimum. We may be reminded of the "pitiably meagre participation" that Milton ordains in "The Readie and Easie Way.''[28] I think Mill's recommendations on this point are as stingy as they are because he really didn't believe that ''average human beings'' (445) possess the requisites for political participation. They cannot, in Mill's view, subordinate their own good to the public good. They cannot pass the republican test.

> A certain amount of conscience, and of disinterested public spirit, may fairly be calculated on in the citizens of any community ripe for representative government. But it would be ridiculous to expect such a degree of it, combined with such intellectual discernment, as would be proof against any plausible fallacy tending to make that which was good for their class interest appear the dictate of justice and of the general good. (445)

Caught between a profound distrust of the many and a strong belief that such abilities as we possess require to be called into play, Mill reconciled his attitudes by issuing an inspiring call for an iota of participation. Richard Arneson accurately paraphrases Mill's position in these terms: ''Given the abysmally low present state of popular participation, we would do well to increase it as much as possible up to that rather minimal level needed for the functioning of a form of government in which rulers are accountable to the citizens.''[29] So it is that Mill's ''expansive ideal of citizenship'' (CW XXVIII, lx) constricts. Where once he recommended ''a large and frequent intervention of the citizens'' in public affairs (CW XVIII, 182), he now seems to recommend a participation that is small, infrequent, closely measured.

In *On Liberty* Mill protests against a social tyranny that has all but extinguished the power of action. In *Considerations on Representative Government* he himself puts a fairly tight check on popular participation. Similarly, while Mill protests against censorship (''In our times, from the highest class of society down to the lowest, every one lives as under the eye of a hostile and dreaded censorship'' [OL 264]), he himself espouses an ethereal republicanism, a politics that has the dangerous passages taken out and is too good to be true. The moral gambling of virtù; the intensely masculine cult of armed vigilance; the risks of energetic participation—all such things drop away, and what is left is mostly a tale about a many who learn to defer to a few who are wise and good, learn, that is, to make the right use of their liberty.[30] Mill so purges the republican concept of the public good that *On Liberty*—the author's political testament and the work he supposed would outlive all his others, except perhaps the *Logic*—reads rather like a philosophical charter of the pursuit of *private* good. Attempting, as it seems, to detoxify the republican ideal, to cleanse it of the "errors" of Machiavelli and Milton, Mill ended with a republicanism that was practically sterile. I don't mean he lacked the love of civic virtue that is the sign and test of a republican. I mean his own "passionate love of virtue" was kept in check by "the sternest self-control," although, like everything repressed, it found expression all the same. The more ominous aspects of Mill's love of virtue (virtù) come out in his defense of virtuous despotisms over "backward" peoples; but to a Victorian audience, that would have been perfectly respectable.

At the beginning of this chapter I cited the opinion that Mill feared people would give themselves up to private pursuits, to the injury of their performance as citizens. This was Tocqueville's fear too. As he saw it, "The middle class's concentration on profits and private pleasures eroded the active and disinterested participation in public affairs that kept a society free."[31] Tocqueville's work has been judged the last great expression of civic humanism.[32] I would argue that John Stuart Mill's work is the last great expression of civic humanism, last not just because it follows Tocqueville's, but because it (all but) liquidates civic virtue into the pursuit of private happiness. Like Tocqueville, Mill is pained at the thought of the enfeebled citizen "centered in himself and forgetful of the public," and like Tocqueville he fears that human beings will wither away "within the narrow circle of domestic interests";[33] but the effect of his argument in *On Liberty* is precisely to center us on ourselves (as in self-regarding acts) and to entrench us in the private sphere. In this sense, *On Liberty* abets the same tendency of commercial society that Tocqueville says it is his intent to "combat."[34] Like an epitaph, *On Liberty* both commemorates and writes an end to the republican tradition.

In "Utilitarianism," for all his defense of the high disinterested character of that school of thought, Mill argues that only perhaps one act out of 100, and one person out of 1,000, need be public-spirited (CW X, 220). The same trajectory, from expansive to narrow, is seen in *On Liberty*.

NOTES

1. Bernard Semmel, *John Stuart Mill and the Pursuit of Virtue* (New Haven, Conn.: Yale University Press, 1984), p. 116.

2. On this subject, see Sissela Bok, *Lying: Moral Choice in Public and Private Life* (New York: Vintage, 1978), ch. 12.

3. Mill himself discusses some of the dangers of the republican ideal in "Armand Carrel." See CW XX, 199.

4. H. Remsen Whitehouse, *The Life of Lamartine* (London: T. Fisher Unwin, 1918), bk. 1, pp. 414–15.

5. Semmel, *Mill and the Pursuit of Virtue*, p. 116.

6. Again, Semmel, *Mill and the Pursuit of Virtue*, p. 116.

7. Thomas Babington Macaulay, *Critical and Historical Essays*, vol. 1 (New York: Dutton, 1966), pp. 177–78. In *Jane Eyre* (1847) the saintly Helen Burns declares, "I like Charles—I respect him—I pity him, poor murdered king! Yes, his enemies were the worst: they shed blood they had no right to shed. How dared they kill him!" (Charlotte Brontë, *Jane Eyre* [New York: Modern Library, 1950], pp. 58–59.) The comment passes unrebutted.

8. See *Culture and Anarchy* in *Poetry and Criticism of Matthew Arnold*, ed. A. Dwight Culler (Boston: Houghton Mifflin, 1961), p. 425.

9. The defensive character of Mill's thought is suggested by a comment by Noel Annan, "John Stuart Mill" in *The English Mind: Studies in the English Moralists Presented to Basil Willey*, eds. Hugh Sykes Davies and George Watson (Cambridge, U.K.: Cambridge University Press, 1964), p. 228: "Mill works away plugging holes, reorganizing his defenses, admitting defects, modifying virtues, patching and darning."

10. In his Inaugural Address to St. Andrews, Mill remarks that men of passionate virtue who are devoted to the public good "permit themselves to do wrong things" (CW XXI, 253), a comment that conflicts with his claim in *On Liberty* that strong passions and strong scruples go together.

11. Robert M. Adams, *Ikon: John Milton and the Modern Critics* (Ithaca, N.Y.: Cornell University Press, 1955), p. 173.

12. Adam Smith, *The Wealth of Nations* (New York: Modern Library, 1937), p. 376.

13. Alexis de Tocqueville, *Democracy in America*, tr. Henry Reeve; rev. Francis Bowen and Phillips Bradley (New York: Vintage, 1945), vol. 2, p. 131.

14. J. G. A. Pocock, *Politics, Language and Time: Essays on Political Thought and History* (New York: Atheneum, 1973), p. 113.

15. J. G. A. Pocock, *The Machiavellian Moment: Florentine Political Thought and the Atlantic Republican Tradition* (Princeton, N.J.: Princeton University Press, 1975), p. 500.

16. On this point, see for example *On Liberty*, p. 242: "But the price paid for this sort of intellectual pacification, is the sacrifice of the entire moral courage of the human mind. . . . The sort of *men* who can be looked for under [these conditions] are either mere conformers to commonplace, or time-servers for truth" (my emphasis).

17. Hanna Fenichel Pitkin, *Fortune Is a Woman: Gender and Politics in the Thought of Niccolò Machiavelli* (Berkeley: University of California Press, 1984), p. 75.

18. Judith N. Shklar, "Jean-Jacques Rousseau and Equality," *Daedalus* (Summer 1978), 17.

19. Pitkin, *Fortune Is a Woman*, p. 50.

20. See the introduction to volume 21 of Mill's *Collected Works*, p. xv.

21. I quote from the second edition of "The Readie and Easie Way" in *Complete Prose Works of John Milton*, vol. 7 (New Haven, Conn.: Yale University Press, 1980), p. 455.

22. *Complete Prose Works of John Milton*, vol. 4, ed. Don M. Wolfe (New Haven, Conn.: Yale University Press, 1966), p. 684.

23. The argument of *On Liberty* culminates on this point; what follows is "Applications."

24. Eric Stokes, *The English Utilitarians and India* (Oxford, U.K.: Clarendon Press, 1959), p. 321.

25. Mill agitated to bring Governor Eyre to justice after he had committed atrocities in Jamaica.

26. Charles Taylor, "What's Wrong with Negative Liberty" in *The Idea of Freedom*, ed. Alan Ryan (New York: Oxford University Press, 1979), pp. 175–76.

27. An idealized version of this principle is Kant's dictum that virtue consists in the "participation . . . [of] the rational being in making universal laws." See *Foundations of the Metaphysics of Morals*, tr. Lewis White Beck (New York: Macmillan, 1990), p. 52. The citizen of the republic of ends is subject to laws of his own enactment.

28. *Complete Prose of Milton*, vol. 7, p. 187.

29. Richard Arneson, "Democracy and Liberty in Mill's Theory of Government," *Journal of the History of Philosophy* (January 1982), 53.

30. Wordsworth's evocation of a pastoral commonwealth, a "perfect republic of shepherds and agriculturists," is twice quoted by Mill. CW II, 253; XXIV, 941.

31. Robert O. Paxton, "The Divided Liberal," *New York Review of Books*, March 2, 1989, p. 17.

32. See Paxton, "Divided Liberal," p. 17, citing Jean-Claude Lamberti.

33. Tocqueville, *Democracy in America*, vol. 2, pp. 270, 277.

34. Tocqueville, *Democracy in America*, vol. 2, p. 310.

4

Mill and His Muse

"I WAS BORN in London, on the 20th of May 1806," Mill records in his *Autobiography*, "and was the eldest son of James Mill, the author of *The History of British India*" (CW I, 5; see the Introduction of this book, note 17). As others have noted, this is a curious statement. It omits Mill's mother.[1] It seems to say that Mill came into the world in the way *The History of British India* did, as the result of an act of generation unmediated by woman. Bruce Mazlish observes cannily that the father's *History of British India* was "conceived around the same time as John Stuart"; book and boy "developed into maturity together."[2] Perhaps Mill's sense during his mental crisis that he wasn't an animate being at all owed something to the fact that he grew up next to a paper double. In James Mill, in any case, was instanced the power to give birth, figuratively the same power that founds cities, institutes laws, and creates artifacts of culture, all without the aid of women. Milton refers to this sort of asexual reproduction in "Areopagitica" when he reminds Parliament,

> That our hearts are now more capacious, our thoughts more erected to the search and expectation of greatest and exactest things, is the issue of your owne vertu [virtù; living power] propagated in us; ye cannot suppresse that unlesse ye reinforce an abrogated and mercilesse law, that fathers may dispatch at will their own children.[3]

Authorship stands as the pure example of womanless birth, and Milton speaks of books, accordingly, as offspring, male-born beings:

> For Books are not absolutely dead things, but doe contain a potencie of
> life in them to be as active as that soule was whose progeny they are; nay
> they do preserve as in a violl the purest efficacie and extraction of that
> living intellect that bred them. ("Areopagitica," p. 492)

Books are mental offspring that themselves possess the power to cause
and create, being, as Milton says, "vigorously productive" (492). In
this realm, reproduction proceeds without women. (Mill's reference to
Bentham and Coleridge as "seminal minds" [CW X, 77] takes on
added meaning in the present context.) In *Paradise Lost* God authors
the Son. This kind of power, the power to author being, John Stuart
Mill disclaimed.

The power of originality that Mill denied he possessed, he attributed
to Harriet Taylor, later Harriet Mill. (For the sake of simplicity, I will
just call her Harriet.) *On Liberty* is dedicated to Harriet, whom Mill
eulogizes in terms few but himself have ever perhaps been able to
credit, terms much too good to be true:

> Were I but capable of interpreting to the world one half of the great
> thoughts and noble feelings which are buried in her grave, I should be the
> medium of a greater benefit to it, than is ever likely to arise from anything
> that I can write, unprompted and unassisted by her all but unrivalled
> wisdom. (OL 216)

To be sure, other writers have disclaimed their originality, but never
more insistently than Mill, who represents Harriet as the begetter of
his ideas. In his *Autobiography* Mill claims that "the most valuable
ideas and features" of the works he wrote during his association with
Harriet "originated with her; were emanations from her mind" (CW I,
251). In *The Subjection of Women* Mill asks, "Who can tell how many
of the most original thoughts put forth by male writers, belong to a
woman by suggestion, to themselves only by verifying and working
out? If I may judge from my own case, a very large proportion indeed"
(CW XXI, 316). Thus the traditionally male power to give birth to
mental offspring is made over to Harriet. As much as this is, Mill
bestows on Harriet more. If Lycurgus was legislator of Sparta, if James
Mill aspired to be legislator of India and Jeremy Bentham legislator of
Venezuela, Harriet is represented by John Stuart as a sort of seer with
the power to envision and create the future, one of those poets who
Shelley says are "the unacknowledged legislators of the World."[4] Mill
acknowledged her. He ascribed the power of creation to her. He made

over to her the tradition of the divinity of the pen that runs from medieval humanism to Sidney to Shelley,[5] her favorite poet. So entirely did Mill renounce the male principle that he did not claim paternity of his ideas and did accept as a daughter a woman he did not father, Helen Taylor.

Can a woman beget? Can a man give birth? What is the relation of pen to penis? As exotic as these questions may seem, they lay near the center of the seventeenth-century debate on regicide, with the royalists arguing that the killing of a king strikes at the paternal principle itself and Milton (the voice of the regicides) impugning the manhood of the royalists and accusing them of hermaphroditism and other perversions of nature. In that context, such claims as that Parliament cannot beget and that Milton's opponent is "as fit to give birth as to beget"[6]—such claims aren't mere aberrations of discourse but actual political arguments, however desperate and scurrilous.[7] In beatifying Harriet, Mill was surely obeying some obscure psychological motive, but he was also arguing with Western political discourse, even if in ways not fully known to himself. In effect, Mill attempted to free his own discourse from the outdated structures of a universe vertically ordered, from men (rulers and authors of being) on down. As the opening paragraphs of *On Liberty* attest, Mill did consider that the model of rulers above and subjects below no longer applied to his society. Milton couldn't finally free his thinking of hierarchical constructs and traditional gender values; in making Harriet his Beatrice, Mill in some sense worked within the tradition he would break with. Stationing Harriet above and himself below, elevating Harriet as fantastically as women had ever been debased by the tradition of male supremacy, Mill repeated that tradition in parody wise. He did not leave it clear behind him.

IT IS DISMAYING to see Mill prostrate himself before Harriet in a way he might have found slavish in anyone else. It particularly pains a reader to see Mill, a critic of censorship, appoint her the censor of his work. Harriet seems to have reviewed some of Mill's manuscripts phrase by phrase and ordered the corrections she deemed necessary, and Mill learned not only to submit but to like it. In her study of Mill, Gertrude Himmelfarb assembles evidence from Mill's correspondence with Harriet that all too plainly demonstrates the powers she wielded:

If *you* do not think so, I certainly will not print it.

The sentence which you objected to in toto of course has come quite out.

It is necessary that something should be decided immediately without waiting for the decision of my only guide and oracle.

I will answer [the publisher] as you say.

I wrote to [the publisher] in the manner you wished.

I shall not attempt any alterations till I hear from you.[8]

These statements are in reference to Mill's *Political Economy*. *On Liberty* itself seems to have been written under the censorship of Harriet, although Mill laments that the text "never underwent her final revision" (CW I, 259). In his *Autobiography* Mill records that he and his wife scrutinized every sentence of *On Liberty* many times over, but since he also records that "the whole mode of thinking of which the book was the expression, was emphatically hers" (CW I, 259), it may be that scrutiny wasn't so much a joint labor as a ceremony in which Mill made submission to Harriet. He was "penetrated with" Harriet's way of thinking, he says (259), a phrase that rather vividly illustrates his renunciation of those pro/creative powers that a male tradition had assigned to men and that his father had drawn on to author a book and a boy at once.

It is as though Mill took the old tale of the man with the power to give birth ("Abraham begat Isaac; and Isaac begat Jacob") and made of it a new tale of a woman with the power to inseminate. In any case, there is something highly unrealistic about Mill's account of how his books came into the world. In *On Liberty* Mill uses Victorianisms to denote how children come into the world. Is a marriage that "has . . . called third parties into existence" (OL 300)[9] dissoluble at the pleasure of husband and wife? After "summoning a human being into the world" (OL 302), do not parents bear a responsibility to educate him or her? According to the story told by this denatured diction, children aren't physically begotten and born but invoked. They come into being almost as if the stork brought them. And I want to say that Mill's story that his writings sprang from Harriet's brain is a stork tale itself. In it, his writings become an expression not of his own conflicting values and intentions—his own humanness—but of Harriet's superhuman genius. A transcendent mind, as Mill portrays Harriet's to be, doesn't know confusion and conflict. (Harriet seems to have been very positive in her assertions.) If *On Liberty* had sprung from the brain of such an immortal, it wouldn't have affirmed private interests and discredited "personal and family selfishness" (OL 305); it wouldn't have told us to mind our own business (OL 286) and also told us to concern ourselves with affairs beyond our own (OL 276–77); it wouldn't have blessed "joint concerns" (OL 305) and sneered at the English "habit of combining" (OL 272); it wouldn't have chained Miltonic passions in priggish language. In some credible way it would have reconciled an antique republicanism with the conditions of modernity.

In reality, Harriet seems to have been not only Mill's muse but his censor, and not an original mind so much as an imitator of the Shelleyan style. Like her favorite poet, Harriet is someone of high feeling, a celebrant of love, an enemy of tyrants, a seer. Shelley in turn had said of Milton, "The sacred Milton was, let it ever be remembered, a Republican, and a bold enquirer into morals and religion."[10] An extreme prude, Harriet was perhaps less bold in her inquiries, and even if she radicalized Mill in some respects, in one case she seems to have muted his republicanism. In March 1849 Mill reported to Harriet that he had seen proofs of his defense of the February 1848 revolution in France (a warm affirmation of his republican ideals) and that "There seems very little remaining in it that could be further softened without taking the sting out entirely—which would be a pity" (CW XIV, 15): a statement that reads like a petition to Harriet to approve his text as it stands.[11] The very depth of Mill's republican feeling may have hidden it from the view of those who find no feeling, nothing but arid intellection, in Mill; and those like Basil Willey who see in him "a certain spinsterish dryness of thought and style."[12] While Mill did present himself as the "feminine" mind Willey portrays him as being, there exists a sort of secret brotherhood between Mill and Milton, who strikes no one as spinsterish. Perhaps Harriet had a hand in suppressing the resemblances between *On Liberty* and the "Areopagitica" of Milton, famed as an antifeminist. This is conjectural. What does seem clear is that Mill's passion for Harriet was intellectualized and his passion for the republican ideal tempered. Mary Wollstonecraft (whose daughter became the second wife of Shelley) urged men and women to master their passions and to put marriage on a more rational basis than romantic love, and in effect, Mill followed this advice on both heads.

It seems clear too that in his withdrawal from public life during the years of his marriage (another index of the completeness of his dedication to Harriet), Mill didn't live out the ideal of public virtue. While he wrote busily, even urgently, during his married years (from 1851 to 1858), Mill published almost nothing except revised editions of earlier works—this as opposed to his Herculean labors of the 1840s—and, when he wasn't traveling, virtually withdrew from society into the bower of intimate life.[13] That change of direction was the more significant in a man as public-spirited as Mill, and it prepares for *On Liberty* and its conflicting attitudes toward "the idea of obligation to the public" (OL 256). We turn now to a consideration of *On Liberty* itself, which tames the dangerous waters of the republican tradition by funneling them into the "Dutch canal" (OL 268) of the single principle of noninterference.

NOTES

1. Contrast Rousseau's statement in his *Confessions*, "I was born at Geneva in 1712, the son of Isaac Rousseau, a citizen of that town, and Susanne Bernard, his wife." *The Confessions of Jean-Jacques Rousseau*, tr. J. M. Cohen (New York: Penguin, 1953), p. 17.

2. Bruce Mazlish, *James and John Stuart Mill: Father and Son in the Nineteenth Century* (New York: Basic, 1975), p. 60.

3. *Complete Prose Works of John Milton*, vol. 2 (New Haven, Conn.: Yale University Press, 1959), p. 559.

4. "A Defence of Poetry," in *Shelley's Poetry and Prose*, eds. Donald H. Reiman and Sharon B. Powers (New York: Norton, 1977), p. 508.

5. On this tradition, see Alice S. Miskimin, *The Renaissance Chaucer* (New Haven, Conn.: Yale University Press, 1975), p. 63.

6. *Complete Prose Works of John Milton*, vol. 4, ed. Don M. Wolfe (New Haven, Conn.: Yale University Press, 1966), p. 571.

7. On this issue see Bruce Boehrer, "Elementary Structures of Kingship: Milton, Regicide, and the Family," *Milton Studies* 23 (1987), 97–117.

8. These passages from Mill's letters are assembled by Gertrude Himmelfarb, *On Liberty and Liberalism: The Case of John Stuart Mill* (New York: Knopf, 1974), pp. 230–31 (emphasis in the original). The original source-book of Mill/Harriet Taylor material is F. A. Hayek, *John Stuart Mill and Harriet Taylor: Their Correspondence and Subsequent Marriage* (Chicago: University of Chicago Press, 1951).

9. In an exposé written in 1846, Mill and Harriet used the phrase "to call a human being into existence" (CW XXIV, 918).

10. Preface to "Prometheus Unbound" in *Shelley's Poetry and Prose*, p. 134.

11. That Mill and Harriet did not see through the same eyes is suggested by the fact that Mill cites Tocqueville with admiration in his defense of the February 1848 revolution, while Harriet, writing to Mill in July 1849, calls Tocqueville "a notable specimen" of "the gentility class—weak in moral, narrow in intellect, timid, infinitely conceited & gossiping." See Hayek, *Mill and Harriet Taylor*, p. 156.

12. Basil Willey, *Nineteenth Century Studies: Coleridge to Matthew Arnold* (London: Chatto & Windus, 1949), p. 141.

13. Cf. Himmelfarb, *On Liberty and Liberalism*, pp. 212–13, 251–52. See also p. xxxiv of the introduction by Francis E. Mineka and Dwight N. Lindley to volume 14 of Mill's *Collected Works*: "To the end Harriet was the all-sufficient centre of his existence. If Harriet could have lived, [Mill] would gladly have foregone the public fame he was later to achieve." In fairness it should be said, too, that Mill's withdrawal from public life was at times forced on him by ill health.

5

The Hidden Dimension of
Mill's *Liberty*

SCATTERED THROUGHOUT THIS book have been any number of quotations from *On Liberty*, most of them intended to bring out republican motifs in the text. It is only too easy to read *On Liberty* as what Mill called "a kind of philosophic text-book of a single truth" (CW I, 259; see the Introduction of this book, note 17): the "truth" of noninterference. But texts, like textiles, are weavings, and in *On Liberty* Mill weaves republican concepts into a libertarian argument. If *On Liberty* really were a univocal text, a text of one counsel, it would have less interest for us than it does. It would simply establish the notion of free choice that has since become the commonplace of a consumer society, a notion marketed by the mass media themselves. It would hallow our clichés. Not *On Liberty* so much as Adam Smith's *Wealth of Nations* is a textbook of a single truth—that it is best to leave people free to act on their own interests according to their own lights. In *On Liberty*, indeed, Mill broadens Smith's argument to mandate noninterference with private conduct generally. But as dedicated as Mill was to the idea of noninterference, he also thought that we urgently need to relearn the meaning of an "obligation to the public" (OL 256)—the republican principle. And these two positions he "reconciled" by arguing, in effect, that the best way to arouse a sense of obligation to the public is to emphatically secure a private sphere within which people can concentrate on their own happiness, knowing they are not answerable to the public at all. I find that this argument doesn't really make sense and that *On Liberty* is less clear, but also richer and more "manysided," than we would expect a primer of "a single truth" to be. If Mill was concerned to promote the "energetic Pursuit of Good" (OL 255) as the antidote to a craven morality of conformity, then what has the consuming or the not consuming of x to do with the energetic pursuit of good? In what conceivable sense can the consumer be said to carry forward the republican tradition that affirms moral courage and the public sphere itself, the tradition that charges Mill's language with power when he speaks of such things as the energetic pursuit of good? What makes the morality of pleasing-ourselves-provided-that-we-abstain-from-hurting-others so much better than (or even different from) the morality of innocuousness and abstention that Mill detests?

In fact *On Liberty* isn't the exposition of a single "truth."[1] We need only attend to the stark contradiction between Mill's defense of good despotisms over "backward" peoples (OL 224) and his ridicule of the notion of civilizing a community by force—between his advocacy of "joint concerns" (OL 305) and his contempt of the English "habit of combining" (OL 272)—to see that *On Liberty* isn't the single-minded text he made it out to be. Perhaps at this point in my argument it is time to address *On Liberty* in a more consecutive way—not to plod through it clause by clause, assuredly, but to take up each of its chapters in turn, noting some of the sites where republicanism lies buried in the text. I will hold repetition of points already made to a minimum.

The introduction to *On Liberty* presents, first of all, a historical synopsis of the rise of liberty. Mill reviews "the struggle between Liberty and Authority" (OL 217) and the evolution of the understanding of liberty, first as a limit on the power of rulers; later as parliamentary government (a point reached in England in the constitutional settlement of 1688); and finally as a security against the intolerance of the community, which itself holds sway now that the struggle between subjects and rulers has been closed. These introductory paragraphs lay the groundwork for the argument to follow. I mean that all of *On Liberty* follows from the thesis that the once-lively conflict between subjects and rulers has expired, and with it the energy necessary to sustain and succor freedom. *On Liberty* pictures a pacified society in which the political majority use their hard-won freedom to no better end than to make slaves of themselves. Having gained securities against "the tyranny of the magistrate" (OL 220)—a phrase with seventeenth-century resonances—people now give themselves up to a

soft social tyranny "enslaving the soul itself" (220), a phrase stamped
with the republican belief that only the uncorrupt can maintain their
liberty. In this sense the gain of freedom proved to be the loss of
freedom. The republican tradition both recognized and struggled
against the "mortality" of liberty.[2] So did Mill, who knew the fate of
the English Commonwealth, who twice saw his hopes for a French
Republic miscarry, and who viewed his own society as the miserably
ironic outcome of a historic struggle for freedom. We can only surmise
how Mill would have regarded the triumph of the free choice he
contended for, and the reduction of political liberty to consumer
appetite, in our own day.[3]

The latest threat to liberty, in Mill's view, is the tyranny of the
majority—not the subjection of a people by the authorities, but the
subjection of the individual by society itself. The example of America
(says Mill) has impressed this threat on thinking minds, and of course
it was Tocqueville, meditative observer of America, who introduced
Mill to the notion of the tyranny of the majority. Yet Tocqueville makes
it plain that the same Americans who have invented this form of
oppression also practice the philosophy of "to each his own" that Mill
recommends as the medicine against it. For example, Americans hold
that "no one has the right of constraining his fellow creatures to be
happy." Again, "That Providence has given to every human being the
degree of reason necessary to direct himself in the affairs that interest
him exclusively is the grand maxim upon which civil and political
society rests in the United States."[4] If the Americans seek their own
good and yet are preparing new forms of tyranny, then perhaps Mill's
liberty principle offers no security against the novel kind of tyranny he
dreads. Can it be that Mill's "one very simple principle" of noninterference (OL 223) provides no defense against the maiming of the
individual? Not a possibility Mill is willing to contemplate. He prefers
to vest his argument in the principle of noninterference.

Concerned as he is to settle the limits of authority over the individual, Mill proposes a rational test to decide what is and what is not an
encroachment on the sovereignty of the person. Customarily, he tells
us, the question is decided by such sub-rational determinants as
personal preference, class interest, and custom itself. Mill cuts through
all of this (rather as Bentham cut through the thickets of English law)
by

> assert[ing] one very simple principle, as entitled to govern absolutely the
> dealings of society with the individual in the way of compulsion and

control. . . . That principle is, that the sole end for which mankind are
warranted, individually or collectively, in interfering with the liberty of
action of any of their number, is self-protection. (OL 223)

When Mill called *On Liberty* a textbook of a single truth, this "one
very simple principle" must have been the truth he was referring to.
The same paragraph goes on to argue that in matters of private
decision—what Mill calls self-regarding matters—there may be "good
reasons for remonstrating with [the individual], or reasoning with him,
or persuading him, or entreating him, but not for compelling him" (OL
224). In "Areopagitica" Milton had struck the very same distinction
between persuasion and compulsion; it is a distinction of capital
importance in that argument. But neither here nor in his review of the
fight for religious liberty nor anywhere else in *On Liberty* does Mill
cite Milton, a republican. Similarly, Mill shuns the kind of appeal to
"abstract right" (OL 224) that revolutionaries make use of. The
language of right lends itself to loose thinking, declamation, and
indiscriminate usage; more than this, it lends itself to the oratory of
revolution. Mill chooses not to play on, or panic his audience with, the
Jacobinical slogan of the Rights of Man. One reason why *On Liberty*
doesn't acknowledge the work of Mary Wollstonecraft, which Mill
must have known or known of, might be that she posts the language of
abstract right in her very titles.

Republicanism is a dangerous ideal—dangerous for its bold enterprise, its stress on political creation and the power of action, its
obsession with virtue. It is perhaps as an attempt to contain the risks
of his own republican values that, in the introduction to *On Liberty*,
Mill holds up the ancient republics as examples *not* to be emulated.
This passage is the more noteworthy in that it so markedly conflicts
both with Mill's paean to Athens in his review of George Grote's
history of Greece and with his belief that the first article of good
government is to cultivate the character of the citizen. Claiming that
his doctrine of noninterference cuts contrary to existing opinion and
that society likes to impose its "notions of personal, as of social
excellence" (OL 226), Mill refers to the bad precedent of

> the ancient commonwealths [which] thought themselves entitled to prac-
> tise . . . the regulation of every part of private conduct by public authority,
> on the ground that the State had a deep interest in the whole bodily and
> mental discipline of every one of its citizens. (OL 226)

These lines seem to me to be a denial of Mill's own republican beliefs,
which don't consist in any "very simple" way with the laissez-faire

argument of *On Liberty*, just as compulsory service in a citizen army (OL 225) doesn't on the face of it accord with the pursuit of one's own good in one's own way. (No one should be punished simply for being drunk, but no soldier should be drunk on duty [OL 282]—and every citizen, at least every male citizen, should serve as a soldier.) Anyway, it would seem that Mill himself believed the state has a deep interest in its citizens, for he asserts as much in *Considerations on Representative Government*, in a passage we have already encountered:

> The first element of good government . . . being the virtue and intelligence of the human beings composing the community, the most important point of excellence which any form of government can possess is to promote the virtue and intelligence of the people themselves. (CW XIX, 390)

As to the oppressive authority of the ancient republics, Mill in his review of Grote's history of Greece rebuts the charge that individual liberty was sacrificed to the good of the Athenian state. I would surmise too that Mill believed that "excellence" can be fostered only in a republic—a polity where the people are sovereign; where hereditary distinctions are at an end; where a natural and not a born aristocracy holds sway; where no one is above the law; where civic virtue is a religion—and that Victorian society, far from imposing norms of excellence, imposed norms of mediocrity. This last point is made outright in chapter 3 of *On Liberty*.

In brief, Mill ensnares himself in problems in the introduction to *On Liberty*. The reason, I think, is that he was less simple than the argument he set himself to write. As a result, he had not only to argue out the principle of noninterference but to keep a check on his republican beliefs, which were deeply held and which complicated and played tricks on his argument. In February 1848, in the heat of excitement following the proclamation of a republic in France (which he interpreted as practically a millennial event, auguring a new era for all of Europe), Mill wrote to a correspondent that the French republicans had succeeded "because *at last* they had the good sense to raise the standard not of a republic but of something in which the middle classes could join" (CW XIII, 731; Mill's emphasis). The muteness of Mill's republicanism in *On Liberty* also argues a certain tactical caution. In this work Mill criticizes the middle class in the name of a principle the class itself recognizes—the principle of dutifully attending to your own business—and he presents his republicanism without oratory and in a way that doesn't call up vivid mental images of armed mobs, the desecration of churches, or the guillotine. Nor is Mill's prose intended to bring up these images of the 1848 revolution in France:

> From every window, from every balcony, from the roofs of surrounding buildings, demagogues and political orators of every shade of opinion, delegates from the secret societies, socialists and anarchists, were haranguing the crowds, and scattering lists of governments they desired to form. Yet in all the Babel of political mouthings, one word was universally echoed to the sky: "The Republic!"[5]

Mill had much to be cautious of, for as he observes in his homage to Armand Carrel, "by professing republicanism, there [is] danger of alarming the timid" (CW XX, 200). (That essay opens with an allusion to Milton.) In his *Autobiography* Mill records that years of experience in the East India Company taught him to dress his views carefully in order to make them acceptable to "minds not prepared for [them] by habit" (CW I, 87)—a strategy of accommodation arguably at work in *On Liberty*, with its "studied moderation of language" (OL 259). Nor was Mill himself above the timidity he despised in others; in particular, he seems to have been fearful of the dangers besetting the republican ideal of an active citizenry. In any event, he curbs his own republicanism in the introduction to *On Liberty*. In his thesis that the pacification of society has been achieved at the expense of the courage to act, he draws on the republican maxim that only the strong can maintain their liberty. In his dream of virtuous empire over barbarian races (OL 224), he draws on the republican ideal of a new Rome.[6] Distinguishing between persuasion and compulsion, he follows Milton. And yet he disparages the ancient republics, prohibits civilizing people by force (this later in *On Liberty*), and makes no reference to Milton. We are ready to proceed to chapter 2.

THE FRENCH REPUBLICANS whose part Mill took had to contend with censorship under Louis Philippe and later under Louis Napoleon; the repressive September Laws of 1835 outlawed the very designation "republican." Mill had to contend with censorship of a different variety—less official, less brutal, more even in its enforcement, and possibly more effective.[7] I have reasoned that Mill muted his republicanism in *On Liberty*, in part so that the essay wouldn't stir up latent anti-Jacobinical passions and prejudices that could overwhelm rational debate. "The popularity of Queen Victoria," it has been said, "made republicanism virtually unthinkable.''[8] Mill thought it, although he spoke of it guardedly. The idea that Mill might have censored himself in framing his protest against censorship has been put forward by Basil Willey, who advises the reader of *On Liberty* to bear in mind that Mill's father warned him against incautiously avowing his lack of Christian faith. (Mill refutes at length the argument that "certain beliefs" [OL 233] are so necessary to society that they must be protected from challenge; without question, he means Christianity, the traditional guarantor of order.) Elsewhere Willey notes astutely that *On Liberty* has something of "the heroic tone of 1789" about it, and he implies that it has something of the tone of 1644 as well, for he describes the text as "a veritable *Areopagitica*."[9] Digging still deeper into the subsoil under *On Liberty*, we might say that, with his stress on active contest and original creation as opposed to passive inheritance of tradition, Mill draws on the memory of the "pushy and revolutionary burghers"[10] who first established the merchant republics of the Middle Ages—those townsmen who didn't inherit their liberties but had to create them in the first place, which meant taking them. *On Liberty* looks back to spots of time when practices were created and truth hadn't yet settled into commonplace and views hadn't yet narrowed, much as though the author had in mind revolutionary moments in which people were able to act with one another in the name of principles more expansive than self-interest. If Mill was cautious of rousing the anti-revolutionary sentiments of the English middle class, he had reason to be so, for *On Liberty* is underwritten by the European revolutionary tradition. In fact, chapter 2 opens with a literal instance of underwriting: a footnote the subject of which is the killing of tyrants.

No sooner does Mill write at the start of chapter 2 that state-enforced censorship has lapsed than he inserts a footnote under his text acknowledging that events have seemed "to give [his claim] an emphatic contradiction" (OL 228n). The footnote goes on to justify, in a rather more conflicted and circumspect way than Milton did, "the lawfulness of Tyrannicide."[11] (Maybe Mill didn't want to be perceived as speaking what Macaulay, in an essay Mill knew well—the refutation of James Mill's theory of government—calls "the old republican cant . . . about . . . the duty of killing tyrants.")[12] After observing that tyrannicide "has been accounted by whole nations, and by some of the best and wisest of men, not a crime, but an act of exalted virtue," Mill goes on to defend criminal penalties for "instigation" to the act. As cautious as it is, Mill's language is redder than Kant's, who depicts regicide as the worst of crimes. The "formal *execution* of a monarch," writes Kant, must arouse dread in any soul imbued with ideas of human right, and this feeling will recur whenever one thinks of events like the fate of Charles I or Louis XVI. . . . [Regicide] amounts to making the people, who owe their existence purely to the legislation of the sovereign, into rulers over the sovereign, thereby brazenly adopting violence as a deliberate principle and exalting it above the most sacred canons of right.[13]

Yet Kant himself was moved to wonder and admiration by the French Revolution; he held a republican ideal and even "expressed hope for a future republic of England."[14] Kant affirms the ideal of a republican constitution but opposes revolution in principle; Mill celebrates original creation but settles for the quiet pursuit of happiness.

The prosecutions that had embarrassed Mill's argument were directed at publications calling for the assassination of Napoleon III.[15] He it was who had put an end to the Second Republic in France by a coup d'état in 1851—the republic for which Mill had entertained such extravagant hopes. A year before the publication of *On Liberty* Mill wrote to the Italian republican agitator Giuseppe Mazzini of the scorn he felt that the English were seeming to connive with Louis Napoleon to "hunt . . . down all foreigners (& indeed English too) who have virtue enough to be his avowed enemies" (CW XV, 548). Evidently Mill thought better of too forcibly expressing his love of virtue in this sense in *On Liberty*. In 1854 he suffered pangs of regret over sending the third edition of his *Political Economy* through the French mails to Harriet, because in that immensity was one sentence damning Louis Napoleon. Thus, as soon as Mill commences the argumentation proper of *On Liberty* (for the first chapter was "Introductory"), republicanism breaks in and draws us into issues of censorship and self-censorship, while drawing the author into a highly guarded defense of tyrannicide, an act that has little enough to do with laissez-faire.

This aside, the second chapter of *On Liberty* sets us in an improved society that has even improved the enforcement of censorship. No longer the indictment for seditious libel, the cell, the fine, bodily mutilation; now the expression of dissident opinion is subject to merely social penalties and discouragements. No longer do the authorities and the Vice Societies, together, prosecute; now the Vice Societies proceed by themselves, outside the courts.[16] Having thrown off their masters in the process described in the introduction to *On Liberty*, the people have become their own censors. Censorship is no longer imposed *on* the public so much as administered *by* the public, now a moral police (as when publishers advised authors against saying things the reading public wouldn't stand for). Not that Victorian censorship was any the less effective than the more brutal censorship of old. According to one student of the subject, "There may have been more censorship, self-imposed or otherwise, in England or in the United States [in the nineteenth century], than during all the preceding centuries of printed literature."[17] In this context, then, Mill undertakes to defend "Liberty of Thought and Discussion," a defense extending equally to opinions that are true, opinions that are untrue, and opinions that are true in part. To this list Mill might have added opinions that once were true but are true no longer, and opinions that may yet be true, for the fact is that Mill sees the Victorian age as a time of transition and implies more or less broadly that Victorian intolerance is grounded in people's fear of discovering that the truth has gone out of their truths. We may be sure Mill takes a historical view of these questions: he speaks of the Reformation as an outbreak of the truth, while he himself, writing in the nineteenth century, was no Christian. This can only mean that *in its time* the Reformation carried the truth.

But what if *On Liberty* itself is judged historically? Some two and a half centuries before *On Liberty*, when a London pamphleteer hazarded the opinion that women should not be "the Bond slaue of Time, the Hand-maid of opinion, or the strict obseruer of euery frosty or cold benummed imagination," this indeed had the audacity of a new doctrine. The same pamphlet argues women should have "freedome of election [choice]"—for example, in matters of fashion and style.[18] By comparison, Mill's argument reads like a codification of doctrines not original with the author, just as his emphatic distinction between the public and private spheres reflects the hardening of that distinction perhaps a century before. For by the eighteenth century there had emerged a "distinction between public life, which was the business of the state, and private life, which individuals were entitled to conceal from others and to shape as they pleased"[19]—the distinction on which *On Liberty* rests, and that it writes as it were into law. To my mind, the merit of *On Liberty* is that the author's thinking is not totally codified, that he pleads for the private sphere in the language of public spirit. And in its unsettled character it suits, perhaps, the temper of the times.

As I have noted, the present was to Mill a time of transition, an interregnum in which old truths had lost their force (in effect, their truth) and new ones hadn't yet arisen to take their place. Like Machiavelli, Mill found himself in a world in which ancient verities had given way, so that passive inheritance and common usage would no longer serve and people must have recourse to their capacity to create and to act. Since the old regime of opinion has lost its legitimacy—"people feel sure, not so much that their opinions are true, as that they should not know what to do without them" (OL 233)—Mill calls on his readers to take an active part in the reconstruction of knowledge, as one might call on people to create a republic on the strength of their political capacities, upon the breakdown of traditional authority. Milton sounded such a call. But Mill doesn't agitate for political revolution in *On Liberty*. Or rather, he sublimates revolution into the "improved" form of the quest for knowledge, exalting an intellectual valor—mental daring and skill in argumentative combat—in lieu of the more risky political valor, which issues perhaps in acts like tyrannicide.

In the course of his defense of opinions in part true, Mill instances Rousseau's opinion that modern civilization is degenerate. According to Mill, this view, while certainly distorted, nevertheless provided a just corrective to the prejudices of Rousseau's day.

> There lay in Rousseau's doctrine, and has floated down the stream of opinion along with it, a considerable amount of exactly those truths which the popular opinion wanted; and these are the deposit which was left behind when the flood subsided. The superior worth of simplicity of life, the enervating and demoralizing effect of the trammels and hypocrisies of artificial society, are ideas which have never been absent from cultivated minds since Rousseau wrote. (OL 253)

Mill doesn't mention Rousseau's view that Christianity is incompatible with civic virtue.[20] He doesn't remark that Rousseau's cherished aim, that of maintaining the integral self, is also his own. He says nothing of their common affirmation of the citizen militia.[21] He passes over the fact that Rousseau's *Discourse on Inequality* ends, in the spirit of *On Liberty*, with a derisive attack on the individual whose life is regulated by the opinions of society—the individual who "knows how to live only in the opinion of others."[22] He also passes over the fact that the *Discourse on Inequality* opens with a paean to the republic of Geneva. (A paean commended by the author of the great textbook of the doctrine of noninterference, Adam Smith.)[23] An autonomous city of autonomous citizens, Geneva stands as a noble exception to the degeneracy of modern societies.[24] Being securely founded, capable of supporting its own freedom, and subject neither to the love of conquest nor the fear of being conquered, the republic of Geneva is an autonomous entity, much like a self at a higher level. And it is the citizenry of a republic—"not only free but fit to be free," as Rousseau says of the citizens of Geneva[25]—against whom the vitiated selves of *On Liberty* are measured. Yet Mill chooses not to affirm the republicanism he held in common with Rousseau, whether because of the predominance in Geneva of the same Calvinism that comes under attack in *On Liberty*; or because Rousseau would compel people to be free; or because Mill thought the real meaning of Rousseau was Robespierre (CW X, 123); or because Rousseau and Geneva later fell out. For whatever reason, here as elsewhere in *On Liberty* Mill chooses not to placard the republican principles in whose name he speaks whenever he depicts a debilitated society unequal to the exertions that are necessary if freedom is to be preserved.

Chapter 2 of *On Liberty* does refer to republicanism, but under the denatured name of "the idea of obligation to the public" (OL 256). The phrase figures in Mill's attack on Christianity, an attack that is moderate in tone but still succeeds in saying Christianity has at last reduced people to such selfishness that they are unable to exert themselves for the public good. Under the Christian regime of the nineteenth century, people are both privatized and deprived as it were of their own being—"cramped," "cowed," and so forth (OL 242). Like the republicans before him, Mill looks back to "Greek and Roman sources" (OL 256) of the idea of public virtue. Like the impassioned republican Victor Hugo, Mill scorns the doctrine of passive obedience. To Hugo, passive obedience is the obedience shown by French soldiers who massacre French citizens on command; active obedience is the obedience shown by citizens erecting barricades to defend the Constitution.[26] The latter know what it is to exert themselves for the public good. And in doing so, they have had to lay aside the morality of passivity and submission. For his part, Mill distinguishes the "energetic Pursuit of Good" from the Christian morality of abstention from evil (OL 255). The foremost of the modern republicans, Machiavelli, is notorious for breaking with the Christian morality of abstention from evil, and Mill himself has been condemned as a teacher of evil, but the argument of *On Liberty* can hardly be called Machiavellian. So abstract and moralized—so "improved"—is the republicanism of *On Liberty* that it too, perhaps, bears only a weak and outward relation to the "truth" republicanism once was.

The fact is that, for all of his contempt for the morality of abstinence, Mill himself in the end recommends that very thing: we are to be free to do as we like, provided we scrupulously abstain from treading on the interests of others; and in accordance with the doctrine of voluntary deference we are to abstain from the exercise of the political power in our hands. Mill doesn't attempt to work out these knots in his argument. Nor does he explain how an obligation to the public can be squared with the pursuit of one's own good in one's own way; as I have said, if the word "obligation" *means* obligation, then these values conflict. Perhaps if Mill had voiced his republican convictions more forcibly, these problems and self-conflicts would have come more clearly into view. As it is, he uses a policy of "studied moderation" (OL 259) that serves not only to mollify his audience somewhat, but also perhaps to keep his own republican passions from confounding his argument.

WHERE CHAPTER 2 of *On Liberty* defends freedom of speech and opinion, chapter 3 encourages freedom of action (within limits) and the unfolding of human manyness. These things stand in need of encouragement because, as Mill sees it, the improved manners and morals and the advancing equality of an age of commerce have had the side-effect of snuffing out the courage to act (virtù). We are shown an England made up not of men but of mannikins. In one of the few passages of *On Liberty* that sound like oratory, Mill warns, "It was men of another stamp than [men of the present] that made England what it has been; and men of another stamp will be needed to prevent its decline" (OL 272). Presumably, what the heroes of the past had was the power to act. In the ideal case, Mill would like to see that power diffused as widely as possible, so that ordinary people too, not just heroes, may achieve their full measure. Underlying Mill's defense of freedom of action is an Aristotelian-republican concept of human beings as choicemakers whose nature is fulfilled in the employment of their capacities. In calling as he does for the education and exercise of our abilities (particularly, it seems, such political abilities as we still possess), Mill speaks as a republican. He seems to envision citizens who are individually unlike, yet alike capable of action, dedicated to the public good, vigilant of liberty. The incarnation of these virtues Mill found in Armand Carrel, the "conservative republican," a title that nicely expresses the balance of forces in Mill's own position. If on reading Mill's accounts of mutilated persons and mannikins we wonder what his conception of a whole and living person is, we will find one example in the republican Carrel, described by Mill as "a human being complete at all points" (CW XX, 213). (Carrel died in a duel, a practice that has been stamped out but that probably comes under the libertarian provisions of Mill's essay. While mourning the loss of Carrel, Mill honored him for dying by his own principles. Here then is an illustration of what Mill means by choosing one's own principles of conduct.)

Ideally, as I say, Mill hopes to see the power of action that Carrel possessed, diffused widely through society. That prospect lies far off, however. For the present, it is enough if the many recognize and respect such a one as Carrel, who was so powerfully distinguished by his passion for virtue (virtù) and by his mastery of his passions. The heroism of Carrel, a man fully realized, is not for everyone. We might say indeed that *On Liberty* pacifies the republican ideal of self-realization, the very ideal on whose power Mill draws. In *On Liberty* Mill abstracts the notion of self-realization from a republican context stressing citizenly duty and political engagement, as in Milton's advocacy of active virtue; as in the revolutionary ideal of a republic where human nature will finally be accomplished. While using something of the language of republicanism, and using it feelingly, Mill nevertheless dilutes republicanism in *On Liberty* to the point where it asks little more of us than to pursue happiness as seems best to us and leave others free to do the same. Thus the struggle for public liberty turns into the pursuit of private happiness, and the heroic idiom of republicanism is written over with more prudent counsels and more modest aspirations. So it is that Mill's conception of choicemaking and self-realization, while indebted to republican sources, finds illustration in the anti-heroic narrative of Dickens's *Great Expectations* (1860–61). Where liberalism is "organized around respect for decisions made by individual men and women as they are in ordinary life,"[27] Mill commits himself to tolerance while being gravely critical of human beings as they are (in that they fall so far short of the ideal of a flourishing human life); *Great Expectations* is the narrative of an undistinguished human being who after long travail comes to make his own decisions.

"He who lets the world, or his own portion of it, choose his plan of life for him," Mill writes,

> has no need of any other faculty than the ape-like one of imitation. He who chooses his plan for himself, employs all his faculties. He must use observation to see, reasoning and judgment to foresee, activity to gather materials for decision, and when he has decided, firmness and self-control to hold to his deliberate decision. (OL 262–63)

These are the things Pip needs to learn, and in some sort does learn. For 20-odd years, Pip didn't choose his plan of life for himself. From his early years it was understood that he was destined to work in the

forge; then for some time he enacted the plan of life scripted for him
by Magwitch. (He is used as a sort of mannikin by Magwitch to show
up respectable society.) Indeed, for a long time Pip lacks just those
character-assets listed by Mill. He fails to "use observation to see"
what should be plain to him: that he will not have Estella. He reasons
poorly, jumping to the conclusion that Miss Havisham is his sponsor,
in spite of Jaggers' admonition to stick to the facts. In London he lives
a life of sloth, not activity, falling into debt, a condition synonymous
with moral dissolution. He lacks discrimination, failing to set people at
their true worth. He lacks firmness and self-control; when Pip asks,
" 'What shall I say I am—to-day?' " Herbert answers, " 'Say a good
fellow . . . with impetuosity and hesitation, boldness and diffidence,
action and dreaming, curiously mixed in him.' "[28] And yet this weak
character, exposed to exploitation and ill usage and lacking powers of
decision, becomes not only the most integrated character in *Great
Expectations*, but someone capable of defying polite opinion. Still, Pip
isn't a citizen vigilant of liberty, and the virtues he certifies to us aren't
republican in character, but pertain entirely to the conduct of private
life. Private concerns engross Pip; and in some sense, the pursuit of
private happiness engrosses the language of republicanism in Mill's
Liberty. I mean to say that Mill's republicanism is so laundered in the
text of *On Liberty* that in practical terms it differs not too widely from
the morality of Pip—who ends *Great Expectations* in the shipping
business, an agent of the very forces of commerce and improvement
that Mill holds responsible for the spread of a pestilential sameness
(OL 274–75). Just so, Mill's lofty thesis of the organic character of
human nature somehow comes down to Pip. "Human nature," writes
Mill,

> is not a machine to be built after a model, and set to do exactly the work
> prescribed for it, but a tree, which requires to grow and develope itself on
> all sides, according to the tendency of the inward forces which make it a
> living thing. (OL 263)

Pip requires to grow and develop, rather than performing the tasks
prescribed for him by adult bosses and programmers. He does grow
and develop—advancing, for example, in the course of experience (not
all of a sudden) from a loathing of Magwitch to an unconditional
acceptance of the man. Pip's very name suggests growth, denoting as
it does a seed. Somehow "the stuff of which heroes are made" (OL
264) comes down to the antiheroic Pip.

The concern with self-realization that was carried by republicanism and that surfaces in Mill appeared in striking form in the political thought of Kant, who looked to a republican constitution to bring out the nobler capacities of men and induct them in time into moral freedom. The first proposition of Kant's "Idea for a Universal History with a Cosmopolitan Purpose" (1784) reads, "All the natural capacities of a creature are destined sooner or later to be developed completely and in conformity with their end."[29] Clearly Mill concurs with Kant's thesis that our capacities are far from realized at present and can come to realization only in a particular order of law—namely, a republic. Kant conceives of a constitution that will make men virtuous in spite of themselves,[30] nursing them until they come into the full possession of their moral freedom. Mill seems to envision men (and women) being tutored by political experience and habituated to virtue. Perhaps not a very active virtue, though. Where Kant marks a strong distinction between pure duty and considerations of interest, Mill seems to believe that republican duty and private happiness are two sides of one coin, much as though we could fulfill an obligation to the public (fulfilling at the same time our own natures) within the private sphere.

Mill protests the fact that everyone in Victorian society "lives as under the eye of a hostile and dreaded censorship" (OL 264), and yet he censors his own republicanism, presenting it in a guise so moralized and "improved" that it hardly appears to the eye. But I don't want to imply that Mill didn't feel the republican ideal strongly. Rather like those evangelicals who censored secular literature because they felt its power so keenly, Mill checked a republican passion that even so (as in his defense of the French revolution of February 1848, a defense that he claims to have muted) could be militant. He tells us that "the same strong susceptibilities which make the personal impulses vivid and powerful, are also the source from whence are generated the most passionate love of virtue, and the sternest self-control" (OL 263–64).[31] Mill's own most passionate love of virtue—the term is a cipher for republicanism—had to be controlled, the more so because of the risks of the republican ideal itself. (The reduction of passion to socially acceptable levels lies at the heart of the moral theory of Mill's predecessor Adam Smith.) Thus we go from the "exalted virtue" of the tyrannicides (OL 228n) to the little virtues of Pip. As we have seen, Mill commended the French republicans of 1848 for not advertising their republicanism and instead offering "something in which the middle classes could join," that is, electoral reform. Mill doesn't advertise his republicanism in flying colors in *On Liberty*, instead appealing to the middle-class maxim of closely attending to your own business. He offers something in which the middle classes—and later, consumer society—could join.

THE CONCEPT OF action is so broad that anything from picking up a spoon to killing a king can be accounted an action. The republican concept of action, as the exercise of civic virtue, is more determinate. At least action in the republican sense has a public character. (Consider how closely action and the public realm are joined in the thought of Hannah Arendt.) Chapter 4 of *On Liberty*, "Of the Limits to the Authority of Society over the Individual," shrinks action to "purely personal conduct" (OL 283). In this chapter Mill dedicates his argument to a defense of self-regarding acts, which by definition have no real public dimension. Granted that temperance societies and other evangelical pressure-groups had power when *On Liberty* was written, still it is ironic that Mill, a republican, should have made so much of acts at the very vanishing point of political life, such as purely subjective choices of consumption. (By contrast, Mill argues in *Considerations on Representative Government* that one has no option, no subjective preference to exercise, in the giving of one's vote.) With his talk of differences of taste and the liberty of the consumer, Mill looks forward to consumer society, where the public realm, far from having the high standing accorded to it by republicanism, is left without standing at all, and where political confidence artists try to claim for themselves as individuals all the credibility that has disappeared from the public world as such.

Tightening the sphere of action as he does, Mill commits, as it seems to me, the very fault he wants to protest: the stifling of action. I don't mean that individuals shouldn't be free to eat pork or abstain from eating pork, but that Mill should have put the emphasis on forms of action "which unite [people] instead of isolating them from one another" (OL 305)—action with a public dimension. He should have developed a point he made in the *Political Economy*: that free people need to range outside the private sphere and combine for common ends (CW III, 943). He should have followed the example of Tocqueville in *Democracy in America*, laying stress on civic action while still arguing for constitutional protections of individual rights.[32] Indeed, republican discourse itself afforded a place to the idea of self-regarding acts. In a manifesto of Mill's acquaintance William James Linton—the more significant in that Linton was not a great or original thinker, so that these were not his ideas alone—appears a distinction between "the act which immediately injures only the actor and that which directly assails another's rights."[33] The problem I find in *On Liberty* is not that Mill allows for self-regarding acts (an idea as old as Pericles), but that he emphasizes those pursuits rhetorically to the point where they bury republican values like civic action and public spirit. The same thing occurs more openly in "Utilitarianism," where the claim is made that perhaps in one act out of 100 we are accountable to the public (CW X, 219)—a proportion that suggests not two equally weighted principles (halves of the truth), but one principle crushing another. Considering how many of the topics of *On Liberty*, from self-realization to the citizen militia, Mill owed to republican discourse; considering how much the spirit of his argument owes to the republican tradition; considering how much power that tradition imparts to his language—it is much as though Mill bit the hand that fed him. So it is that *On Liberty* has come to be read virtually as a refutation of republican principles. Finding people given to a morality with "an essentially selfish character"—one that "disconnect[s] each man's feelings of duty from the interests of his fellow-creatures" (OL 255)—Mill devotes a large block of his text to defending acts that concern no one but the agent. It seems an odd method of raising a person up from the morality of selfishness to sanctify conduct that he or she alone has an interest in, and to sanctify it for that very reason. By privatizing action, Mill has conceded the greater part of the republican ideal, in particular the image of the citizen "constantly involved with his fellows in the making of public decisions."[34]

At the same time, Mill makes a large compromise with his Victorian readers in chapter 4 of *On Liberty*, calling for so much disapprobation of bad conduct that anyone but an evangelical might be tempted to cry coercion.

> We have a right . . . in various ways, to act upon our unfavourable opinion of any one, not to the oppression of his individuality, but in the exercise of ours. We are not bound, for example, to seek his society; we have a right to avoid it (though not to parade the avoidance), for we have a right to choose the society most acceptable to us. We have a right, and it may be our duty, to caution others against him, if we think his example or conversation likely to have a pernicious effect on those with whom he associates. We may give others a preference over him in optional good offices. (OL 278)

As though this sort of blackballing weren't enough, Mill adds that disapproval may rise to the pitch of "abhorrence," and that not necessarily of bad conduct, but of bad *attitudes*. As critical as he is of moral police-actions, Mill is willing to impose these stiff penalties because "they are the natural, and, as it were, the spontaneous consequences of the [churlish individual's] faults themselves" (278)—which is a little like the argument that retribution naturally follows sin, or the argument that capital punishment is the natural penalty appointed for murder. (Then too there are those who say that a majority may, in the exercise of *its* free speech, restrict forms of expression it doesn't like, and that if it is barred from doing so, then *it* is censored. Certainly Mill would have rejected this argument, but some of the language I have just quoted does present itself to those who would make it.) In this chapter of *On Liberty*, Mill has diminished the republican concept of action and diminished, too, the distance between himself and his Victorian readers. To those readers, the very word "republican" would have been incendiary.[35]

BY THE END of *On Liberty*, we are once again aware of the republican tradition of civic virtue underlying the text. Even so, it can be said that the final chapter of *On Liberty* ("Applications") hushes the author's republican convictions. Much of the chapter impresses on us not "the idea of obligation to the public," but the value of unhindered private consumption, an entirely different thing. In this sense, the "Applications," like chapter 4, lay the philosophical foundations for consumer society—such a society as our own, where people are inclined to identify freedom with private consumption itself. The "idea of obligation to the public" withers under these conditions, for the public realm is left without standing or credit. It is left a sham. American political speech, which is widely perceived to be a sham, accurately records a consumer society's verdict on the public sphere itself. Given Mill's abiding concern with the integrity of public discussion, it is bitterly ironic that he should have had anything, however distant, to do with these proceedings. Ironic too is the fate of the private sphere that Mill was at pains to close against society, like a sanctuary. Where tens of millions view the same television show in private or make the same private choice as consumers, clearly the meaning of privacy has been mooted.

Mill opposes restraints on trade that infringe the liberty of "the buyer" (OL 293). He urges that poisons, for example, not be put off limits to "the buyer" (OL 294, 295). He gives philosophical sanction to advertising with the words, "Whatever it is permitted to do, it must be permitted to advise to do" (OL 296). (A rule not strictly kept in

American society, generally so receptive to the libertarianism of *On Liberty*. We are permitted to drink and smoke, yet advertisements for liquor and tobacco are prohibited on television.) He asserts that our "choice of pleasures" is our own concern (OL 298). He upholds the individual's right to "please himself without giving pain to any one" (OL 305). Again, I don't mean we have no right to innocuous pleasures. The point is that this argument is itself innocuous. Having denounced a conventional morality enjoining mere "Abstinence from Evil" (OL 255), Mill goes on to recommend that we do as we like provided we abstain from evil. This libertarian thesis—the thesis that *On Liberty* is remembered for—represents nothing so much as a retraction of the author's own powerful critique of the morality of innocuousness. Mill has misplaced his emphasis on consumer values that he doesn't seem to perceive lame his own republican principles.

As iconoclastic as some have found *On Liberty* to be, it would have been more controversial if Mill had devoted whole pages to spelling out public forms of endeavor in which liberty is realized. Not just considerations of strategy but surely his own profound distrust of the people stayed him from doing so. Yet Mill *did* cherish republican values, and specifically the value of action-in-concert. Toward the end of *On Liberty* he recognizes the need for forms of action that draw people out of the private sphere (which he has fenced round with fortifications) and into their identity as citizens: forms of action that put into practice that "liberty . . . of combination among individuals" which is asserted in the introduction (OL 226). It is characteristic of the way in which Mill tempers and suppresses his own "most passionate" love of the republican ideal that he insists this subject doesn't really belong in *On Liberty*. It is characteristic of the tangles of this text that Mill claims issues of civic action "are not questions of liberty" (OL 305) but then almost at once subjoins the remark that, where people don't possess the power and the habit of civic action, liberty dies. After recommending jury service, political participation, and the formation of voluntary associations, Mill says,

> These are not questions of liberty, and are connected with that subject only by remote tendencies; but they are questions of development. It belongs to a different occasion from the present to dwell on these things as parts of national education; as being, in truth, the peculiar training of a citizen, the practical part of the political education of a free people, taking them out of the narrow circle of personal and family selfishness, and accustoming them to the comprehension of joint interests, the man-

agement of joint concerns—habituating them to act from public or semi-
public motives, and guide their conduct by aims which unite instead of
isolating them from one another. Without these habits and powers, a free
constitution can neither be worked nor preserved. (OL 305)

Mill believed that English liberties derived from the ability of the
feudal barons to concert their actions, to make one of many;[36] here in
On Liberty, for a moment at least, he envisions the commons practic-
ing the same political art and coming to a comprehension of themselves
as acting beings. (Not that Mill had anything to teach the working class
on this point. The Chartists knew all about it.) In Tocqueville's esti-
mation, the Americans' habit of acting in concert, even in minor
concerns, counteracted the tendency of their society to estrange individuals from the past, from the future, and from one another (a
tendency working today with powerful effect). By comparison, Mill
has strangely little to say in *On Liberty* about the issue of civic action,
an issue on which he himself deems the existence of liberty to depend.
Indeed, earlier in the essay he deprecated the English "habit of
combining" in pursuit of large ends (OL 272). It seems civic action is
a sore point in Mill's thinking, for he speaks of it in contradictions and
asides.[37] He fails to incorporate the theme of civic action into the
rational structure of his argument, instead digging a sort of moat
around each individual (like the moat around Wemmick's castle in
Great Expectations) and enforcing the very solitude that, according to
Tocqueville, saps the strength and indeed the individuality of the
citizen.

In the final pages of *On Liberty* Americans appear as virtuous
citizens, capable of maintaining their own freedom, conducting their
civic affairs for themselves, and re-inventing government itself if they
have to. True republicans, they possess more than the passive ability
to keep within the law; they possess the ability to institute government
in the first place. Let Americans be without a government, Mill says,
and they are able

> to improvise one, and to carry on that or any other public business with
> a sufficient amount of intelligence, order, and decision. This is what every
> free people ought to be: and a people capable of this is certain to be free.
> (OL 307–8)

Yet in the introduction to *On Liberty* Mill holds up the "democratic
republic" (OL 219) of the United States not as a model of civic virtue,

but as an infamous case of the tyranny of the majority. Mill makes no effort whatever to reconcile these positions, which perhaps serve as one more index of his mixed feelings toward the republican ideal of a politically alive citizenry. He retreats from that risky ideal to the program for which he is better known: that of minding our own business (in conformity with the suggestions of common prudence) and privately pursuing happiness. If, according to classical republicanism, corruption is the enfeeblement suffered by the citizenry that sacrifices public to private interests, then Mill decries the corruption of his society (mainly the middle class) at the same time that he raises private concerns to a new level of philosophical dignity and so reinforces the very conditions responsible for the enfeeblement in the first place. If the antidote to corruption is

> preservation or renewal of the public spirit or "virtue" of the citizenry, typically by subordinating private concerns to the public good, encouraging active participation in public affairs, and preventing the pursuit of personal luxury from undermining such essential citizenly qualities as martial valour,[38]

then Mill makes the same recommendations, but only in passing, or in ways that receive small or no argumentative emphasis.

Freedom cannot be preserved where people lack public spirit and political ability: this is a version of the republican argument that freedom depends on active virtue. *On Liberty* ends with a warning of a society in which action has died out, or rather where all ability, all power of doing, has been soaked up by the state, leaving nothing to the citizens themselves. Apparently Mill never considered that the individuals thus debilitated might still be perfectly free to eat or not eat pork, and otherwise please themselves. Stephen Spender imagines a sort of prison

> in which the prisoners were free to write graffiti on the prison walls, write and circulate their own "adult" pornography, smoke pot, paint abstract art, watch videos, and drink large quantities of alcohol without at any moment any of them harboring a thought which threatened Big Brother.[39]

In Western liberal societies there exists no Big Brother, but in all other respects this scenario isn't just conjecturally, but really and historically possible. Mill wouldn't be surprised at all to see today's bureaucrats and managers writing a prose without actions and agents (the extinction of agency that *On Liberty* warns of), but he never imagined that these worthies would preside over a society where people freely pursue their own happiness.

NOTES

1. If *On Liberty* really were the exposition of a single "truth," it would in effect repeat and weaken an earlier argument against the tyranny of the majority: Thoreau's essay on civil disobedience.

2. J. G. A. Pocock, *The Machiavellian Moment: Florentine Political Thought and the Atlantic Republican Tradition* (Princeton, N.J.: Princeton University Press, 1975), p. 53.

3. "Consume. Grow. Do what you want. Amuse yourselves"—these now seem to be the dictates of liberty. See Susan Sontag, "AIDS and Its Metaphors," *New York Review of Books*, October 27, 1988, p. 95.

4. Alexis de Tocqueville, *Democracy in America*, tr. Henry Reeve; rev. Francis Bowen and Phillips Bradley (New York: Vintage, 1945), vol. 1, pp. 409, 435–36. Tocqueville does fear the state draining away people's powers—which is not the same thing as people trespassing on one another's privacy.

5. H. Remsen Whitehouse, *The Life of Lamartine*, vol. 2 (London: T. Fisher Unwin, 1918), p. 230.

6. See Zera S. Fink, *The Classical Republicans: An Essay in the Recovery of a Pattern of Thought in Seventeenth Century England* (Evanston, Ill.: Northwestern University Press, 1945), p. 81.

7. On censorship in France, see Charles F. Ramus, *Daumier: 120 Great Lithographs* (New York: Dover, 1978), esp. p. xiv.

8. See W. J. Mc Cormack's notes to Anthony Trollope, *The Eustace Diamonds* (New York: Oxford University Press, 1983), bk. 2, p. 398.

9. Basil Willey, *Nineteenth Century Studies: Coleridge to Matthew Arnold* (London: Chatto & Windus, 1949), pp. 144, 164. On James Mill's self-censorship, see Joseph Hamburger, *Intellectuals in Politics: John Stuart Mill and the Philosophic Radicals* (New Haven, Conn.: Yale University Press, 1965), pp. 36–37. On Charles Molesworth's public unbelief, see William Thomas, *The Philosophical Radicals: Nine Studies in Theory and Practice, 1817–1841* (Oxford, U.K.: Oxford University Press, 1979), p. 191. See also Mill's *unpublished* letter to the unbeliever G. J. Holyoake, CW XXIV, 1082–84. Contrast Mill's policy of caution with Henry Hetherington's avowal of atheism in his last will and testament (1849): "I calmly and deliberately declare that I do not believe in the popular notion of the existence of an Almighty, All-wise and Benevolent God" (cited in *From Cobbett to the Chartists*, ed. Max Morris [London: Lawrence & Wishart, 1948], p. 237). A radical printer and publisher, Hetherington infuses the language of his will with a kind of Shelleyan republicanism.

10. Robert S. Lopez, *The Commercial Revolution of the Middle Ages, 950–1350* (Cambridge, U.K.: Cambridge University Press, 1976), p. 149.

11. The footnote reads in part: "It would . . . be irrelevant and out of place to examine here, whether the doctrine of Tyrannicide deserves [to be called immoral]. I shall content myself with saying that the subject has been at all times one of the open questions of morals; that the act of a private citizen in striking down a criminal, who, by raising himself above the law, has placed himself beyond the reach of legal punishment or control, has been accounted by whole nations, and by some of the best and wisest of men, not a crime, but an act of exalted virtue" (OL 228n). Nevertheless, Mill goes on to justify criminal penalties for "instigation" to tyrannicide.

12. Thomas Babington Macaulay, *Prose and Poetry*, ed. G. M. Young (London: Rupert Hart-Davis, 1952), p. 609. In a speech in the House of Commons in 1830, Macaulay himself invoked the liberty principle: one "must use all his rights so as not to infringe the rights of others." See Macaulay, *Selected Writings*, eds. John Clive and Thomas Pinney (Chicago: University of Chicago Press, 1972), p. 186.

13. See *Kant's Political Writings*, ed. Hans Reiss; tr. H. B. Nisbet (Cambridge, U.K.: Cambridge University Press, 1971), pp. 145n–146n. The source is Kant's *Metaphysics of Morals*. Emphasis in the original.

14. Hannah Arendt, *Kant's Political Philosophy*, ed. Ronald Beiner (Chicago: University of Chicago Press, 1982), p. 48.

15. On this point, see the note by David Spitz in his edition of Mill's *On Liberty* (New York: Norton, 1975), p. 17.

16. On this subject, see Joel H. Wiener, *Radicalism and Freethought in Nineteenth-Century Britain: The Life of Richard Carlile* (Westport, Conn.: Greenwood Press, 1983), ch. 3.

17. Ann Ilan Alter, "An Introduction to the Exhibition" in *Censorship: 500 Years of Conflict* (New York: Oxford University Press, 1984), p. 19.

18. Excerpts from this pamphlet, entitled *Haec-Vir* (1620), appear in Louis B. Wright, *Middle-Class Culture in Elizabethan England* (Ithaca, N.Y.: Cornell University Press, 1965; orig. pub. 1935), pp. 495–97. Wright calls the pamphlet "the *Areopagitica* of the London woman" (p. 497). On *Haec-Vir*, see ch. 6 of Linda Woodbridge, *Women and the English Renaissance: Literature and the Nature of Womankind, 1540–1620* (Urbana, Ill.: University of Illinois Press, 1984).

19. See Keith Thomas, "Behind Closed Doors," *New York Review of Books*, November 9, 1989, p. 18. On the partitioning of public and private, see also Edmund Burke's "Thoughts and Details on Scarcity" (1795) in *The Works of Edmund Burke*, vol. 5 (London: Bell & Sons, 1893), pp. 83–109.

20. See Judith N. Shklar, *Men & Citizens: A Study of Rousseau's Social Theory* (Cambridge, U.K.: Cambridge University Press, 1985), p. 18.

21. On Rousseau and the citizen militia, see Shklar, *Men & Citizens*, p. 189.

22. Jean-Jacques Rousseau, *A Discourse on Inequality*, tr. Maurice Cranston (New York: Penguin, 1984), p. 136.

23. See John Rae, *Life of Adam Smith* (London: Macmillan, 1895), p. 124.

24. On Rousseau's concept of autonomy, see Lionel Trilling, *Sincerity and Authenticity* (Cambridge, Mass.: Harvard University Press, 1971).

25. Rousseau, *Discourse on Inequality*, p. 59.

26. See Victor Hugo, *History of a Crime* (New York: A. L. Burt, n.d.).

27. Jeremy Waldron, "Theoretical Foundations of Liberalism," *Philosophical Quarterly* 37 (1987), 133.

28. Charles Dickens, *Great Expectations* (New York: Penguin, 1965), p. 269.

29. *Kant's Political Writings*, p. 42.

30. On this point, see Kant's "Perpetual Peace," included in his *Political Writings*.

31. In his tribute to Armand Carrel, which is in some respects an idealized portrait of himself, Mill pictures a republican at once highly principled, passionate in his love of virtue, and master of his passions. As to this last, he quotes the view that Carrel "den[ied] himself rigidly the innocent aid of all the language of passion" (CW XX, 210).

32. See Tocqueville, *Democracy in America*, bk. 2, p. 347: "To lay down extensive but distinct and settled limits to the action of the government; to confer certain rights on private persons, and to secure to them the undisputed enjoyment of those rights . . . these appear to me the main objects of legislators in the ages upon which we are now entering."

33. See F. B. Smith, *Radical Artisan: William James Linton, 1812–97* (Manchester, U.K.: Manchester University Press, 1973), p. 235.

34. Pocock, *Machiavellian Moment*, p. 49.

35. Following a speech by Mill to a citizens' association in 1871, a group of protesters burst in and unfurled a flag "bearing the word 'republic' "—such was the charge the word carried. See CW XXIX, 415.

36. See Mill's essay on *Guizot's Essays and Lectures on History*, CW XX, 291–92.

37. On Thomas Carlyle's scorn of people who make common cause, and the seemingly more measured critique of associations by one W. E. Channing (in a pamphlet known to Mill), see John C. Rees, *John Stuart Mill's* On Liberty (Oxford, U.K.: Clarendon Press, 1985), pp. 72–74.

38. Donald Winch, *Adam Smith's Politics: An Essay in Historiographic Revision* (Cambridge, U.K.: Cambridge University Press, 1978), p. 30.

39. Stephen Spender, "Thoughts on Censorship in the World of 1984" in *Censorship*, p. 126.

6

Lessons of *On Liberty*

MANY ISSUES RAISED in *On Liberty* remain topical at this hour—big government, competence testing, child support, and evangelical zealotry, to name a few. The lesson of tolerance is still timely; large numbers of people still haven't learned its first principles. Even so, as an argument for free choice, *On Liberty* has been outdated. Consumer culture has carried private preference to lengths not contemplated by John Stuart Mill. The early pages of *Habits of the Heart*, a 1985 status report on American values, introduce us to a Californian who doesn't need to be instructed that there is such a thing as a self-regarding act. "By and large," he says,

> the rule of thumb out here is that if you've got the money, honey, you can do your thing as long as your thing doesn't destroy someone else's property, or interrupt their sleep, or bother their privacy, then that's fine. If you want to go in your house and smoke marijuana and shoot dope and get all screwed up, that's your business, but don't bring all that out on the street, don't expose my children to it, just do your thing. That works out kind of neat.[1]

Here Mill's "one very simple principle" (OL 223; see the Introduction of this book, note 17), the principle of noninterference, is made even simpler—turned into a jingle—banalized. Language of this order discourages thought, but if we make an effort to think about it in spite of itself, some questions may form. For example, is there a money qualification for the right to do your own thing? Is it all right for users to expose their own children to drugs? And how are drugs to get into the privacy of your California home except by way of the street? How can you consume drugs in the discreet privacy of your home unless there is a traffic in drugs? If it should happen that this traffic menaces the public, will it then be good enough to continue to talk about the neat way things work themselves out if only we don't meddle in each other's private affairs? Clearly, this man's language, unlike Mill's, is not equal to the issues it proposes to discuss.

Our California philosopher has already voyaged beyond the thought of John Stuart Mill and might see no point in going back to read *On Liberty*; but if he did, he would (I imagine) read it as a text that doesn't ask anything of him except not to infringe on the rights of others— itself not a taxing requirement. He would understand it as a call to self-fulfillment, but would have no sense whatever of the tradition (still extant in Mill) that holds that "self-fulfillment is possible only when the individual acts as a citizen."[2] Practically without exception, students in my experience have read *On Liberty* in just this light, as a text that reaffirms and philosophically dignifies what they as members of a consumer society already believe. If *On Liberty* merely asked us not to persecute or interfere, it would ask little. In order not to interfere with my neighbor, I need do nothing at all. I can satisfy the requirements of noninterference while I sit watching television, or for that matter while I sleep. One of Mill's precursors, Adam Smith, made a similar point. "Mere justice," he wrote,

> is, upon most occasions, but a negative virtue, and only hinders us from hurting our neighbour. The man who barely abstains from violating either the person, or the estate, or the reputation of his neighbours, has surely very little positive merit. He fulfils, however, all the rules of what is peculiarly called justice. . . . We may often fulfil all the rules of justice by sitting still and doing nothing.[3]

Like the "negative virtue" of justice in Adam Smith's sense, toleration is of the nature of a minimum, not a maximum: it is the least that a people intent on freedom ought to be capable of. Free citizens do more than formulate their various lifestyles and leave one another in peace: they stand up to oppression; they expose corruption; they act in common cause; they resist; they decline to bow, scrape, bribe, charm, manipulate. While Mill would probably be content if people just tolerated, *On Liberty* is nourished by the republican ideal of the citizen and reminds us of the responsibilities of the active life. Mill's most deeply held ideal was that of free citizens who manifest "nobility of thought and forcefulness of action"—those excellences that so impressed Mill's contemporary Margaret Fuller during her visit to the Roman republic.[4] Nobility of thought and forcefulness of action: in consumer society, this is a fossil language, as dead as the love of classical antiquity in which Mill's republicanism was rooted.

For years Mill maintained a liaison with Harriet Taylor that was illicit in the eyes of the world and that he for his part believed was not the world's business. In *On Liberty* he argued out his opinion that society has no jurisdiction over certain areas of conduct. Yet it is not as an argument admonishing people to "mind their own business" (OL 286) that *On Liberty* has its real value today (if only because this maxim commits us to nothing more than business-as-usual), but rather as an argument challenging people to learn to act in concert and "guide their conduct by aims which unite instead of isolating them from one another" (OL 305). This latter principle so apparently disagrees with the first that Mill banished it to the margin of his text (where readers miss it entirely), saying that it is scarcely connected to the issue of liberty. Learning to act in concert is necessary not only because there is strength in union, but because our choices are already coordinated for us, by default, by such "invisible" agencies as the mass media. Mill hoped people could come together as intentional agents and free citizens, not as mannikins whose behavior is driven by the gears and wheels of mass conformity. "Comparatively speaking," he writes, people now "read the same things, listen to the same things, see the same things, go to the same places, have their hopes and fears directed to the same objects" (OL 274). This in 1859. Today the power of mass society is incalculably greater than it was in Mill's time, and we face that much more acute a decision between leaving it to an Invisible Hand to coordinate our free choices and taking it upon ourselves to do so. Isolated, attending to our own business, consuming drugs in privacy, we are not much of a match for powerful agencies like the corporation or the state. "Individuals should be free, indeed, in all sorts of ways, but we don't set them free by separating them from their fellows."[5] Americans today are good at baking brownies for the PTA, less good at forming, say, small associations that give sanctuary to political refugees, or make purchases in common (as of snow-throwers or other goods wasted unless they serve a number of households), or go into business, or interview political candidates, or provide for mutual aid.[6]

I don't seriously imagine that the United States is going to cease being a mass society. But by the same token I can't take seriously the fiction that consumers are each of us sovereigns making independent choices, thinking our own thoughts, expressing the unique reserves of being that are inside us. The market provides efficiently for the coordination of the "perceptions" and indeed the acts of many millions of sovereign individuals. It is practically a definition of mass society that, in it, millions who don't feel themselves to be co-laborers in a common purpose or inheritors of a common past nevertheless have the same responses—agree in a way that they don't seem able to achieve for themselves.

In our society, political choice is patterned after the most weightless and inconsequential of all judgments: consumer preferences. But if everyone is left to his or her own choice, and if the marketplace presents a vast emporium of choices (as we are constantly told), then that would seem to raise the possibility of 1,000 people making 1,000 different choices. We know from experience this doesn't happen. In spite of the fact that we cannot either in theory or in practice argue out choices of consumption, in spite of the fact that we share neither in common endeavor nor in a common past, millions of us succeed in choosing the very same things. I believe Alasdair MacIntyre goes wrong on this point in *After Virtue*, a provocative anti-liberal work of moral philosophy that begins with the claim that public discourse has broken down into barking.

In contemporary America MacIntyre finds no consensus to speak of, not even the dubious and ill-founded consensus represented by public opinion. Public speech he judges to be a babel: arguments without issue. MacIntyre believes consensus doesn't exist for us because the modern self is an "emotivist" brat, a sort of private king whose only law is his own wholly undetermined choices. What distinguishes our debates today, he says, is just their interminability: the fact that they can't be brought to resolution. (Herbert Marcuse used to take the contrary position: that our arguments are terminated before they begin.) MacIntyre gives several examples of the sort of confusion of tongues that he has in mind, including these three "rival moral arguments":

(a) . . . [I]n a modern war calculation of future escalation is never reliable and no practically applicable distinction between combatants and non-combatants can be made. Therefore no modern war can be a just war and we all now ought to be pacifists.

(b) If you wish for peace, prepare for war. The only way to achieve peace is to deter potential aggressors. Therefore you must build up your armaments and make it clear that going to war on any particular scale is not necessarily ruled out by your policies.

(c) . . . [W]ars waged to liberate oppressed groups, especially in the Third World, are a necessary and therefore justified means for destroying the exploitative domination which stands between mankind and happiness.

MacIntyre goes on to say that these arguments and their variants are heard everywhere in American society, "in newspaper editorials and high-school debates, on radio talk shows and letters to congressmen, in bars, barracks and boardrooms."[7]

I don't know where MacIntyre drinks his beer, but it can't be in a neighborhood bar where pacifists and revolutionaries put forward their views on equal terms with the majority. Nor can I imagine a boardroom—much less a barracks—where wars of liberation are debated hotly. If a debate among (a), (b), and (c) ever did take place, it is over for now, having been decided in (b)'s favor. (In point of fact, the United States built atomic weapons before the people ever knew about it, before the question could be put to a public determination.) To most, the doctrine of nuclear deterrence is common sense itself, and we hear 1,000 repetitions of it in the mass media for every defense of the pacifist or revolutionary position. I don't mean nuclear deterrence is indefensible. The point is that a powerful apparatus of conformity and consent keeps real argument, on these issues as on others, from ever quite coming about. We do not in fact hear too many of the debates MacIntyre seems to hear. If our public discourse is sham, this isn't because it has turned into an argumentative anarchy, but because of the measures taken to make it overwhelmingly likely that millions of people will make the same "emotivist" choices. It seems to me that political and economic actors possess many strategies, from scaremongering to the arts of bribery, for coaxing people to choose in the same way, as they couldn't possibly do if their decisions were really as undetermined and individual as MacIntyre makes them out to be. Consumerism both reduces judgment to the inarguable (there is no disputing points of taste or subjective preference) and gives us ways to get around differences that couldn't conceivably be argued out.

Both Mill and Milton urged citizens to take the burden of choice on themselves, but both understood choice as having a public dimension in the sense that, unlike a taste-preference, it can be put into words and actually defended. The supreme act of moral life, choice is too important a thing not to be brought to language; or so I imagine Mill and Milton would have believed. "I cannot praise thy Marriage choices, Son," says Manoa to Samson, referring to choices which, no matter how personal and inward they may have been, are acts of political import and therefore subject, like all other acts of that kind, to praise, blame, and misconstrual.[8] Choice has since been radically privatized, with the result that this most celebrated of acts in a consumer society is of all things the one about which the least can intelligently be said. Where candidates are marketed like candy, political choice is reduced to a wholly inarguable sort of liking or not liking, trusting or not trusting. At the same time, more and more of politics passes outside of the precincts of language altogether. In "debates" between presidential candidates, for example, the disputants are judged by learned commentators less on what they say than on the way they carry themselves. Image, which as the word suggests doesn't really have a language basis, now has a force at least equal to that of any other political consideration. Sworn as Americans are to the pursuit of private happiness, we leave the public realm little to be *but* invalid and fictitious; so it is, perhaps, that our public space comes to be dominated by images that really are invalid and fictitious. Typical of the working of images is the consciousness-altering political ad on television, which serves

> not to stimulate thought but to prevent it; not to communicate information, but to conceal or trivialize it; not to persuade but to placate and entertain; not to move but to enlarge quiescence; ultimately, not to use language at all if cinematic artifice and a musical sound-track can be used to conjure the desired image and elicit the favourable emotion.[9]

Such ads coax political consumers to make this or that choice, at the same time that they "establish . . . an embargo on public discourse."[10] So it is that we are able to choose the same things in great numbers without being able to discuss our choices even in principle.

In this context, Mill's *On Liberty*, which has the sovereign merit of stimulating and not preventing thought, reminds us of the distinction between active and passive consensus. It recalls us to the conception of human beings as capable of acting, not just responding. Liberty asks of us something more difficult than just keeping out of the business of others: it asks us to find out how to act in concert, isolated as we already are. Although he made this issue a sort of footnote to his text (as he did more literally with the issue of tyrannicide), Mill would have agreed. He held that unless a people possesses political ability—that is, the ability to form common intentions and concert their actions—"a free constitution can neither be worked nor preserved" (OL 305). I believe we do not possess that ability. With us the experience of common deliberation and joint action is largely missing, nor do we possess so much as the concept of the adjudication of differing "preferences." So privatized are American lives, so bounded within "the narrow circle of personal and family selfishness" (OL 305) that *On Liberty* both rings with fortifications and beckons us out of, that most of us know nothing of what it is to deliberate and act with others for public ends.

Mill defended consumer choice but insisted that a citizen, unlike a consumer, cannot exercise a merely private preference in the giving of a vote; indeed Mill would have made voting a public act.[11] The front of consumerism has now advanced to the point where candidates themselves are marketed as products and political choice is one more act of consumption, as radically inarguable ("I just *like* Reagan") as any other decision about what to swallow. At the same time, the ethical standard of disinterest that was of such solemn importance to Mill has been put to sale. In court, tobacco companies with a fierce interest in the sale of cigarettes defend the consumer's right to free choice. They defend it on the high ground of philosophical principle, and, I suppose, with a straight face. But conceivably Mill would say that, if the right to smoke is important to consumers, they ought to defend it *themselves*, rather than leaving it to the tobacco interests to defend it for them. To default to the tobacco companies, to look to them to do your own work for you, is to succumb to the same paternalism that the companies pretend to oppose.

Like everyone else with something on the market, the tobacco companies claim to be serving the public interest. But if anything and everything is "in the public interest," then the meaning of the term has been gutted. If the National Association of Birdfood Packagers stands to gain from a given bill, then its publicists will celebrate that bill as being sacred to the public interest. "Voluntary associations" on the order of this one fill the American landscape and sound their ludicrously narrow views throughout the land. A pirated copy of the republican principle of the common good has flooded the market, like one more consumer article. Americans imitate the language of republicanism. We have that much in common with the republic of Albania.

The principle on which *On Liberty* stands—every individual's title

to pursue happiness—was not invented by Mill. It was part of the
intellectual currency of Europe and America. In his essay "On the
Common Saying: 'This May be True in Theory, but it does not Apply
in Practice,' " Kant had laid it down that "each may seek his happiness in whatever way he sees fit, so long as he does not infringe upon
the freedom of others to pursue a similar end." The same work
prefigures other themes and even clauses in *On Liberty*, for example,
its rejection of paternalistic government, and its invalidation of any
contract in which the individual signs away sovereignty over him- or
herself. For all this, Kant marks an emphatic distinction between the
dictates of duty and the pursuit of happiness. He disputes

> the erroneous assumption that a motive derived from the idea of duty in
> itself is far too subtle for the common understanding, whereas a cruder
> motive based on advantages which can be expected either in this or in a
> future world from obedience to duty . . . would act more forcibly upon
> the mind.[12]

No doubt Mill grasped Kant's distinction between duty and interest
(as he despised the idea of purchasing advantages in the next world).
Nevertheless, the whole tendency of *On Liberty* is to "reconcile" the
two by making it appear that in attending to our own happiness we are
carrying out the daring tradition of republicanism. Where Kant—a
declared republican—affirms that "the rights of men" stand "above
all utilitarian values,"[13] Mill declines to use militant language like "the
rights of men," grounds his argument on the principle of utility, and
somehow resolves the ideals of republicanism into private happiness.
Kant condemns the man who looks around him at the struggles of
others and decides

> "What concern of mine is it? Let each one be as happy as heaven wills,
> or as he can make himself; I will not take anything from him or even envy
> him; but to his welfare or to his assistance in time of need I have no
> desire to contribute."[14]

In spite of Mill's generous sentiments, in spite of his Kantian concern
for agents in themselves and not just their acts, the let-alone argument
of *On Liberty* readily degrades into this kind of isolationism. Unintentionally, Mill helps to prepare for a political order in which people
"reconcile" republican obligation and private interest by representing
anything that benefits them as being in the public good. Mill's language

is on the way to becoming our own fossilized republicanism. At length, *On Liberty* declines into the argument that the consumer who "knowingly" decides for Coca-Cola ranks above the one who makes his or her choice without reflection: the first is autonomous, the second not.[15]

"The bourgeois," we read, "comes into being when men no longer believe that there is a common good."[16] In keeping with his practice of "reconciling" clashing values, Mill attempted to recover the morality of duty to the common good and wed it to the morality of private happiness. I would argue that public duty and private happiness must conflict at some point; that it is good to be clear about this; and that when they do conflict, the second principle ought to give way to the first. In consumer society, the second principle triumphs over the first. In a small way, Mill himself contributed to that victory. As intensely public-spirited as he was, he is better known for having dug a defensive trench around the private sphere, and his most enduring work helps to justify consumer values that negate the public realm. Consumer society has created a reality-poor public language and has given rise to political performers who campaign against the public sphere itself, trying to win for themselves all the credibility that has gone out of it. But *On Liberty* possesses enough inconsistency and enough power to criticize the same kind of isolationism to which it has given a philosophical sanction. Mill never did reconcile public spirit and private interest; we ourselves are far from being able to do so. The language of private consumption—one of the languages of *On Liberty*—we speak with spirit, and we believe not just in free consumption but in consumption without end; the language of public responsibility—another of the languages of *On Liberty*—is for us a sort of Latin to be used on ceremonial occasions. The idea of noninterference comes readily to most of us; the idea of "requiring everyone to help clean up a deteriorating neighborhood"—which perhaps comes under Mill's "obligation to the public" (OL 256)[17]—has hardly any following at all, to judge by the condition of inner cities. I doubt that consumer values and public responsibility can be reconciled either in practice or in principle.

NOTES

1. Robert N. Bellah, Richard Madsen, William M. Sullivan, Ann Swidler, and Steven M. Tipton, *Habits of the Heart: Individualism and Commitment in American Life* (Berkeley: University of California Press, 1985), p. 7.

2. J. G. A. Pocock, *Politics, Language and Time: Essays on Political Thought and History* (New York: Atheneum, 1973), p. 85.

3. Adam Smith, *The Theory of Moral Sentiments*, eds. D. D. Raphael and A. L. Macfie (Indianapolis: Liberty Classics, 1982), p. 82.

4. Ann Douglas, *The Feminization of American Culture* (New York: Avon, 1977), p. 344.

5. Michael Walzer, "Liberalism and the Art of Separation," *Political Theory* 12 (1984), 325.

6. On forms of "voluntary collectivism," see F. M. L. Thompson, "Social Control in Victorian Britain," *Economic History Review* 34 (1981), 207–8.

7. Alasdair MacIntyre, *After Virtue: A Study in Moral Theory* (Notre Dame, Ind.: University of Notre Dame Press, 1981), pp. 6–7.

8. Line 420 of *Samson Agonistes* in Milton's *Complete Poems and Major Prose*, ed. Merritt Y. Hughes (Indianapolis: Odyssey Press, 1957), p. 562.

9. Paul E. Corcoran, *Political Language and Rhetoric* (Austin: University of Texas Press, 1979), p. 175.

10. Corcoran, *Political Language and Rhetoric*, p. 175.

11. A splendid article on Shelley's conception of public voting as a stimulus to civic virtue is Gerald McNiece, "Shelley, John Stuart Mill, and the Secret Ballot," *Mill News Letter* (Spring 1973).

12. *Kant's Political Writings*, ed. Hans Reiss; tr. H. B. Nisbet (Cambridge, U.K.: Cambridge University Press, 1971), pp. 74, 72.

13. "The Contest of Faculties" in *Kant's Political Writings*, p. 184n.

14. Immanuel Kant, *Foundations of the Metaphysics of Morals*, tr. Lewis White Beck (New York: Macmillan, 1990), p. 40.

15. See Lawrence Haworth, "Autonomy and Utility," in *The Inner Citadel: Essays on Individual Autonomy*, ed. John Christman (New York: Oxford University Press, 1989), p. 162.

16. See Allan Bloom's introduction to his own translation of Jean-Jacques Rousseau, *Emile* (New York: Basic, 1979), p. 5.

17. Paula Rothenberg Struhl, "Mill's Notion of Social Responsibility," *Journal of the History of Ideas* 37 (1976), 157.

Bibliography

Abrams, M. H. *The Mirror and the Lamp: Romantic Theory and the Critical Tradition*. New York: Oxford University Press, 1953.

Adams, Robert M. *Ikon: John Milton and the Modern Critics*. Ithaca, N.Y.: Cornell University Press, 1955.

Alter, Ann Ilan. "An Introduction to the Exhibition." In *Censorship: 500 Years of Conflict*. New York: Oxford University Press, 1984.

Annan, Noel. "John Stuart Mill." In *The English Mind: Studies in the English Moralists Presented to Basil Willey*. Eds. Hugh Sykes Davies and George Watson. Cambridge, U.K.: Cambridge University Press, 1964.

Anspach, Ralph. "The Implications of the *Theory of Moral Sentiments* for Adam Smith's Economic Thought." *History of Political Economy* 4 (1972), 176–206.

Appleby, Joyce. *Capitalism and a New Social Order: The Republican Vision of the 1790s*. New York: New York University Press, 1984.

———. "Republicanism in Old and New Contexts." *William and Mary Quarterly* 3rd Series, 43 (1986), 20–34.

Arendt, Hannah. *Between Past and Future: Eight Exercises in Political Thought*. New York: Penguin, 1978.

———. *Kant's Political Philosophy*. Ed. Ronald Beiner. Chicago: University of Chicago Press, 1982.

———. *The Life of the Mind*. 2 volumes. New York: Harcourt Brace Jovanovich, 1978.

———. *On Revolution*. New York: Viking, 1963.

Arneson, Richard. "Democracy and Liberty in Mill's Theory of Government." *Journal of the History of Philosophy* 20 (1982), 43–64.

———. "Mill versus Paternalism." *Ethics* 90 (1980), 470–89.

Aron, Raymond. "Tocqueville and Marx." In *History, Truth, Liberty: Selected Writings of Raymond Aron*, Ed. Franciszek Draus. Chicago: University of Chicago Press, 1985.

Ashcraft, Richard. *Revolutionary Politics and Locke's* Two Treatises of Government. Princeton, N.J.: Princeton University Press, 1986.

Bailyn, Bernard. *The Ideological Origins of the American Revolution*. Cambridge, Mass.: Harvard University Press, 1967.

Barber, Benjamin. "Rousseau and the Paradoxes of the Dramatic Imagination." *Daedalus* 107 (1978), 79–92.

Barker-Benfield, G. J. "Mary Wollstonecraft: Eighteenth-Century Commonwealthwoman." *Journal of the History of Ideas* 50 (1989), 95–115.

Bellah, Robert N., Richard Madsen, William M. Sullivan, Ann Swidler, and Steven M. Tipton. *Habits of the Heart: Individualism and Commitment in American Life*. Berkeley: University of California Press, 1985.

Berlin, Isaiah. *Four Essays on Liberty*. New York: Oxford University Press, 1969.

———. "On the Pursuit of the Ideal." *New York Review of Books*, March 17, 1988.

Bloch, Ruth H. "The Gendered Meanings of Virtue in Revolutionary America." *Signs* 13 (1987), 37–58.

Boehrer, Bruce. "Elementary Structures of Kingship: Milton, Regicide, and the Family." *Milton Studies* 23 (1987), 97–117.

Bok, Sissela. *Lying: Moral Choice in Public and Private Life*. New York: Vintage, 1978.

Briggs, Asa. *The Making of Modern England: 1783–1867*. New York: Harper and Row, 1959.

———. *Victorian People: A Reassessment of Persons and Themes, 1851–1867*. Chicago: University of Chicago Press, 1972.

Bush, Douglas. *John Milton: A Sketch of His Life and Writings*. New York: Macmillan, 1964.

Cobbett, William. *Advice to Young Men*. London: Routledge, 1892.

Coleridge, Samuel Taylor. *On the Constitution of Church and State*. Volume 10 of *The Collected Works of Samuel Taylor Coleridge*. Princeton, N.J.: Princeton University Press, 1976.

Comte, Auguste. *A General View of Positivism*. Tr. J. H. Bridges. New York: Robert Speller, 1957.

Corcoran, Paul E. *Political Language and Rhetoric*. Austin: University of Texas Press, 1979.

Cropsey, Joseph. *Polity and Economy: An Interpretation of the Principles of Adam Smith*. The Hague: Martinus Nijhoff, 1957.

Defoe, Daniel. *Moll Flanders*. New York: Crowell, 1970.

Dickens, Charles. *Great Expectations*. New York: Penguin, 1965.

Douglas, Ann. *The Feminization of American Culture*. New York: Avon, 1977.

Elias, Norbert. *The History of Manners*. (Volume 1 of *The Civilizing Process*.) Tr. Edmund Jephcott. New York: Pantheon, 1978; orig. pub. 1939.

Epstein, James. "Understanding the Cap of Liberty: Symbolic Practice and Social Conflict in Early Nineteenth-Century England." *Past and Present* 122 (1989), 75–118.

Fink, Zera. *The Classical Republicans: An Essay in the Recovery of a Pattern of Thought in Seventeenth Century England*. Evanston, Ill.: Northwestern University, 1945.

Fish, Stanley. *Self-Consuming Artifacts: The Experience of Seventeenth-Century Literature*. Berkeley: University of California Press, 1972.

———. *Surprised by Sin: The Reader in Paradise Lost*. London: Macmillan, 1967.

Flathman, Richard E. *The Philosophy and Politics of Freedom*. Chicago: University of Chicago Press, 1987.

Forster, E. M. *Two Cheers for Democracy*. New York: Harcourt, Brace, 1951.

Franklin, Benjamin. *Autobiography*. Eds. J. A. Leo Lemay and P. M. Zall. New York: Norton, 1986.

Frye, Northrop. *The Return of Eden: Five Essays on Milton's Epics*. Toronto: University of Toronto Press, 1965.

Grazia, Sebastian de. *Machiavelli in Hell*. Princeton, N.J.: Princeton University Press, 1989.

Griffiths, A. Phillips, ed. *Of Liberty*. Cambridge, U.K.: Cambridge University Press, 1983.

Halévy, Elie. *The Growth of Philosophic Radicalism*. Tr. Mary Morris. London: Faber and Faber, 1928.

Hamburger, Joseph. *Intellectuals in Politics: John Stuart Mill and the Philosophic Radicals*. New Haven, Conn.: Yale University Press, 1965.

Hayek, F. A. *John Stuart Mill and Harriet Taylor: Their Correspondence and Subsequent Marriage*. Chicago: University of Chicago Press, 1951.

Hill, Christopher. *Milton and the English Revolution*. New York: Viking, 1977.

Hill, Melvyn A., ed. *Hannah Arendt: The Recovery of the Public World*. New York: St. Martin's, 1979.

Himmelfarb, Gertrude. *The Idea of Poverty: England in the Early Industrial Age*. New York: Knopf, 1984.

———. *On Liberty and Liberalism: The Case of John Stuart Mill*. New York: Knopf, 1974.

Hirschman, Albert O. *The Passions and the Interests: Political Arguments for Capitalism before Its Triumph*. Princeton, N.J.: Princeton University Press, 1977.

Hobsbawm, E. J. *The Age of Capital: 1848–1875*. New York: New American Library, 1984.

———. *The Age of Revolution: 1789–1848*. New York: New American Library, 1962.

Howe, Irving. *Celebrations and Attacks: Thirty Years of Literary and Cultural Commentary*. New York: Harcourt Brace Jovanovich, 1979.

Hugo, Victor. *History of a Crime*. New York: Burt, n.d.

Kant, Immanuel. *Kant's Political Writings*. Ed. Hans Reiss. Tr. H. B. Nisbet. Cambridge, U.K.: Cambridge University Press, 1971.

Kuhn, Thomas. *The Structure of Scientific Revolutions*. Chicago: University of Chicago Press, 1970.

Locke, John. *The Second Treatise of Government*. Indianapolis: Library of Liberal Arts, 1952.

Long, Douglas G. *Bentham on Liberty: Jeremy Bentham's Idea of Liberty in Relation to His Utilitarianism*. Toronto: University of Toronto Press, 1977.

Lopez, Robert S. *The Commercial Revolution of the Middle Ages, 950–1350*. Cambridge, U.K.: Cambridge University Press, 1976.

Macaulay, Thomas Babington. *Critical and Historical Essays*. New York: Dutton, 1966.

———. *Prose and Poetry*. Ed. G. M. Young. London: Rupert Hart-Davis, 1952.

Machiavelli, Niccolò. *The Discourses*. Tr. Christian Detmold. New York: Modern Library, 1950.

MacIntyre, Alasdair. *After Virtue: A Study in Moral Theory*. Notre Dame, Ind.: University of Notre Dame Press, 1981.

McNiece, Gerald. "Shelley, John Stuart Mill, and the Secret Ballot." *Mill News Letter*, Spring 1973, 2–7.

Macpherson, C. B. Review in *Mill News Letter*, Winter 1976, 21–23.

Malcolmson, Robert W. *Popular Recreations in English Society, 1700–1850*. Cambridge, U.K.: Cambridge University Press, 1973.

Mazlish, Bruce. *James and John Stuart Mill: Father and Son in the Nineteenth Century*. New York: Basic, 1975.

Melville, Herman. *Selected Tales and Poems*. New York: Holt, Rinehart and Winston, 1950.

Mill, John Stuart. *Collected Works*. Toronto: University of Toronto Press. 29 volumes. Volume 29 published 1988.

Milner, Andrew. *John Milton and the English Revolution: A Study in the Sociology of Literature*. Totowa, N.J.: Barnes and Noble, 1981.

Milton, John. *Complete Poems and Major Prose*. Ed. Merritt Y. Hughes. Indianapolis, Ind.: Odyssey, 1957.

———. *Complete Prose Works of John Milton*. 8 volumes. New Haven, Conn.: Yale University Press, 1953–82.

Packe, Michael St. John. *The Life of John Stuart Mill*. London: Secker and Warburg, 1954.

Paxton, Robert O. "The Divided Liberal." *New York Review of Books*, March 2, 1989.

Pitkin, Hanna Fenichel. *Fortune Is a Woman: Gender and Politics in the Thought of Niccolò Machiavelli*. Berkeley: University of California Press, 1984.

Place, Francis. *Autobiography*. Ed. Mary Thale. Cambridge, U.K.: Cambridge University Press, 1972.

Plamenatz, John. *The English Utilitarians*. Oxford: Basil Blackwell, 1958.

———. "Liberalism." In *Dictionary of the History of Ideas*, Volume 3, pp. 36–61. New York: Scribner's, 1973.

Pocock, J. G. A. *The Machiavellian Moment: Florentine Political Thought and the Atlantic Republican Tradition*. Princeton, N.J.: Princeton University Press, 1975.

———. *Politics, Language and Time: Essays in Political Thought and History*. New York: Atheneum, 1973.

———. *Virtue, Commerce, and History: Essays on Political Thought and History, Chiefly in the Eighteenth Century*. Cambridge, U.K.: Cambridge University Press, 1985.

Rae, John. *Life of Adam Smith*. London: Macmillan, 1895.

Ramus, Charles F. *Daumier: 120 Great Lithographs*. New York: Dover, 1978.

Rees, John C. *John Stuart Mill's* On Liberty. Oxford, U.K.: Clarendon Press, 1985.

Richards, David A. J. "Autonomy in Law." In *The Inner Citadel: Essays on Individual Autonomy*. Ed. John Christman. New York: Oxford University Press, 1989.

Richmond, Hugh. *The Christian Revolutionary: John Milton.* Berkeley: University of California Press, 1974.

Robson, John M. *The Improvement of Mankind: The Social and Political Thought of John Stuart Mill.* London: Routledge and Kegan Paul, 1968.

Rousseau, Jean-Jacques. *The Confessions.* Tr. J. M. Cohen. New York: Penguin, 1953.

———. *A Discourse on Inequality.* Tr. Maurice Cranston. New York: Penguin, 1984.

———. *Emile.* Tr. Allan Bloom. New York: Basic, 1979.

Ryan, Alan, ed. *The Idea of Freedom.* New York: Oxford University Press, 1979.

Scott, John A. *Republican Ideas and the Liberal Tradition in France, 1870–1914.* New York: Columbia University Press, 1951.

Semmel, Bernard. *John Stuart Mill and the Pursuit of Virtue.* New Haven, Conn.: Yale University Press, 1984.

Sennett, Richard. *The Fall of Public Man: On the Social Psychology of Capitalism.* New York: Vintage, 1978.

Shelley, Percy Bysshe. *Poetry and Prose.* Eds. Donald H. Reiman and Sharon B. Powers. New York: Norton, 1977.

Shklar, Judith N. "Jean-Jacques Rousseau and Equality." *Daedalus* 107 (1978), 13–25.

———. *Men & Citizens: A Study of Rousseau's Social Theory.* Cambridge, U.K.: Cambridge University Press, 1985.

Skinner, Quentin. "The idea of negative liberty: philosophical and historical perspectives." In *Philosophy in History· Essays on the Historiography of Philosophy.* Eds. Richard Rorty, J. B. Schneewind, and Quentin Skinner. Cambridge, U.K.: Cambridge University Press, 1984.

Smith, Adam. *The Theory of Moral Sentiments.* Eds. D. D. Raphael and A. L. Macfie. Indianapolis: Liberty Classics, 1982.

———. *The Wealth of Nations.* New York: Modern Library, 1937.

Smith, F. B. *Radical Artisan: William James Linton, 1812–1897.* Manchester, U.K.: Manchester University Press, 1973.

Spender, Stephen. "Thoughts on Censorship in the World of 1984." In *Censorship: 500 Years of Conflict.* New York: Oxford University Press, 1984.

Steiner, George. *On Difficulty and Other Essays.* New York: Oxford University Press, 1978.

Stokes, Eric. *The English Utilitarians and India.* Oxford, U.K.: Clarendon Press, 1959.

Struhl, Paula Rothenberg. "Mill's Notion of Social Responsibility." *Journal of the History of Ideas* 37 (1976), 155–62.

Thomas, Keith. "Behind Closed Doors." *New York Review of Books*, November 9, 1989.

Thomas, William. *The Philosophical Radicals: Nine Studies in Theory and Practice, 1817–1841*. Oxford, U.K.: Oxford University Press, 1979.

Thompson, F. M. L. "Social Control in Victorian Britain." *Economic History Review* 34 (1981), 189–208.

Tippens, Darryl. "The Kenotic Experience of *Samson Agonistes*." *Milton Studies* 22 (1986), 173–94.

Tocqueville, Alexis de. *Democracy in America*. Tr. Henry Reeve; rev. Francis Bowen and Phillips Bradley. New York: Vintage, 1945.

Trilling, Lionel. *Sincerity and Authenticity*. Cambridge, Mass.: Harvard University Press, 1971.

Waldron, Jeremy. "Mill and the Value of Moral Distress." *Political Studies* 35 (1987), 410–23.

———. "Theoretical Foundations of Liberalism." *Philosophical Quarterly* 37 (1987), 127–50.

Walzer, Michael. *Exodus and Revolution*. New York: Basic, 1985.

———. "Liberalism and the Art of Separation." *Political Theory* 12 (1984), 315–30.

———. *The Revolution of the Saints: A Study in the Origins of Radical Politics*. Cambridge, Mass.: Harvard University Press, 1965.

Whitehouse, H. Remsen. *The Life of Lamartine*. London: T. Fisher Unwin, 1918.

Wiener, Joel H. *Radicalism and Freethought in Nineteenth-Century Britain: The Life of Richard Carlile*. Westport, Conn.: Greenwood, 1983.

Willey, Basil. *Nineteenth Century Studies: Coleridge to Matthew Arnold*. London: Chatto & Windus, 1949.

Winch, Donald. *Adam Smith's Politics: An Essay in Historiographic Revision*. Cambridge, Mass.: Cambridge University Press, 1978.

Wolin, Sheldon. *Politics and Vision: Continuity and Innovation in Western Political Thought*. Boston: Little, Brown, 1960.

Wollstonecraft, Mary. *A Vindication of the Rights of Woman*. Ed. Carol H. Poston. New York: Norton, 1988.

Wood, Gordon S. "The Fundamentalists and the Constitution." *New York Review of Books*, February 18, 1988.

————. "Politics without Party." *New York Review of Books*, October 11, 1984.

Wright, Louis B. *Middle-Class Culture in Elizabethan England*. Ithaca, N.Y.: Cornell University Press, 1935.

Index

181

About the Author

STEWART JUSTMAN has a Ph.D. from Columbia University and is Professor of English at the University of Montana. He is at work on a revisionary reading of Chaucer's Wife of Bath.